Sanna Turoma, Kaarina Aitamurto,
Slobodanka Vladiv-Glover (Eds.)

RELIGION, EXPRESSION, AND PATRIOTISM IN RUSSIA
Essays on Post-Soviet Society and the State

Bibliografische Information der Deutschen Nationalbibliothek
Die Deutsche Nationalbibliothek verzeichnet diese Publikation in der Deutschen Nationalbibliografie; detaillierte bibliografische Daten sind im Internet über http://dnb.d-nb.de abrufbar.

Bibliographic information published by the Deutsche Nationalbibliothek
Die Deutsche Nationalbibliothek lists this publication in the Deutsche Nationalbibliografie; detailed bibliographic data are available in the Internet at http://dnb.d-nb.de.

ISBN-13: 978-3-8382-1346-0

© *ibidem*-Verlag, Stuttgart 2019
Alle Rechte vorbehalten

Das Werk einschließlich aller seiner Teile ist urheberrechtlich geschützt. Jede Verwertung außerhalb der engen Grenzen des Urheberrechtsgesetzes ist ohne Zustimmung des Verlages unzulässig und strafbar. Dies gilt insbesondere für Vervielfältigungen, Übersetzungen, Mikroverfilmungen und elektronische Speicherformen sowie die Einspeicherung und Verarbeitung in elektronischen Systemen.

All rights reserved. No part of this publication may be reproduced, stored in or introduced into a retrieval system, or transmitted, in any form, or by any means (electronical, mechanical, photocopying, recording or otherwise) without the prior written permission of the publisher. Any person who does any unauthorized act in relation to this publication may be liable to criminal prosecution and civil claims for damages.

Printed in the EU

Soviet and Post-Soviet Politics and Society (SPPS)   Vol. 213
ISSN 1614-3515

General Editor: Andreas Umland,
Institute for Euro-Atlantic Cooperation, Kyiv, umland@stanfordalumni.org

Commissioning Editor: Max Jakob Horstmann,
London, mjh@ibidem.eu

EDITORIAL COMMITTEE*

DOMESTIC & COMPARATIVE POLITICS
Prof. **Ellen Bos**, *Andrássy University of Budapest*
Dr. **Gergana Dimova**, *University of Winchester*
Dr. **Andrey Kazantsev**, *MGIMO (U) MID RF, Moscow*
Prof. **Heiko Pleines**, *University of Bremen*
Prof. **Richard Sakwa**, *University of Kent at Canterbury*
Dr. **Sarah Whitmore**, *Oxford Brookes University*
Dr. **Harald Wydra**, *University of Cambridge*

SOCIETY, CLASS & ETHNICITY
Col. **David Glantz**, *"Journal of Slavic Military Studies"*
Dr. **Marlène Laruelle**, *George Washington University*
Dr. **Stephen Shulman**, *Southern Illinois University*
Prof. **Stefan Troebst**, *University of Leipzig*

POLITICAL ECONOMY & PUBLIC POLICY
Dr. **Andreas Goldthau**, *Central European University*
Dr. **Robert Kravchuk**, *University of North Carolina*
Dr. **David Lane**, *University of Cambridge*
Dr. **Carol Leonard**, *Higher School of Economics, Moscow*
Dr. **Maria Popova**, *McGill University, Montreal*

FOREIGN POLICY & INTERNATIONAL AFFAIRS
Dr. **Peter Duncan**, *University College London*
Prof. **Andreas Heinemann-Grüder**, *University of Bonn*
Prof. **Gerhard Mangott**, *University of Innsbruck*
Dr. **Diana Schmidt-Pfister**, *University of Konstanz*
Dr. **Lisbeth Tarlow**, *Harvard University, Cambridge*
Dr. **Christian Wipperfürth**, *N-Ost Network, Berlin*
Dr. **William Zimmerman**, *University of Michigan*

HISTORY, CULTURE & THOUGHT
Dr. **Catherine Andreyev**, *University of Oxford*
Prof. **Mark Bassin**, *Södertörn University*
Prof. **Karsten Brüggemann**, *Tallinn University*
Dr. **Alexander Etkind**, *University of Cambridge*
Dr. **Gasan Gusejnov**, *Moscow State University*
Prof. **Leonid Luks**, *Catholic University of Eichstaett*
Dr. **Olga Malinova**, *Russian Academy of Sciences*
Dr. **Richard Mole**, *University College London*
Prof. **Andrei Rogatchevski**, *University of Tromsø*
Dr. **Mark Tauger**, *West Virginia University*

ADVISORY BOARD*

Prof. **Dominique Arel**, *University of Ottawa*
Prof. **Jörg Baberowski**, *Humboldt University of Berlin*
Prof. **Margarita Balmaceda**, *Seton Hall University*
Dr. **John Barber**, *University of Cambridge*
Prof. **Timm Beichelt**, *European University Viadrina*
Dr. **Katrin Boeckh**, *University of Munich*
Prof. em. **Archie Brown**, *University of Oxford*
Dr. **Vyacheslav Bryukhovetsky**, *Kyiv-Mohyla Academy*
Prof. **Timothy Colton**, *Harvard University, Cambridge*
Prof. **Paul D'Anieri**, *University of Florida*
Dr. **Heike Dörrenbächer**, *Friedrich Naumann Foundation*
Dr. **John Dunlop**, *Hoover Institution, Stanford, California*
Dr. **Sabine Fischer**, *SWP, Berlin*
Dr. **Geir Flikke**, *NUPI, Oslo*
Prof. **David Galbreath**, *University of Aberdeen*
Prof. **Alexander Galkin**, *Russian Academy of Sciences*
Prof. **Frank Golczewski**, *University of Hamburg*
Dr. **Nikolas Gvosdev**, *Naval War College, Newport, RI*
Prof. **Mark von Hagen**, *Arizona State University*
Dr. **Guido Hausmann**, *University of Munich*
Prof. **Dale Herspring**, *Kansas State University*
Dr. **Stefani Hoffman**, *Hebrew University of Jerusalem*
Prof. **Mikhail Ilyin**, *MGIMO (U) MID RF, Moscow*
Prof. **Vladimir Kantor**, *Higher School of Economics*
Dr. **Ivan Katchanovski**, *University of Ottawa*
Prof. em. **Andrzej Korbonski**, *University of California*
Dr. **Iris Kempe**, *"Caucasus Analytical Digest"*
Prof. **Herbert Küpper**, *Institut für Ostrecht Regensburg*
Dr. **Rainer Lindner**, *CEEER, Berlin*
Dr. **Vladimir Malakhov**, *Russian Academy of Sciences*

Dr. **Luke March**, *University of Edinburgh*
Prof. **Michael McFaul**, *Stanford University, Palo Alto*
Prof. **Birgit Menzel**, *University of Mainz-Germersheim*
Prof. **Valery Mikhailenko**, *The Urals State University*
Prof. **Emil Pain**, *Higher School of Economics, Moscow*
Dr. **Oleg Podvintsev**, *Russian Academy of Sciences*
Prof. **Olga Popova**, *St. Petersburg State University*
Dr. **Alex Pravda**, *University of Oxford*
Dr. **Erik van Ree**, *University of Amsterdam*
Dr. **Joachim Rogall**, *Robert Bosch Foundation Stuttgart*
Prof. **Peter Rutland**, *Wesleyan University, Middletown*
Prof. **Marat Salikov**, *The Urals State Law Academy*
Dr. **Gwendolyn Sasse**, *University of Oxford*
Prof. **Jutta Scherrer**, *EHESS, Paris*
Prof. **Robert Service**, *University of Oxford*
Mr. **James Sherr**, *RIIA Chatham House London*
Dr. **Oxana Shevel**, *Tufts University, Medford*
Prof. **Eberhard Schneider**, *University of Siegen*
Prof. **Olexander Shnyrkov**, *Shevchenko University, Kyiv*
Prof. **Hans-Henning Schröder**, *SWP, Berlin*
Prof. **Yuri Shapoval**, *Ukrainian Academy of Sciences*
Prof. **Viktor Shnirelman**, *Russian Academy of Sciences*
Dr. **Lisa Sundstrom**, *University of British Columbia*
Dr. **Philip Walters**, *"Religion, State and Society", Oxford*
Prof. **Zenon Wasyliw**, *Ithaca College, New York State*
Dr. **Lucan Way**, *University of Toronto*
Dr. **Markus Wehner**, *"Frankfurter Allgemeine Zeitung"*
Dr. **Andrew Wilson**, *University College London*
Prof. **Jan Zielonka**, *University of Oxford*
Prof. **Andrei Zorin**, *University of Oxford*

* While the Editorial Committee and Advisory Board support the General Editor in the choice and improvement of manuscripts for publication, responsibility for remaining errors and misinterpretations in the series' volumes lies with the books' authors.

Soviet and Post-Soviet Politics and Society (SPPS)
ISSN 1614-3515

Founded in 2004 and refereed since 2007, SPPS makes available affordable English-, German-, and Russian-language studies on the history of the countries of the former Soviet bloc from the late Tsarist period to today. It publishes between 5 and 20 volumes per year and focuses on issues in transitions to and from democracy such as economic crisis, identity formation, civil society development, and constitutional reform in CEE and the NIS. SPPS also aims to highlight so far understudied themes in East European studies such as right-wing radicalism, religious life, higher education, or human rights protection. The authors and titles of all previously published volumes are listed at the end of this book. For a full description of the series and reviews of its books, see www.ibidem-verlag.de/red/spps.

Editorial correspondence & manuscripts should be sent to: Dr. Andreas Umland, Institute for Euro-Atlantic Cooperation, vul. Volodymyrska 42, off. 21, UA-01030 Kyiv, Ukraine

Business correspondence & review copy requests should be sent to: *ibidem* Press, Leuschnerstr. 40, 30457 Hannover, Germany; tel.: +49 511 2622200; fax: +49 511 2622201; spps@ibidem.eu.

Authors, reviewers, referees, and editors for (as well as all other persons sympathetic to) SPPS are invited to join its networks at www.facebook.com/group.php?gid=52638198614
www.linkedin.com/groups?about=&gid=103012
www.xing.com/net/spps-ibidem-verlag/

Recent Volumes

205 Ksenia Maksimovtsova
Language Conflicts in Contemporary Estonia, Latvia, and Ukraine
A Comparative Exploration of Discourses in Post-Soviet Russian-Language Digital Media
With a foreword by Ammon Cheskin
ISBN 978-3-8382-1282-1

206 Michal Vít
The EU's Impact on Identity Formation in East-Central Europe between 2004 and 2013
Perceptions of the Nation and Europe in Political Parties of the Czech Republic, Poland, and Slovakia
With a foreword by Andrea Pető
ISBN 978-3-8382-1275-3

207 Per A. Rudling
Tarnished Heroes
The Organization of Ukrainian Nationalists in the Memory Politics of Post-Soviet Ukraine
ISBN 978-3-8382-0999-9

208 Kaja Gadowska, Peter Solomon (Eds.)
Legal Change in Post-Communist States
Progress, Reversions, Explanations
ISBN 978-3-8382-1312-5

209 Paweł Kowal, Georges Mink, Iwona Reichardt (Eds.)
Three Revolutions: Mobilization and Change in Contemporary Ukraine I
Theoretical Aspects and Analyses on Religion, Memory, and Identity
ISBN 978-3-8382-1321-7

210 Paweł Kowal, Georges Mink, Adam Reichhardt, Iwona Reichardt (Eds.)
Three Revolutions: Mobilization and Change in Contemporary Ukraine II
An Oral History of the Revolution on Granite, Orange Revolution, and Revolution of Dignity
ISBN 978-3-8382-1323-1

211 Li Bennich-Björkman; Sergiy Kurbatov (Eds.)
When the Future Came
The Collapse of the USSR and the Emergence of National Memory in Post-Soviet History Textbooks
ISBN 978-3-8382-1335-4

212 Olga R. Gulina
Migration as a (Geo-)Political Challenge in the Post-Soviet Space
Border Regimes, Policy Choices, Visa Agendas
With a foreword by Nils Muižnieks
ISBN 978-3-8382-1338-5

Table of Contents

Sanna Turoma and Kaarina Aitamurto
Contesting Cultural and Religious Identities in Russia:
An Introduction 7

Boris Knorre
The Culture of War and Militarization within Political
Orthodoxy in the Post-Soviet Region 25

Mikhail Suslov
The Russian Orthodox Church in Search of the Cultural Canon 57

Irina Kotkina
We Will ROC You! 'Tannhäuser' Opera Scandal and the
Freedom of Artistic Expression in Putin's Russia 93

Susan Ikonen
The Reception of *Leviathan* in Light of Two Soviet "Cultural
Scandals": A Revival of Soviet Rhetoric and Values? 125

Andrey Makarychev
The War in Chechnya in Russian Cinematographic Representations. Biopolitical Patriotism in "Unsovereign" Times 153

Tomi Huttunen and Jussi Lassila
Zakhar Prilepin, the National Bolshevik Movement and
Catachrestic Politics 177

Elena Ostrovskaya
The Religious Identity of Modern Orthodox and Hasidic
Jewry in St. Petersburg 203

About the Contributors 227

Contesting Cultural and Religious Identities in Russia: An Introduction

Sanna Turoma and Kaarina Aitamurto
University of Helsinki

Keywords: identity politics, nationalism, patriotism, masculine identities, Russian Orthodox Church, religious communities, state cultural policies

This edited volume is a revised reprint of a 2016 special issue, which gathered a group of specialists to analyze recent developments in Russian politics of religion and culture for *Transcultural Studies: A Journal in Interdisciplinary Research*. Compiling the special issue took place in the immediate aftermath of the events, which shaped Russia's civil society in the first years of the 2010s: the protests during the 2011–2012 election cycle and the subsequent tightening of political control, the anti-Maiden frenzy, and the annexation of Crimea, followed by the intense anti-Westernism of the Kremlin rhetoric. All this underscored the "conservative turn", which many analysts observed as the major shift in Russian domestic and foreign policy with two watersheds: President Vladimir Putin's 2007 "Munich speech" and the nomination of Metropolitan Kirill (Gundiaev) of Smolensk as the head of the Russian Orthodox Church in 2009.[1]

These conservative developments and trends, however, are not unique to Russia. Only a year after the special issue was published, Donald Trump was inaugurated as the president of the United States, embodying what his opposition sees as a change toward an increasingly nationalist, isolationist, racist, and misogynist society. Incidentally, the common thread between Western and

---

1 See M. Suslov and D. Uzlaner "Dilemmas and Paradoxes of Contemporary Russian Conservatism: Introduction" in M. Suslov and D. Uzlaner (eds.), *Contemporary Russian Conservatism: Problems, Paradoxes and Dangers* (Leiden: Brill, forthcoming 2019).

Russian far-right movements has also drawn scholarly attention.[2] The rise of radical conservatism and rightist ideology has become an acknowledged and researched fact worldwide.[3] In various European countries, nationalist and ultraconservative parties have gained significant victories in recent elections. These parties share a common populist rhetoric, which juxtaposes the common, "good" people with impudent minorities claimed to threaten the majority by compromising their every-day sense of security as well as economic and cultural stability. This kind of populist rhetoric extolls the nation and idealizes the people, and imagines both as curiously homogeneous. The essentialist conceptualization of a national identity at the center of far-right political programs, puts the "protecting" of that identity from outside influences high on the agenda.

In Russia, these rightwing views have found their way into a legislative document, which incorporates cultural policies into a "national security strategy". This strategy, launched in 2009, has emerged as an overarching matrix of Russia's social and political reforms.[4]

The turn toward conservative values in Russia has been reinforced by introducing legislative initiatives on religion, sexuality, and culture, which politicize areas of life commonly perceived as private and expected to be free of state control. Writing as recently as 2017 in response to Misha Gabowitsch's research on non-(or anti-) governmental social networks, Alexander Etkind foresaw the "full shut-down of the Internet in Russian territory" as the only threat to this grassroots political activism; yet, the idea seemed like "an apocalyptic project... discussed in semi-official circles".[5] However, the

---

2 See M. Laruelle *Entangled Far Rights: A Russian-European Intellectual Romance in the Twentieth Century* (Pittsburgh: University of Pittsburgh Press, 2018).
3 J.F. Drolet and M. C. Williams, 'Radical conservatism and global order: international theory and the new right', *International Theory* 10(3), (2018).
4 'Strategiia natsional'noi bezopasnosti Rossiiskoi Federatsii do 2020 goda'. Kremlin.ru, 13 May 2009
http://www.kremlin.ru/supplement/424 (accessed 17 June 2019).
5 A. Etkind 'Genres and genders of protest in Russia's petrostate', in *Cultural Forms of Protest in Russia*, eds. B. Beumers, A. Etkind, O. Gurova, and S. Turoma (Farnham: Routledge, 2017), p. 9.

plan to restrict citizens' access to Internet services, more specifically to foreign service providers, took a step toward official realpolitik in May 2019. The Russian government's plan to establish an alternative domain name system in case Russia is cut off from the World Wide Web – either by its own initiative or by foreign forces – was backed up by a legislative act signed by President Putin.[6] The law, presented as a security strategy, will ensure the continuing governmental investment in planning and building an infrastructure for isolating *Runet* (Russian-language Internet) from the global web. Considered for a long time a platform for maintaining freedom of expression in Russia, digital and social media are now the targets of a new legislation, which gives the government potentially limitless means for controlling digitally mediated political opinion.

In 2013, the new law on "insulting religious feelings," was introduced. This law makes all criticism of the "traditional" religions or "traditional" religious institutions susceptible to criminalization and thus sets restrictions to freedom of speech. At the same time, it does not necessarily work to the advantage of the religious communities. It is seldom applied to protect minority religions and in the case of such bigger confessions as Orthodox Christianity or Islam, it may block critical discussion that is vital for their development. Further restrictions for criticism and expressions of dissent are set by the law that penalizes expressions that can be claimed to show "disrespect toward the authorities". This law, which came into force in 2019, effectively restricts political discussions, but also jeopardizes the accountability of the officials.

Cultural Policies as Conservative Identity Politics

The legislative text, which captures the ideational foundation of the current leadership's promotion of conservatism, and which, as such, deserves a more detailed analysis, is the presidential decree for a new cultural policy. Publicized as a draft in the spring of 2014 on the Russian Ministry of Culture website, the guidelines for "state

---

6   For the text in Russian, see http://publication.pravo.gov.ru/Document/View/0001201905010025 (accessed 5 June 2019).

cultural policies" caused a fierce debate among Russians involved in the cultural and intellectual production.[7] The fact that the document subjugated "family relations" to state policies received particularly harsh criticism from liberal Russians. Despite the debate, however, the document formed, with some revisions, the basis of a decree (*ukaz*) signed by President Vladimir Putin on Dec 24, 2014.[8]

The president's decree understands culture as a system of values and institutions, which produce and preserve these values. Moreover, Russia's culture is seen on a par with Russia's natural resources. This naturalized conceptualization delivers culture as a fundamental force for Russia's civilizational authenticity (*tsivilizatsionnaia samobytnost'*).[9] Culture is a foundation of a unified "mentality of the Russian people" (*mentalitet rossiiskogo naroda*), the production of which is the goal of Russia's cultural policy, as outlined by the decree. The document uses the term "Russian people" but not in the form familiar, for instance, from the 19th century sources, i.e. *russkii narod*. Instead, the document speaks of *rossiiskii narod*, expanding the symbolic field of national significations

---

[7] See, for instance, I. Kalinin 'Kul'turnaia politika kak instrument demodernizatsii', Neprikosnovennyi zapas 98(6) (2014): http://www.nlobooks.ru/node/5648 (accessed June 15, 2016); the writer D. Bykov 'Zelenye chelovechki rossiiskoi kul'tury', Novaia gazeta (9 April 2014) http://www.novayagazeta.ru/columns/63084.html (accessed 15 June 2016); on the response of the Institute of Philosophy at Russia's Academy of Science, R. Saakov, 'Filosofy protiv Medinskogo: novaia kul'turnaia politika', BBC Moscow (16 April 2014) http://www.bbc.com/russian/society/2014/04/140416_russia_new_culture_concept (accessed 15 June 2016); and an interview with Mikhail Shvydkoi, the special advisor to the President of the Russia Federation on International Cultural Relations on Ekho Moskvy, an independent radio station: Kseniia Larina and Vitalii Dymarskii, 'Kul'turnaia politika kak novaia ideologia?' Ekho Moskvy (2 May 2014) http://echo.msk.ru/programs/year2014/1310258-echo/ (accessed 15 June 2016).

[8] 'Osnovy Gosudartvennoi kul'turnoi politiki', http://static.kremlin.ru/media/events/files/41d526a877638a8730eb.pdf (accessed 15 June 2016).

[9] For the uses of "culture" in this naturalized sense in the political speech of Russia's leading politicians, see I. Kalinin, 'Carbon and Cultural Heritage: The Politics of History and the Economy of Rent' in 'Modernization and Russian Culture', Special Issue of *Baltic Worlds*, eds. S. Turoma and K. Lehtisaari, 2–3 (2014): 65–74. http://balticworlds.com/wp-content/uploads/2014/10/BW-2-3-2014-TEMA-uppslag.pdf (accessed 15 June 2016).

to relocate the Russian people in the realm of geopolitical identity building.

The "Guidelines" make great claims about the ability of culture to unify Russia's multinational citizens and instill a sense of Russian national pride in them across ethnic and religious boundaries. At the same time, echoing the 1960s Soviet concept of the Soviet people (*sovetskii narod*), the "Guidelines" emphasize the role of the Russian nationality as a cornerstone of this imagined community by identifying "the Russian language and the great Russian culture (*russkaia kul'tura*)" as a "unifying factor of the historical consciousness of the multinational Russian people (*rossiiskii narod*)".[10] For the "great Russian culture" the document uses the traditional *russkii* evoking *russkaia kul'tura* as an ethnocultural totality, whereas the people are, again, imagined as forming a transnational *rossiiskii* community.

The vacillation between *russkii* and *rossiiskii* in the "Guidelines" is symptomatic of the "ambiguous terminology," which Marlene Laruelle has recently recognized as the Russian leadership's strategy for avoiding "a definite stance on the national identity of Russia".[11] It supports those analysts who maintain that Vladimir

---

10　*Osnovy*, p. 2. On the concept of the "Soviet people", sovetskii narod, in the 1960s, see S. Turoma, 'Imperiia re/constructed narratives of space and nation in the 1960's Soviet culture,' in *Empire De/Centered: New Spatial Histories of Russia and the Soviet Union*, eds. S. Turoma and M. Waldstein (Farnham: Ashgate, 2013), 245 et seq; for more on the topic, see F. Hirsch, *Empire of Nations: Ethnographic Knowledge ad the Making of the Soviet Union* (Ithaca: Cornell University Press, 2005), pp. 316–318. On Benedict Anderson's influential concept "imagined community", see B. Anderson, *Imagined Communities: Reflections on the Origins and Spread of Nationalism* (London: Verso, 1991).

11　See Marlene Laruelle's recent deliberation on Russian nationalism in 'Russia as an anti- liberal European civilization', in *The New Russian Nationalism*, eds. P. Kolstø and H. Blakkisrud (Edinburgh: Edinburgh University Press, 2016), 276. Pål Kolstø, on the other hand, has interpreted the shift in Putin's speeches from the state-centered rossiiskii to the ethnocultural russkii as a change in his position toward ethnonationalism. The turning point, according to Kolstø, was the President's speech at the Russian Federal Assembly on March 18, 2014 after the annexation of the Crimea. See P. Kolstø, 'The ethnification of Russian nationalism', in *The New Russian Nationalism*, eds. P. Kolstø and H. Blakkisrud (Edinburgh: Edinburgh University Press, 2016), pp. 18–45, esp. pp. 18–19, pp. 38–39.

Putin has not made nationalism his main agenda, but who claim that his popular appeal draws on the promotion of conservative values, which aims at delegitimizing Russian liberals and nationalists alike. Meanwhile, the terminological ambivalence leaves room to invoke, and possibly, operationalize the construct of a value-based community of Russians beyond the Russian state borders, the Russian-speaking *russkii mir*—"Russian world"—without subscribing to the diverse ethnonationalist causes voiced by various intellectuals and/or radical mass movements.[12]

The agencies whose practices the "Guidelines" will direct include a wide range of administrative bodies, which govern a broad spectrum of Russian life including education, science, arts and cultural production, civil activities, community and youth services. It remains to be seen how the decree is implemented in the long run by Russian policy-makers at national or regional levels and how it will affect the work of administrative units, institutions, and state organizations. It is clear, however, that in addition to setting a framework for preserving, developing, and disseminating the value-based understanding of *russkaia kul'tura*—Russian culture—the Kremlin policies establish state patriotism as a foundation for Russia's cultural production, including the educational system. The policies offer tools for practicing conservative identity politics in the name of "traditional Russian values". The policies will most likely be reinforced by a federal law, as the Ministry of Culture has launched an initiative for introducing new legislation "On Culture", which, according to the Ministry's website, will draw on the 2014 decree.[13]

This kind of conservative identity politics promoted by the state leaves little room for the idea of intersectional categories such as gender or sexual orientation to be considered as a justifiable subject position in the making of the "mentality of the Russian people".

On the distinction of state-centered and ethnocultural nationalism, see, for instance, B. Rogers, *Citizenship and Nationhood in France and Germany* (Cambridge: Harvard University Press, 1992), pp. 98–101.
12   Laruelle 2016, p. 275
13   https://www.mkrf.ru/press/current/kontseptsiya_proekta_federalnogo_zakona_o_kulture/ (accessed 5 June 2019).

The Orthodox Christian religion, on the other hand, is granted a large space to maneuver within cultural policies. The guidelines acknowledge Islam, Buddhism, Judaism, and "other religions and faiths traditional for our Fatherland" as having an "impact on the formation of national and cultural self-understanding of the peoples in Russia". At the same time, however, the document highlights the primary role of Russian Orthodoxy (*pravoslavie*) in "the formation of the system of Russia's values".[14] In other words, it singles out the Russian Orthodox Church (ROC) as the leading institution among the religious communities in the country and establishes it as the main religious authority on the conservative value agenda.

Orthodoxy and Orthodox Culture Contested

The representatives of the Orthodox Church often use the concept of Symphony to describe the harmonious nature of the co-existence and cooperation between the Russian state and the Church. Historians generally agree that the close alliance of Imperial power and the Orthodox Church made the latter vulnerable in the early Bolshevik years, as the Church was associated with the oppression of the Czarist regime. In the later Soviet period, yielding to cooperation with the state became a survival strategy, which was manifest, for example, in the way the Church promoted Soviet interests in international arenas. Again, the cooperation was a disadvantage for the Church after the change of regime, and even today the ROC has not carried out a process of lustration as many of the Churches in ex-Socialist Europe have done. The late Patriarch Aleksi II aimed at keeping the Church independent of the state and separate from state politics. The new Patriach Kirill has adopted a more active role in the Church's relations with the Russian state.[15]

Since the end of the 2000s, the status and political influence of the ROC has become stronger in Russian society. This is usually

---

14 Osnovy, p. 2.
15 For this, see E. Namli, 'Pravoslavnoe bogoslovie i iskushenie vlast'iu', *Gosudarstvo, religiia, tserkov' v Rossii i za rubezhom* 32(3) (2014).

seen as a result of two developments: on the one hand, the political elite has expressed increasing keenness to affiliate itself with the Church; on the other hand, the Church has projected its authority more forcefully into the spheres of education, social services, military, and the penal system. However, there is a scholarly debate about the nature of the Church and state relations: how much does the ROC ultimately influence political decision-making, or is the state taking advantage of the increasingly close ties to achieve its own goals?[16] The Ukrainian crisis has definitely not been in the interests of the ROC, which has lost ground in the area.

At the same time, as Boris Knorre demonstrates in his article on the culture of war and militarization within political Orthodoxy, there are powerful actors in the ROC, who have not only actively supported but even promoted the war in Ukraine. As the contributions to this volume attest, there are diverse voices within the Orthodox Christian community and even inside the institution of the ROC. In his contribution Boris Knorre argues that those engaged with questions of militarized Orthodoxy do not represent the highest elite of the Church and have occasionally been rejected by the Church, as in the dismissal of the ultra-conservative Archpriest Vsevolod Chaplin. Yet, the militaristic interpretation of Orthodox Christianity and the mission of the Church are influential not only within the ROC, but also in Kremlin politics.

Surveys indicate that even though around 70% of the citizens identify themselves as Orthodox Christians, only a small minority of Russians go to church regularly, participate in religious services or consider religion to have a significant role in their life. According to a Levada Center survey, only 24% of Russians think that the Church should influence decision-making on the governmental

---

16   For this, see E. Namli, 'Pravoslavnoe bogoslovie i iskushenie vlast'iu', *Gosudarstvo, religiia, tserkov' v Rossii i za rubezhom* 32(3) (2014).

level.[17] In other words, there are those who consider themselves Orthodox Christians but do not identify with its official institutions or support the ROC's close ties with the Russian state.

In addition to the "cultural conflicts" between secularists and religious traditionalists, or the resistance to the clericalization of Russian society, several recent debates can also be seen as a struggle for the right to re-interpret and reinvigorate religious traditions. The (in)famous Pussy Riot trial is one such case. In the closing statement of the trial, Yekaterina Samutsevich stated that the aim of their performance was to suggest that "Orthodox culture belongs not only to the Russian Orthodox Church, the Patriarch and Putin, but that it may also side with civic rebellion and protest in Russia".[18] Nevertheless, judging by the response in Russian mainstream media, Samutsevich or Pussy Riot are not generally recognized as legitimate participants in the public negotiation of the essence of Orthodox Christianity.

In his contribution to this volume, Mikhail Suslov recognizes a conservative core within the Orthodox Christian community, since, as he argues, "the Church's supply of traditional values has met with increasing demand from a conservative majority from below, as well as from the conservative elite from above."[19] Suslov

---

17 'Religioznaia vera v Rossi', *Levada-tsentr* (26 September 2011) http://www.lev ada.ru/2011/09/26/religioznaya-vera-v-rossii/ (accessed 24 May 2016): 'Tserkov' i gosudarstvo', *Levadatsentr* (19 February 2016) http://www.levada.ru/2016/02/19/tserkov-i-gosudarstvo-2/ (accessed 24 May 2016).
18 "Yekaterina Samutsevich: Closing Statement at the Pussy Riot Trial", (8 August 2012) http://eng-pussy-riot.livejournal.com/6352.html (accessed 24 May 2016).
19 This is supported by Vyacheslav Karpov and Rachel L. Schroeder's recent assertion that the repressive reactions by the ROC and state in the Pussy Riot case, for instance, "were congruent with an intolerant public sentiment towards opponents of the ROC", in R. L. Schroeder and V. Karpov, 'The crimes and punishment of the "enemies of the Church" and the nature of Russia's desecularising regime', *Religion, State and Society* 41 (3) (2013). Meanwhile, Vyatcheslav Karpov and Elena Lisovskaya, for instance, argue that the current "desecularization" of Russian society is mainly operated "from above". V. Karpov and E. Lisovskaya, 'Orthodoxy, Islam, and the desecularization of Russia's state schools', *Politics and Religion* 3 (2) (2010). See also K. Aitamurto, 'Protected and controlled. Islam and "desecularisation from above" in Russia', *Europe-Asia*

analyzes Orthodox Christian cultural production, concluding that the Church has failed in its attempts to create cultural products with Orthodox content for the popular taste, and, thus, the ROC is in a position where it has "dominance without hegemony". Moreover, as Suslov demonstrates, within the ROC there are diverse views about the relationship between religion and culture and about understanding of what religious or "Orthodox culture" should entail.

Despite the dissonance within the ROC about an understanding of what "Orthodox culture" is or how it could be capitalized as a viable strategy to display and produce religious identity, the Church and Orthodox Christian activists often seem to agree on what Orthodox culture should **not** be. This becomes apparent in Irina Kotkina's and Susan Ikonen's contributions, which address conflicts triggered among Christian audiences by recent products of visual culture and performing arts. As these contributions manifest, the ROC and Orthodox activists have been successful in attempts to censor what they consider to be anti-religious cultural products. Analyzing the scandal around the production of Wagner's *Tannhäuser* in Novosibirsk in 2014 — this was Timofei Kuliabin's controversial production which made the national news and created an extensive media hype — Kotkina argues that the ROC was instrumental in causing a moral panic, which the state officials could use for censorious claims.[20] Discussing the reception of *Leviathan*, Andrei Zvyagintsev's award-winning 2014 film, Susan Ikonen claims that the Orthodox-minded activists, complaining about the "anti-Russian" or "anti-orthodox Christian" nature of the film, have a

---

Studies 68 (1) (2016): 182–202. Gulnaz Sharafutdinova uses the term "sovereign morality" to describe the discursive turn of the new "morality politics" in Russia and argues that the phenomenon is orchestrated by the Kremlin. G. Sharafutdinova, 'The Pussy Riot affair and Putin's démarche from sovereign democracy to sovereign morality', *Nationalities Papers* 42(4) (2014): 615–621.

20 Cf. fn. 12 with references to research that indicates that there are efforts to manipulate the Russians' religious sensibilities from above.

"growing self-assurance that their voice will be heard by the highest authorities". Both contributions point to the quintessential role of social media and digital communication in mobilizing patriotic and religious sensibilities in today's Russia.[21]

Patriotism and Masculine Identity Formations

Andrei Makarychev's as well as Tomi Huttunen and Jussi Lassila's contributions address questions of patriotism and nationalism, and the disputed line between the two. In political philosophy, definitions of patriotism often distinguish it from nationalism as an alternative ethos for "a stable, well-functioning polity."[22] Nationalism is seen as a political doctrine, which can mobilize masses and destabilize society, whereas patriotism is an unmobilized sentiment of loyalty and affection. Nationalism implies political agency, whereas patriotism renders citizens as objects. Readjusted to George Orwell's classic formula, nationalism is aggressive, patriotism is defensive. This, again, conjures another dichotomy typical of patriotic and nationalist discourse: it is always about us vs. them, our patriotism is their nationalism.[23] States can also mobilize patriotic sensibilities to utilize them for the needs of state-centered nationalism.[24]

Research on post-Soviet nationalism is a burgeoning field which privileges conceptualizations of state-centered and ethnocultural nationalisms. Both are crucial for understanding contemporary Russian society, as is what Rogers Brubaker has termed "homeland nationalism".[25] By this he means state-centered nationalism, which bases its claims on the idea of an ethnonational unity

---

21 For more on this, see *Digital Orthodoxy in the Post-Soviet World: The Russian Orthodox Church and Web 2.0*, ed. M. Suslov (Stuttgart: ibidem-Verlag, 2016).
22 See Stanford Encyclopedia of Philosophy, http://plato.stanford.edu/entries/patriotism/ (accessed 15 June 2016).
23 See M. Billig, *Banal Nationalism* (London: Sage Publications, 1995), pp. 55–59.
24 Pål Kostlø's recent analysis of Vladimir Putin's speeches points to the President's turn toward ethnonationalism from the earlier statist position. Cf. fn. 5.
25 R. Burbaker, *Nationalism Reframed: Nationhood and the National Question in the New Europe.* (Cambridge: Cambridge University Press, 1996), p. 5.

beyond the state borders. "Russian world" (*Russkii mir*) is an example of this.

In critical close-readings of popular films about the Chechen wars of 1994–1996 and 1999–2000, Andrei Makarychev shows how people in these films are represented in battlefields in conditions to which he adapts Giorgio Agamben's concept of "bare life" that is "a life without any mediating role of public institutions or legal mechanisms". To conceptualize the state's role in the patriotic production of culture, Makarychev makes the Foucaultian distinction between sovereign and bio-political power, with the former referring to territory and the latter to population. The Russian state has successfully capitalized on the "bio-political solidarity" between people in crisis, and this, according to Makarychev, forms the "core element of quasi-ideological constructs of patriotism, transformable to the vague and loosely articulated ideas of the 'Russian world' as a family-like organic community, or Russia's civilizational self-sufficiency."

Despite some female characters being present in the films Makarychev analyzes, the world in these war films is predominantly masculine. The same can be said about the materials Tomi Huttunen and Jussi Lassila analyze in their discussion of Zakhar Prilepin and the National Bolshevik movement. Coining the concept of "catachrestic politics", Huttunen and Lassila attempt to make sense of the paradoxes of the movement and its political practices and identifications, which blur the distinctions of established political activity. The authors' thesis is that the dislocated significations at the core of catachrestic politics had their roots in the 1990s social and political turmoil and stemmed from "Russia's weak socio-political institutions, which facilitate and sustain the space for the self-purposeful radicalism and non-conformism". Huttunen and Lassila's article, like Makarychev's, identifies the same crucial moment for the post-Soviet masculine identity formation.

Shunning the use of "nationalism" in his analysis of war films, Andrei Makarychev refers to the well-researched fact of Russia's historical oscillation between national/ist and imperial/ist politics and identity formation, expressed in the semantic difference of *russkii* and *rossiiskii*, as discussed above.²⁶ Instead, Makarychev prefers Serguie Oushakine's concept of "patriotism of despair," which Oushakine uses to describe the first post-Soviet generation and the sense of loss and abandonment felt acutely in identity formation and cultural practices of the time. It is this patriotic despair, i.e. the sense of affection in the absence of its object, which in addition to aphasia has engendered both nostalgia and radical nationalism in post-Soviet Russia. All these also contribute to the disjointed and volatile "catachrestic politics" and its masculine identification processes, described by Huttunen and Lassila in their discussion of Prilepin's literary and political activity.

Religious Minority Identities

In recent years, Russian authorities have tightened their religious policies, especially concerning minority religions. Religious publications form a majority in the list of banned literature while numerous religious organizations have been closed down on the basis of anti-extremist laws.²⁷ Such evaluative dichotomies as "traditional" and "non-traditional," or "official" and "non-official" are widely used by authorities to differentiate organizations seen to cooperate with the state from those that are regarded as potentially dangerous. Though suppressing grass-root religious activism seems to be

---

26 For the semantic differences of *russkii* and *rossiiskii*, see also S. Franklin and E. Widdis, "'All the Russias...?'" in *National Identity in Russian Culture*, eds. S. Franklin and E. Widdis (Cambridge: Cambridge University Press, 2004), p. 5, and Laruelle 2016, pp. 275–76. For discussions of Russian identity formations on the national vs. imperial axis, see R.G. Suny, 'The Empire Strikes Out: Imperial Russia, "National identity", and Theories of Empire', in *A State of Nations: Empire and Nation-Making in the Age of Lenin and Stalin,* Eds. R. G. Suny and T. Martin (Oxford: Oxford University Press, 2001), pp. 23–66; S. Turoma and M. Waldstein, 'Empire and Space: Russia and the Soviet Union in Focus', in *Empire De/Centered: New Spatial Histories of Russia and the Soviet Union*, eds. S. Turoma and M. Waldstein (Farnham: Ashgate, 2013), pp. 1–28.
27 M. A. Ledovskikh. (ed.) *Ostorozhno, ekstremizm! Analiz zakonodatel'stva o protivodeistvii ekstremistskoi deiatel'nosti i praktiki ego primereniia.* (Voronezh: Tsentr zashchity prav smi, 2013).

in line with the centralization of power and other processes that undermine the development of Russia's civil society, Geraldine Fagan argues that the oppressive religious politics is not necessarily coherently planned and managed from the top, but an outcome of the administrative culture and the legacies of the Soviet period.[28]

The changes in legislature as well as its implementation, and the repudiation of the rulings by the European Court of Human Rights, give evidence to the fact that in managing religious diversity, the Russian state has chosen the traditionalist idea of the "Russian world" over liberal governance.[29] However, this politics is inefficient, as Marat Shterin argues, since the anti-constitutional trends in religious policies and the tendency to see diversity as a social problem point to the weakness of the state's institutions rather than the strength of its centralized power. Thereby, Shterin draws attention to the role of different political and religious elite groups, which claim to have state authority, but whose actions may actually further erode state institutions.[30]

In the political elite's rhetoric, the role of religions is often positively emphasized as safeguarding societal morality. In 2012, the newspaper *Nezavisimaia gazeta* published an article by President Putin, titled 'Russia: The National Question,'[31] in which he wrote that "we are counting on an active involvement in the dialogue of Russia's traditional religions [in the formation of national policies]. The foundations of the Christian Orthodox Church, Islam, Buddhism, Judaism — with all of their differences and peculiarities — include basic shared moral, ethical, and spiritual values: compassion, reciprocity, truth, justice, respect for elders, family and work values." These attributes exclude many forms of religiosity and, more

---

28 G. Fagan. *Believing in Russia – Religious Policy after Communism* (London: Routledge, 2013).
29 M. Shterin 'Friends and Foes of the "Russian World": The Post-Soviet State's management of Religious Diversity', in *The Politics and Practice of Religious Diversity. National Contexts, Global Issues.* ed. A. Dawson. (Abingdon and New York: Routledge, 2016).
30 Ibid.
31 V. Putin. 'Rossiia: natsional'nyi vopros', *Nezavisimaia gazeta*, 23 January 2012. This article significantly guided the content of the 'The Concept of National Migration Policy until 2025'.

importantly, they advance an instrumental understanding of religion.

Nevertheless, this understanding of religion guides the way religious communities define their identities and strategize their activity. The restrictions imposed by the state's religious policies have numerous consequences for religious organizations. The tightened religious politics compels religions, especially minority religions vulnerable to oppressive measures, to emphasize their loyalty and patriotism. The display of patriotism by religious organizations, for example, may limit the multiplicity of voices within them, while it is used as leverage in negotiations with the state.

Despite the restrictions and the societal pressure for "traditional" forms of religiosity within centralized, hierarchic institutions, the religious life in post-Soviet Russia has been characterized by growing diversity. Elena Ostrovskaya's contribution about Orthodox Jewish and Lubavitch Hassidic communities in St. Petersburg demonstrate this persuasively. These communities have created their own way of life, culture and transnational complexity. The Lubavitchers limit their contacts with the surrounding society, but at the same time, the community is an example of a minority religion, which has been successful in renegotiating its relation with the state.

Despite the fact that Lubavitchers make up a mere five percent of the Russian Jewry, their Chief Rabbi has a high profile in Russian media and is often seen to represent the entire Jewish community at state events.[32] At these official events, the hierarchies and values in Russian religious policy are displayed and reinforced. The ROC, of course, features prominently in all these state events, which reinforces the Russian state's celebration of Russia's culture as a foundation of its civilizational distinctiveness, something the "Guidelines" also underline. The presence of a religious leader of an Orthodox Jewish community does not undermine these celebrations but supports the state leadership's conservative value agenda and the conservative identity politics promoted in the "Guidelines".

---

32   Shterin 2016.

Bibliography

Aitamurto, K., 'Protected and controlled: Islam and 'desecularisation from above' in Russia', *Europe-Asia Studies* 68(1) (2016): 182-202.

Anderson, B., *Imagined Communities: Reflections on the Origins and Spread of Nationalism* (London: Verso, 1991).

Billig, M., *Banal Nationalism* (London: Sage Publications, 1995).

Brubaker, R., *Citizenship and Nationhood in France and Germany* (Cambridge: Harvard University Press, 1992).

Burbaker, R., *Nationalism Reframed: Nationhood and the National Question in the New Europe* (Cambridge: Cambridge University Press, 1996).

Bykov, D., 'Zelenye chelovechki rossiiskoi kul'tury', Novaia gazeta, 9 April, 2014: http://www.novayagazeta.ru/columns/63084.html (accessed 15 June 2016).

Drolet, Jean-François and Williams, M.C., 'Radical conservatism and global order: international theory and the new right', *International Theory* 10(3), (2018): 285-313.

Etkind, A., 'Genres and genders of protest in Russia's petrostate', in *Cultural Forms of Protest in Russia*, eds. B.Beumers, A.Etkind. O.Gurova and S. Turoma (Farnham: Routledge, 2017), 1-15.

Fagan, G., *Believing in Russia – Religious Policy after Communism* (London: Routledge, 2013).

Franklin, S. and Widdis, E., 'All the Russias...?' in *National Identity in Russian Culture*, eds. S. Franklin and E. Widdis (Cambridge: Cambridge University Press, 2004), 1-8.

Hirsch, F., *Empire of Nations: Ethnographic Knowledge and the Making of the Soviet Union* (Ithaca: Cornell University Press, 2005).

Kalinin, I., 'Carbon and cultural heritage: the politics of history and the economy of rent', *Modernization and Russian Culture*, special issue for *Baltic Worlds*, eds. S. Turoma and K. Lehtisaari, 2-3 (2014): 65-74.

Kalinin, I., 'Kul'turnaia politika kak instrument demodernizatsii', *Neprikosnovennyi zapas* 98(6) (2014): http://www.nlobooks.ru/node/5648 (accessed 15 June 2016).

Karpov, V. and Lisovskaya, E., 'Orthodoxy, Islam, and the desecularization of Russia's state schools', *Politics and Religion* 3(2) (2010): 276-302.

Kolstø, P., 'The ethnification of Russian nationalism' in *The New Russian Nationalism*, eds. P. Kolstø and H. Blakkisrud (Edinburgh: Edinburgh University Press, 2016), 18-45.

Larina, K. and Dymarskii, V. 'Kul'turnaia politika kak novaia ideologia?' *Ekho Moskvy* (2 May 2014) http://echo.msk.ru/programs/year2014/1310258-echo/ (accessed 15 June 2016).

Laruelle, M. 'Russia as an anti-liberal Russian civilization' in *The New Russian Nationalism*, eds. P. Kolstø and H. Blakkisrud (Edinburgh: Edinburgh University Press, 2016), 275–294.

Laruelle, M., *Entangled Far Rights: A Russian-European Intellectual Romance in the Twentieth Century* (Pittsburgh: University of Pittsburgh Press, 2018).

Ledovskikh, M. A. (ed.). *Ostorozhno, ekstremizm! Analiz zakonodatel'stva o protivodeistvii ekstremistskoi deiatel'nosti i praktiki ego primereniia.* (Voronezh: Tsentr zashchity prav smi, 2013).

Namli, E. 'Pravoslavnoe bogoslovie i iskushenie vlast'iu', *Gosudarstvo, religiia, tserkov' v Rossii i za rubezhom* 32(3) (2014): 12–41.

Osnovy gosudarstvennoi kul'turnoi politiki (Guidelines for state cultural policies) http://static.kremlin.ru/media/events/files/41d526a877638a8730eb.pdf. (accessed 4 June 2019)

Papkova, I. 'The contemporary study of religion, society and politics in Russia: a scholar's reflections', *Religion, State and Society* 41(3) (2013): 244–53.

'Religioznaya vera v Rossi', Levada-tsentr (26 September 2011) http://www.levada.ru/2011/09/26/religioznaya-vera-v-rossii/ (accessed 24 May 2016).

Richters, K., *The Post-Soviet Russian Orthodox Church: Politics, Culture and Greater Russia* (London: Routledge, 2012).

Saakov, R. 'Filosofy protiv Medinskogo: novaia kul'turnaia politika', BBC Moscow (16 April 2014) http://www.bbc.com/russian/society/2014/04/140416_russia_new_culture_concept (accessed 15 June 2016).

Schroeder, R. L. and Karpov, V. 'The crimes and punishment of the 'enemies of the church' and the nature of Russia's desecularising regime', *Religion, State and Society* 41(3): 284–311.

Sharafutdinova, G. 'The Pussy Riot affair and Putin's démarche from sovereign democracy to sovereign morality', *Nationalities Papers* 42(4) (2014): 615–621.

Shterin, M. 'Friends and foes of the 'Russian world': the post-Soviet State's management of religious diversity'. In *The Politics and Practice of Religious Diversity. National Contexts, Global Issues*, ed. A. Dawson. (London and New York: Routledge, 2016), 29–48.

Simons, G. and Westerlund, D., (eds.) Religion, Politics and Nation-building in Post-communist Countries (Farnham: Ashgate, 2015).

'Strategiia natsional'noi bezopasnosti Rossiiskoi Federatsii do 2020 goda'. Kremlin.ru, 13 May 2009 http://www.kremlin.ru/supplement/424 (accessed 17 June 2019).

Suny, R.G. 'The empire strikes out: imperial Russia, 'national identity', and theories of empire' in *A State of Nations: Empire and Nation-Making in the Age of Lenin and Stalin*, eds. R. G. Suny and T. Martin (Oxford: Oxford University Press, 2001), 23–66.

Suslov, M. (ed.) *Digital Orthodoxy in the Post-Soviet World: The Russian Orthodox Church and Web 2.0*, (Stuttgart: ibidem Verlag, 2016).

'Tserkov' i gosudarstvo', Levada-tsentr, 19 February 2016 http://www.levada.ru/2016/02/19/tserkov-i-gosudarstvo-2/ (accessed 24 May 2016).

Turoma, S. 'Imperiia re-constructed narratives of space and nation in the 1960's Soviet culture', in *Empire De/Centered: New Spatial Histories of Russia and the Soviet Union*, eds. S. Turoma and M. Waldstein (Farnham: Ashgate, 2013), 245–269.

Turoma, S. and Waldstein, M. 'Empire and space: Russia and the Soviet Union in focus'. In *Empire De/Centered: New Spatial Histories of Russia and the Soviet Union*, eds. S. Turoma and M. Waldstein. (Franham: Ashgate, 2013).

'Yekaterina Samutsevich Closing Statement at the Pussy Riot Trial' http://eng-pussy-riot.livejournal.com/6352.html (accessed 24 May 2016).

The Culture of War and Militarization within Political Orthodoxy in the Post-Soviet Region[1]

Boris Knorre
National Research University Higher School of Economics, Moscow

This article is focused on "Political Orthodoxy" as an ideological trend and sociocultural phenomenon and its impact on militarization and the justification of war from a religious point of view. The author elaborates the idea of "Orthodox civilization" as propounded by Orthodox nationalist theoreticians striving to transform Orthodoxy into a "political religion"; he scrutinizes the development of eschatological ideologems and war apologia that have appeared alongside this process. He examines the models of mythological outlook connected with Political Orthodoxy as manifested throughout the last decade, in particular with reference to the Russia-Ukraine conflict. Through the lens of the latter, the author gives examples of the practical embodiment of religiously influenced militaristic discourse, showing some epiphenomena (side effects), in particular, hate, aggravation of the conflicts, separation into "friends" and so on.

Keywords: "Political Orthodoxy", "Orthodox civilization", political religion, nationalism, militarization, culture of war, values, "the sacred", conflict in Ukraine

Introduction

"Political Orthodoxy" has only recently been identified as a phenomenon in academic discourse. Accordingly, it has not yet been fully understood. At the same time, it demands close attention both in the context of the universal process of the politicization of religions generally, and in the context of the politicization and militarization of the ecclesiastical culture in Russia.

---

[1] This study was carried out within a grant of the European Community Mobility Programme Erasmus Mundus Action 2, Strand 1 (ema2) — aurora20121593. The article utilises results of research supported by "The National Research University Higher School of Economics Academic Fund Program", 2013–2014, Research Grant No. 12-01-0233.

Let us remind ourselves that the notion of Political Orthodoxy was first proposed at the beginning of this century by the researchers Alexander Verkhovsky and Anastasiia Mitrofanova, who made an attempt to analyze some forms of renovated Russian Orthodoxy as a kind of political religion. In his treatise *Political Orthodoxy: the Russian Orthodox Nationalists and Fundamentalists, 1995–2001* (Moscow, 2003), Alexander Verkhovsky focuses on identifying those politicized groups in Russia that can be called *"subjects of 'Political Orthodoxy'*,*"* and carries out a comparative analysis of their ideology. He analyzes the views of politically-Orthodox Christians on such positions as geopolitics, party-building, Church/state relations, conspiracy, apocalyptic expectations, the role of the Church in wider society and in the economy, as well as the concepts of sovereignty, ethical and religious identity, human rights, violence and war.[2]

In her book *The Politicization of the Orthodox World*, Anastasiia Mitrofanova gives a picture of social groups in Russia that claim to comprise a social core for the remaking of state laws in accordance with Orthodox moral principles.[3] Mitrofanova also analyzes different Orthodox groups and communities in different countries with regard to their influence in these countries in order to build an argument for conceptualizing the notion of an "Orthodox world" or even "Orthodox civilization" in Samuel Huntington's sense. As is well known, Huntington used this concept in his book *The Clash of Civilizations and the Remaking of World Order*, together with concepts such as "Western", "Confucian", "Japanese", "Muslim", and

---

2 See A. Verkhovsky, *Politicheskoe pravoslavie: Russkie pravoslavnye natsionalisty i fundamentalisty, 1995–2001* [Political Orthodoxy: the Russian Orthodox nationalists and fundamentalists, 1995–2001] (Moscow: Tsentr "Sova", 2003). Verkhovsky has also published a brief version of his monograph, putting his most important conclusions into the article *"Politicheskoe pravoslavie v rossiiskoi publichnoi politike. Podiem antisekuliarnogo natsionalizma"* [Political Orthodoxy in Russian public policy. The rise of anti-secular nationalism], in *Sova-center*, (21 May 2005) http://www.sova-center.ru/religion/publications/2005/05/d4678 (accessed 25 January 2016.)
3 A. Mitrofanova, *Politizatsiia "pravoslavnogo mira"* [Politicization of the Orthodox world]. (Moscow: Nauka, 2004).

"Hindu" civilizations.[4] While scrutinizing political processes related to Orthodoxy, Mitrofanova tries to find similar phenomena in the Islamic world in order to create an analogy with the politicization of the Orthodox world. While reflecting on the essence of Political Orthodoxy, she notes the difference between two groups of scholars. The first group consists of those who are inclined to see the political motivation in political religions as a foundational factor (Tibi, Haynes, Ignatenko, Mirskii, etc.); the second group consists of those scholars who stress religious motivation as a foundation for political religions (Jeurgensmeier, Hussain, Malashenko). In conclusion Mitrofanova offers her own definition of political religion in order to clarify the phenomenon of "Political Orthodoxy" as she sees it. According to her, "political religion is a special form of religion, which justifies political action or is a special form of ideology which motivates political action through appeal to otherworldly forces."[5]

About 15 years have passed since Verkhovsky and Mitrofanova published their extensive and informative monographs. Although further analytical papers focusing on the issue of Orthodoxy and politics appeared subsequently, over the last 15 years there have been no similar works claiming to analyze Political Orthodoxy as a consistent phenomenon. However, Jardar Østbø's monograph *The New Third Rome* (Columbia University Press, 2016) may be considered as an example of a study that continued this line of investigation.

Nevertheless, the development of Political Orthodoxy in Russia and the Post-Soviet space did not stop. Within this framework, a worrying militaristic trend appeared as a feature of political processes, in Russia and in some other parts of the Post-Soviet space. Society faced a phenomenon that can be characterized as a "culture of war", accompanied by attempts to rehabilitate violence and dictatorship from a religious (pro-Orthodox) point of view. It is therefore not by chance that the politicization of Orthodoxy attracts the attention of theologians: it was the subject of critical analysis at the

---

4   See S. Huntington, *The Clash of Civilizations and the Remaking of World Order* (New York: Simon & Schuster, 1996).
5   Mitrofanova, *Politizatsiia "pravoslavnogo mira"*, pp. 19–20.

international theological conference "Political Orthodoxy and Totalitarianism", held in Helsinki in May, 2015.

The main aim of this article is to analyze the forms of militaristic discourse and war apologia that appeared in the rhetoric of ROC priests and lay believers alongside the politicization of Orthodoxy in Russia over the years 2005–2015. My aim is also to develop further the concept of Political Orthodoxy with regard to its militaristic manifestations. This presupposes several tasks.

- To outline the development of the militaristic discourse at different levels of the Church's society, in particular at the level of pro-Orthodox intellectual politicians, the level of ordinary clergy and Church laymen.

- To clarify the position of the senior Church leadership in regard to militaristic discourse.

- To analyze examples of the practical embodiment of the militaristic ideas offered by the political Orthodox representatives. Since the most representative and relevant contemporary case was the Ukraine crisis of 2014–2015, the author pays special attention to it.

- To evaluate the role of the religious background and religious argumentation in the escalation of militarism, aggression, hate, opposition, separation into "friends" and "foes", as well as to examine the models of a mythological outlook that can be found in the phenomenon of Political Orthodoxy as manifested throughout the last decade, in particular with reference to the Russia-Ukraine conflict.

- Finally, the author aims to clarify the notion of Political Orthodoxy with regard to all its militaristic manifestations. This is done by asking what can one say today about Russian Orthodoxy from the viewpoint of *political religion* as a concept? What kind of role can it play in society today? What happened to the Political Orthodoxy groups, which took part in the "Novorossiia" campaign, after 2015?

The Political Position of Senior Church Leadership and Ideas about Changing the Constitution of the Russian Federation

It is worth stating that in the 1990s and early 21st century, the Church establishment did not encourage the activity of Political Orthodox groups. One exception, however, was the Orthodox nationalist metropolitan Ioann (Snychev). Although he died in 1995, he influenced many successors who continued to disseminate his ideas. Verkhovsky notes that Snychev used to be a figure whose ideas triggered appreciable political movements based on the mix of "ethnic-nationalism, Russian imperialism, Orthodox monarchy, Church anti-modernism and anti-ecumenism."[6] However, after 2004 the situation changed. The novelty of this period was bound up with the fact that Metropolitan Kirill (today Patriarch), head of the Department for External Church Relations (DECR) of the Moscow Patriarchate—without ever explicitly using the term Political Orthodoxy—started to loudly proclaim the so-called doctrine of "Orthodox civilization," a Huntington-like term which made way for the later use of Political Orthodoxy. In January 2004, the themes of "Orthodox world" and "Orthodox civilization" formed the basis for the VIII World Russian People's Council (WRPC)[7] that took place at that time. Metropolitan Kirill, when speaking at the Council on the topic "Russia and the Orthodox world", stated:

> The social and political body of the Orthodox world consists of the states of the Orthodox tradition, of the formation of cultures on which Orthodoxy had a decisive influence. These are Bulgaria, Belarus, Greece, Cyprus, Moldova, the Republic of Macedonia, Russia, Romania, Serbia and Montenegro,

---

6   Verkhovsky, 2005; See also Verkhovsky 2003, pp. 21–22.
7   WRPC—an international non-governmental organization, established in May 1993, under the auspices of the Russian Orthodox Church and at the initiative of the then chairman of the Department for External Church Relations of the Moscow Patriarchate, Metropolitan Kirill (Gundyaev) (the current Patriarch). The purpose of WRPC was to consolidate people of Russian culture in Russia and CIS countries, as well in the wider Russian diaspora. WRPC set itself the task of disseminating the Orthodox world outlook in society. For more details, see A. Krasikov, "*Pravoslavie i globalizatsiia*" [Orthodoxy and Globalization], in *Religiia i globalizatsiia na prostorakh Evrazii* [Religion and Globalization across Eurasia]. A. Malashenko and S. Filatov, eds., (Moscow: ROSSPAeN, 2009).

Ukraine ... They are diasporas of Orthodox peoples, as a rule, living in the countries of the Western tradition and the nations who make up religious minorities in the countries of residence, but are stable culturally and ethnically, and correlated with the Orthodox civilization.[8]

The doctrine of "Orthodox civilization" was consistently developed at the highest levels of the Church.[9] The most active ideologist in the actual development of the idea of "Orthodox civilization" from the mid-2000s was the then member of the DECR of the Moscow Patriarchate, Archpriest Vsevolod Chaplin, who was one of the leading and long-term official speaker of the Russian Orthodox Church. In 2006, in the magazine *Political class* (*Politicheskii klass*), he published an article on the "Five tenets of Orthodox civilization", in

---

8 Doklad predsedatelia Otdela vneshnikh tserkovnykh sviazei Moskovskogo Patriarkhata mitropolita Kirilla na VIII Vsemirnom russkom narodnom sobore "Rossiia i pravoslavnyi mir" [Report of the Chairman of the Department for External Church Relations of the Moscow Patriarchate Metropolitan Kirill at the VIII World Russian People's Council, "Russia and the Orthodox world"], Russian Orthodox Church. Archive of the official website of the Moscow Patriarchate 1997–2009. (Moscow, 2004). https://mospat.ru/archive/page/church-and- society/ 30419.html. (accessed 10 December 2015).

9 Let us say a few words about the connection of the concepts "Orthodox Civilization" and "Russkii mir" [Russian World] (sometimes called "Russian Civilization"), which is popular in contemporary Russian political discourse. These notions are very close to each other, they are intertwined and often interchangeable, because they are used to designate belonging to a certain set of values, peculiar to Orthodoxy and Russia in general. Nevertheless, it is necessary to distinguish them. "Russkii mir" appears to be more formally constructed and to have more utilitarian aspects than Orthodox Civilization. According to Kirill, "Russkii Mir" aims to unite and consolidate the people of Russian culture living in CIS, migrants and successors of migrants in the diaspora, while "Orthodox Civilisation" aims to unite pro-Orthodox states, different ethnic or confessional communities, which can extend far beyond the territories of the former USSR and those not inevitably speaking Russian. See: *Doklad predsedatelia Otdela vneshnikh tserkovnykh sviazei* ... (2004) https://mospat.ru/archive/page/churc h-and-society/30419.html (accessed 5 June 2019)
When speaking about "Russkii mir", Church officials place it in the context of "Orthodox Civilization", calling it a "global project of Orthodox civilization". "'Russkii mir' as a global project of Orthodox civilization acts as its representative, the defender and guardian of its values." See E. Moiseev, *Kontseptsiia russkogo mira kak tsivilizatsionnyi proekt XXI veka* [The concept of the Russian world as a civilizational project of the XXI century], *Kurskaia pravoslavnaia dukhovnaia seminariia* [Kursk Orthodox Seminary] (2015), http://kursk pds.ru/articles/ kontseptsiya-russkogo-mira-kak-tsivilizatsionnyy-proekt-khkhi-veka/ (accessed 29 September 2016).

which he spoke out against secularism and the religious neutrality of the state, and expressed the need for society and the government to realize their "religious mission," which had "higher meaning, extending beyond a generation, state, nation and even earthly life." Chaplin also associated this "higher meaning" with the willingness for self-sacrifice (though not necessarily the sacrifice of the *self*). He stated that "the sacrifice of your own (and in terms of defending the faith and the Fatherland *even somebody else's*) *life*, self-restraint, renunciation of your rights, freedom, wealth for the good of thy neighbor, for the sake of the community and your people is the norm of behavior of an Orthodox Christian" (emphasis added).[10]

The leitmotif of the ideas of "Orthodox civilization" expressed by Chaplin was the assertion of priority of the "otherworldly", "eternal life" over "earthly life"; this led to the logical conclusion that one should not prioritize the task of preserving this "life on earth". Thus, for example, during a public debate in early 2007 on the attitude of the Church towards nuclear weapons, Chaplin made the following statement: "For many believers, the eternal life of the soul is far more important than the temporary and to lose it as a result of the enslavement to other faiths or atheists *is much worse than to die in a nuclear war.*" (emphasis added).[11]

Later the same year during another dialogue he said, "for me, there are things that are more important than the destruction of any particular number of people, or even the life of all mankind ...These are sanctities and faith. Human life is less important to me." (emphasis added).[12]

---

10 V. Chaplin, *'Piat' postulatov pravoslavnoi tsivilizatsii'* [Five tenets of Orthodox civilization], *Politicheskii klass* [Political class], 12 December (2006), pp. 16–29.
11 V. Chaplin, *'Istok konflikta – ne v iadernom oruzhii, no v grekhe vlastoliubiia'* [The source of the conflict is not in nuclear weapons, but in the sin of striving for power], in *Index bezopasnosti 81* [Security index] 1 (13) (2007), p. 203.
12 *'Nereligioznyj evrei protiv pravoslavnogo protoiereia. Protoierei Vsevolod Chaplin protiv politika Leonida Gozmana'* [An irreligious Jew against an Orthodox archpriest. Archpriest Vsevolod Chaplin against politician Leonid Gozman] *Portal-Credo.Ru* (8 June 2007), http://www.portal-credo.ru/site/?act=news&id=54730 (accessed 19 September 2015).

It should be noted that such statements about the acceptability of the "sacrifice of someone else's life," or "destruction of any particular number of people" were not just loose statements from Chaplin's mouth, but the declaration of his willingness to change the actual wording of the Russian Constitution. The specific issue concerns the first section of the constitution's chapter "Fundamentals of the constitutional system of the Russian Federation," which states that "A man, his rights and freedoms are a supreme value." However, in the interpretation of the exponents of "Orthodox civilization", the highest declared value is "the Orthodox faith, shrines and Fatherland" over and above the individual.[13] Chaplin stated: "The law can be based on different values. For someone, the most important is the man, and on this basis he is building his law. For another person, sanctities, or the territory of the state or the country are more important, and on this basis he would build his social system."[14] Let there be no doubt that the desire to change basic Russian law — the Constitution of the Russian Federation — was a distinctive and integral goal of the adherents of Political Orthodoxy.

New Orthodox Intellectuals, the Discourse of War and Militaristic Dominance

With respect to further development of Political Orthodoxy among ordinary priests and Church laymen after January 2004, the process was certainly encouraged by the declaration of the doctrine of "Orthodox civilization" at the official level of the Church establishment. The increased intertwining of politics and religion started to be more openly associated with the Church authorities, even

---

13 K. Khamidullina, *'Chelovecheskaia zhizn' radi territorial'noi tselostnosti!'* [Human life for the sake of territorial integrity!] Portal-Credo.Ru (14 June 2007), http://www.portal-credo.ru/site/index.php?act=fresh&id=623 (accessed 18 September 2015).
14 Ibid.

though the latter did not use the term Political Orthodoxy. For example, with Kirill's approval, the brotherhood "Radonezh"[15] and DECR organized a discussion of Orthodoxy and human rights, from the viewpoint of the doctrine of "Orthodox civilization."[16]

Additionally, a new phase of development of Political Orthodoxy was also connected with the above-mentioned publications by Verkhovsky and Mitrofanova, which Political Orthodoxy activists did not fail to notice. Some groups, identified by researchers as "subjects of Political Orthodoxy", were quick to disavow any such identification, stating that their position is nothing other than Church conservatism, and opposed using the political methods of the modern world. The Church establishment, and even Kirill, in spite of his involvement in politics, also preferred not to be identified with Political Orthodoxy, and even on some occasions explicitly rejected it.

However, by contrast, a large set of groups of Orthodox nationalists expressed a desire to try the title Political Orthodoxy — as defined by the researchers — as an ideological self-description. Among them was the Union of Orthodox Citizens (UOC), a social political association of Orthodox imperial nationalists, whom Verkhovsky called a core organization of Political Orthodoxy activists, closest to the Church.[17]

A new development of Political Orthodoxy was manifested through one additional category of Orthodox nationalists — intellectuals who identified with Political Orthodoxy. The prominent Or-

---

15 See A. Verkhovsky, E. Mikhailovskaia and V. Pribylovsky, *"Politicheskaia ksenofobiia. Radikal'nye gruppy. Predstavleniia politikov. Rol' Tserkvi* [Political xenophobia. Radical groups. Views of politicians. The Role of the Church] (Moscow: Panorama, 1999), p. 33.

16 *"'Radonezh' organizoval diskussiiu o pravoslavii i pravakh cheloveka,"* [Radonezh organized a discussion on Orthodoxy and human rights], in *Sova-center.Ru* (13 July 2004), http://www.sova-center.ru/religion/discussions/society/2004/07/d2499/ (accessed 24 January 2016).

17 While being organized in 1997, the UOC stated its main task as "to be an active assistant to every bearer of the Orthodox outlook, involved in politics, exercising the state power." See: Verkhovsky, Mikhailovskaia, Pribylovsky, p, 33; Verkhovsky, 2005.

thodoxy-focused publicists and political thinkers, Egor Kholmogorov, Boris Mezhuyev, Dmitry Volodikhin, as well as the Institute of National Strategy and Agency of Political News, headed at that time by Stanislav Belkovsky and Mikhail Remizov, formed a team who constructed an apologia for Political Orthodoxy. Thanks to their efforts, a special issue of *Strategic Magazine* (*Strategicheskii zhurnal*), titled "Political Orthodoxy" was prepared.[18] The contributors volunteered to work out the concept of Political Orthodoxy systematically, so as to use it as a national, neo-imperial project. They launched a discussion on the national sovereignty of the state, the formation of national consciousness, and the explanation of national values within the context of sacral historical reference points, such as, for example, the dichotomy of the ancient Russian traditions of Josephitism (*iosiflyanstvo*) and Non-possessors (*nestiazhateli*). Some articles appealed to the idea of Lev Gumilev's passionary impulse,[19] promoting ideas of conservative revolution, and offered anti-globalist opinions.

---

18   See *Politicheskoe pravoslvie: strategicheskii zhurnal* [Political Orthodoxy: strategic magazine], 2 (Moscow: Institute of National Strategy, Political News Agency, 2006).
19   See D. Volodikhin, *"Novyi narod"* [The new nation] *Politicheskoe pravoslvie: strategicheskii zhurnal* [Political Orthodoxy: strategic magazine], 2 (Moscow: Institute of National Strategy, Political News Agency, 2006), pp. 39–50. The idea of passionary impulse has been formulated by the Soviet historian-ethnologist Lev Gumilev within his invented passionary theory of ethnogenesis, by which the scholar tried to explain stages and regularities of the historical process. A key notion of his theory—"passionarity"—was defined by Gumilev as "an internal aspiration to action which was stronger than any rational reason of human beings, and which could not be thrown away" (see: *'Ia ne byl odinok'. Interv'iu L'va Gumileva "Leningradskoi pravde"* ['I was not alone'. Interview of Lev Gumilev to "Leningradskaia Pravda"], *Leningradskaia Pravda* (30 December 1990), Retrieved from: http://baznica.info/article/lev-gumilev-ya-ne-byl-odinok/ (accessed 29 September 2016); the concept also entailed a special activity, which was expressed as the aspiration towards a dominant goal and the ability to supertension and sacrifice for the sake of achieving that goal, including the sacrifice of one's own life (see: L. N. Gumilev, *Drevniaia Rus' i Velikaia step'* [Ancient Rus and the Great Steppe] (Moscow: Mysl', 1989), V. N. Demin, *Lev Gumilev* (Moscow: Molodaia Gvrdiia, 2007)). From a biological point of view, the "passionary impulse" is stipulated by micromutations, leading to an increase in the number of "passionaries" — individuals able to make superhuman efforts, the overvoltage. From a socio-historical point of view, the passionary

One should note that the contributors to the issue expressed different approaches to influencing society. In particular, Deacon Andrei Kuraev and Orthodox publicists Vladimir Golyshev and Viktor Militarev, tackled the problem of reorienting the cultural strategy and social position of Russian Orthodoxy in favor of its wider socialization, that is, in favor of broadening the social field of impact or influence of the Russian Orthodox Church.[20] It should be mentioned that since the mid-2000s, Russia has witnessed a fairly consistent discussion of the question of whether the Church should reach beyond the framework of a narrow subculture, which prevents its wider influence on Russian society. This discussion has addressed the creation of a wide network of Orthodox educational establishments at various levels, the deployment of a social ministry ("*sotsial'noe sluzhenie*", "*diakonia*") plus charity and parish philanthropy — leading as a whole to a greater openness of parishes to different forms of social activity.

However, the other side of the policy of Political Orthodoxy gained the upper hand, that is, its militaristic-apocalyptical discourse, as expressed in the articles written by Dmitry Volodikhin,

---

impulse reveals itself in an unprecedented intensification of socio-political activity, including the period of state-building, the rise of economic activity, conquering territories, setting up the national statehood, making breakthroughs in science, technology and art. See Gumilev, 1989; M. Wojnar, 'The west and the great steppe in the history of Rus and Russia', *Studies into the History of Russia and Central-Eastern Europe*. XVII (2012), pp. 5–30.
Gumilev's theory of ethnogenesis appeared to be very attractive for many pro-imperial Orthodox believers in the post-Soviet period, particularly because Gumilev declared a Russian super-ethnos (i.e. a base, sufficient for the formation of civilization), and also determined that this super-ethnos was 500 years younger than the European one, and therefore more promising. Many Orthodox intellectuals liked the concept of "passionarity", which they started to interpret it their own way and to attribute it to Orthodox people as an inherent virtue, which should provide a revival of Orthodoxy and national rise of Russia. In his article "*Novyi narod*" [The New nation], Dmitry Volodihin suggested the hypothesis that Russia had gone through the new passionary impetus in the period of 1945–1980, with the result that the new nation was born, having thus acquired a new great future. Volodokhin 2006, pp. 44–45. See also M. Bassin, *The Gumilev Mystique: Biopolitics, Eurasianism, and the Construction of Community in Modern Russia*, (Ithaca, NY: Cornell UNIVERSITY PRESS, 2016.
20 See *Politicheskoe pravoslvie: strategicheskii zhurnal* [Political Orthodoxy: strategic magazine], 2 (Moscow: Institute of National Strategy, Political News Agency, 2006).

Kirill Frolov, Vadim Tsimbursky and, especially, Egor Kholmogorov who made the most appreciable contribution to developing these trends. Among the authors of that issue, Kholmogorov showed himself to be the most ardent and consistent apologist for Political Orthodoxy, while offering the most conceptual, comprehensive description of the phenomenon, formulating its tasks and mission.

Kholmogorov depicts an Orthodox civilization through the lens of geopolitics. He argues for the role that Political Orthodoxy should play in the clash of civilizations. However, he shows that the said clash should not only have an ordinary religious dimension, but even an apocalyptic one, in which the Orthodox civilization and Russia serve as a *"Kathechon"* ("Keeper"), "one who restrains now" and lawlessness at the End Time (2 Thes. 2:7).[21] Accordingly, he considers the End Time to have actually already come. This idea is expressed in the title of his article—"End Time Religions" (*Religii poslednego vremeni*),[22] in which he gives his most complete conceptual vision of Political Orthodoxy. Thus Kholmogorov writes that "human activities aimed at reaching the Kingdom of Heaven" need a "military cover", and as a *Kathechon*, Russia has to restrain iniquity by all means necessary, including military ones.[23] He states that Orthodoxy at the End Time will inevitably become a political religion in order to serve as a "battle flag for the people who would like to take part in the ultimate battle."[24] Thus Political Orthodoxy should be an "army of the Apocalypse," as he dramatically states.[25] Kholmogorov uses images such as the "Third Rome" and "Holy Rus'", which are connected with the "heavenly army" through the host of Russian angels and saints.[26]

It is clear that, according to Kholmogorov, the participation of the Orthodox Civilization in the clash of civilizations is both an

---

21 E. Kholmogorov, *"Religii poslednego vremeni"* [End Time Religions] *Politicheskoe pravoslvie: strategicheskii zhurnal* [Political Orthodoxy: strategic magazine], 2 (Moscow: Institute of National Strategy, Political News Agency, 2006), p. 68.
22 Ibid., pp. 51–72.
23 Ibid., p. 68.
24 Ibid., p. 70.
25 Ibid., p. 59.
26 Ibid., pp. 68–69.

earthly conflict as well as a projection of some "Heavenly battle", a "Cosmic war." This could serve as an example of the concept of "cosmic" or "sacred" war, presented by anthropologist Mark Juergensmeyer, who considers that earthly wars can be interpreted through the lens of religious conscience as part of more global stand-offs that takes place beyond the "earthly", the "visible world".[27]

Kholmogorov adds a further nuance to the sacred-militaristic rhetoric: this is that the main *"religious task of the End Time"* is *"a joint breakthrough to Heavens"*, *"a breakthrough to the transcendental"* of all individuals who are ready to put "the divine" ahead of "the worldly."[28] Strange as it sounds, such wording is an imitation of special ops military jargon, particular to special ops troops. So Kholmogorov's "theology of war" is in some way a "special ops theology" (*teologiia spetsnaza*) that can also be used by Political Orthodoxy.

In the context of his militaristic and apocalyptic approach, Kholmogorov pays special attention to the justification of atomic weapons: he even manages to construct a bizarre doctrine of "Atomic Orthodoxy", which justifies using a nuclear weapon as a means of protecting "Orthodox civilization."[29] At this point he comes close to Vsevolod Chaplin's ideas of "nuclear apocalypse".[30]

The militaristic and apocalyptic ideas, expressed by Kholmogorov and Chaplin, received a second wind in the pre-election times of autumn 2011, which marked a new cycle of Russian political history. They found a new, passionate advocate in priest Ioann Okhlobystin (at the time he was taken off the Church staff by his own choice, but that did not damage his authority in the Church's

---

27 M. Juergensmeyer, 'Sacrifice and cosmic war, violence and the sacred in the modern world' in: *Violence and the Sacred in the Modern World*, ed. M. Juergensmeyer, (London: Frank Cass & Co., 1992), p. 112.
28 *Politicheskoe pravoslvie: strategicheskii zhurnal*, 2006, p. 51–72.
29 E. Kholmogorov, '*Atomnoe pravoslavie*' [Atomic Orthodoxy], in *Russkii obozrevatel*' [Russian Observer] (31 August 2008), http://www.rus-obr.ru/idea/594 (accessed 4 March 2014).
30 On "nuclear apocalypse", see a recent monograph by Dmitry Adamsky, *Russian Nuclear Orthodoxy. Religion, Politics and Strategy* (Palo Alto, CA: Stanford University Press, 2019).

circles sympathizing with Political Orthodoxy). In the autumn of 2011, Okhlobystin declared a run for the presidency and presented widely his ideologically-strategic doctrine named "Doctrine_77", noting that he saw his support in the electorate firstly among military men.[31]

According to Okhlobystin, the Russian people have two calls: to organized prayer in the church and to battlefield combat. He argues that these two activities share a similar charisma and puts a special emphasis on the latter, even using the phrase "We are created for war" as a chapter title.[32] Okhlobystin openly admits that he was inspired by Kholmogorov's ideas. This inspiration seems to be expressed in the approval of the phenomenon of "Atomic Orthodoxy."[33] Okhlobystin showed himself more radical on this point; he anticipated even more unambiguously than Kholmogorov and Chaplin the possibility of perishing in a global nuclear holocaust in order to prevent ideals hostile to "Orthodox civilization" from prevailing. He states:

> Then we will have no other way out but to destroy the whole world rotten through with its vices and indifference and to commit suicide in the hope that the human individuals managing to escape by some miracle will form the basis of a new, better mankind. Only so will we be forgiven by God.[34]

The 2014 Ukrainian Crisis and the Militaristic Role of Political Orthodoxy

A new chapter of Political Orthodoxy was reached during the Ukrainian crisis of 2014, when a political upheaval took place at the end of February as a result of the Kiev confrontation between Euromaidan protesters and the authorities of Victor Yanukovych.

---

31 *'Doctrina-77 Ivana Okhlobystina'* [Doctrine-77 by Ivan Okhlobystin] *Pravmir.Ru* (13 September 2011), http://www.pravmir.ru/doktrina-77-ivana-oxlobystina-polnyj-tekst/ (Accessed 11 December 2015).
32 See ibid.
33 Kholmogorov, 2008.
34 *"Doctrina-77 Ivana Okhlobystina."*

The authority of the Russian Orthodox Church of the Moscow Patriarchate, of course, did not sympathize with Maidan, but nevertheless abstained from pointed statements. Moreover, several days after the overthrow of Yanukovych, Kirill, the Patriarch of Moscow and All Russia, said that "the Church does not take any sides in the political battle" and that "the children of our Church are still people of different political visions and convictions, including those who today stand on opposite sides of the barricades."[35] As Mikhail Suslov notes, Patriarch Kirill did not support militaristic methods of solving the Ukrainian crisis. It would, after all, lead to the crumbling of his own vision of *"Holy Rus"*, a project which cannot be realized by violent methods.[36]

Nevertheless, the attitude of some apologists for Political Orthodoxy turned out to be different. In January, that is, before the overthrow of Yanukovych, the Archpriest Vsevolod Chaplin urged Russia to intervene in Ukraine, and not only Russia but also the countries of the Russian-speaking world.[37] During the confrontation between Euromaidan and the Yanukovych administration, Archpriest Chaplin coordinated and encouraged the groups of Orthodox activists, such as the Union of Orthodox Citizens, Association of Orthodox Experts and many other Orthodox nationalist associations, who served as an engine of Political Orthodoxy.

---

35 *"Obrashenie Sviateishego Patriarkha Moskovskogo i vseia Rusi Kirilla k mestobliustiteiyu Kievskoi mitropolichiei kafedry mitropolitu Chernovitskomu i Bukovinskomu Onufriiu, arkhipastyriam, pastyriam i vsem vernym chadam Ukrainskoi Pravoslavnoi Tserkvi v sviazi s situatsiei na Ukraine,"* [Appeal of the Patriarch of Moscow and All Russia Kirill to the Deputy to the Locum Tenens of the Metropolitan Diocese of Kiev Metropolitan Onufrii of Chernivtsi and Bukovina, archpastors, pastors and all faithful children of the Ukrainian Orthodox Church with respect to the situation in Ukraine] *Patriarchia.Ru* (2 March 2014) http://www.patriarchia.ru/db/text/3588256.html (accessed 18 December 2015).
36 M. Suslov. *"The Russian Orthodox Church and the crisis in Ukraine,"* in *Churches in the Ukrainian Crisis.* A. Krawchuk and T. Brener. eds. (Basingstone: Palgrave Macmillan, 2016), pp. 139–141.
37 *"Rossiia dolzhna vmeshat'sia v dela Ukrainy i spasti ee, schitaiut v Russkoi tserkvi,"* [Russia must intervene in the Ukrainian affairs and save it—this is what the Russian Church believes] *Interfax-religion* (28 January 2014) http://www.interfax-religion.ru/?act=news&div=54273 (accessed 19 December 2015).

At the end of February these groups were visible. They started to actively agitate for the coercive intervention of Russia into Ukrainian affairs. A press-secretary of the Union of Orthodox Citizens, Kirill Frolov, commented upon any small event connected with Maidan, by urging ecclesiastical people, priests and monks to resort to force in order to confront Euromaidan. *"Monks will die for the faith — monks will tear anyone to pieces for the faith,"*[38] — said Kirill Frolov with much conviction, urging the Orthodox Church members to support the "thugs" (*titushki*) and those who have the strength — to become *titushki*. This is despite the diametrically opposite position taken by the Ukrainian Orthodox Church of the Moscow Patriarchate in Kiev. An employee of the Information Department of the Ukrainian Orthodox Church of the Moscow Patriarchate, Archpriest Georgii Kovalenko, begged: "Dear Russian people, if you have at least a bit of love for us, Ukrainian people, please stop calling us "fascists", "*Banderovtsi*", "Nazis" and "nationalists" even in private conversations! These words kill! Remember the words of the Savior "*But I say unto you, That whosoever is angry with his brother without a cause shall be in danger of the judgment: and whosoever shall say to his brother, Raca, shall be in danger of the council: but whosoever shall say, Thou fool, shall be in danger of hell fire* (Matthew 5, 22)!"[39]

However, the Orthodox political organizations on the Russian side had an absolutely different point of view and ignored the requests of their brothers in faith. For example, Viktor Aksiuchits, a

---

38 "*Pochaevskaia lavra ne sdaetsia. Monakhi umrut za veru. Monakhi 'porvut' za veru*" [Pochayiv Lavra does not capitulate. Monks will die for the faith. Monks will 'tear anyone to pieces' for the faith], 20 February 2014 in *Blog in LiveJournal of Kirill Frolov* (accessed 20 February 2014).

39 "*Glava press-sluzhby UPTS MP prizval rossiian ne nazyvat' ukraintsev 'fashistami', 'banderovtsami', 'natsistami' i 'natsionalistami',*" [Head of The Press-Service of the Ukrainian Orthodox Church of Moscow Patriarchate Archpriest Georgii Kovalenko requested Russians to stop calling Ukrainian people "fascists", "Banderivtsi", "Nazis" and "nationalists"] *PortalCredo.Ru* (24 February 2014) http://www.portal-credo.ru/site/?act=news&id=106355 (accessed 25 February 2014).

CULTURE OF WAR AND MILITARIZATION   41

member of the Political Council of the Rodina party,[40] started to send petitions to the President of the Russian Federation, aimed at using the political situation to expropriate the historical Russian areas from Ukraine. One of the most common petitions was: *"Recognition of independence of the South-Eastern provinces of Ukraine and start of the process of their joining to the Russian Federation."*[41]

To show that such a strategy, made explicit in this petition, was not a chance occurrence, we can quote an earlier, confidential statement made in the late 1990s by the Orthodox historian Vladimir Makhnach, an activist of The Union of Orthodox Citizens (until his death in 2009). During a lecture in the Russian Orthodox University named after St. John the Theologian, he stated that:

> Ukraine is an artificial state, absolutely artificial, tragically separated from Russia. Very serious efforts will be necessary to return these Orthodox lands, belonging to us. Now we cannot quarrel with the West, and then when a Russian ruler comes to power, it will be necessary to quarrel with the West, and efforts will be necessary to divide this artificial state, it will be necessary to somehow pit the Galicians against the Russians, the Ukrainians against the Carpathian Rosses, etc.[42]

Incidentally, in his lecture Makhnach used the term "Novorossia" with reference to the territories adjoining and forming a part of South-Eastern Ukraine. Makhnach's opinion cannot be considered marginal within Political Orthodoxy, since he was an active worker of the Union of Orthodox Citizens. However, one rarely encounters this opinion outside of Political Orthodoxy. This position dovetails with the attitude towards Ukraine that has been characteristic of a considerable number of Orthodox believers who belonged to Orthodox-motivated political circles throughout the 1990s and 2000s, but has not been typical of non-politicized Orthodox believers.

---

40 After Autumn 2011, the Rodina party was reborn in a new incarnation. The party presents itself as officially secular, but according to its views it is related to the "left-wing" supporters of Political Orthodoxy.

41 The petitions were published at http://www.avaaz.org/ru/petition/ (accessed 25, February 2015), but at the moment they are not accessible.

42 U. Makhnach, *'Bor'ba za pravoslavie'* [Struggle for Orthodoxy], in *Predanie.Ru* (audiolectures). http://staroe.predanie.ru/audio/lekcii/mahnach/#istoriya-rossii (accessed 20 December 2015).

It is therefore not far-fetched to suggest that leaders of Political Orthodoxy groups played a role as the ideologists of the "Russian Spring", the term that Kholmogorov used to draw an analogy between the "Arab Spring" of 2010 and the pro-Russian protest actions in Ukraine, and later to refer to the protests in the South-Eastern Ukraine. [43] Kholmogorov gave practical recommendations, pointing to actual cities in the South-Eastern Ukraine where he hoped for rebellion against new, pro-Maidan Ukrainian authorities in the event that Russia would dare to intervene.

It is noteworthy that political-Orthodox ideologists of the alleged "Russian Spring" hoped to solve the situation in Ukraine in a more radical way than the Russian authorities sought to do. Beside archpriest Vsevolod Chaplin, some other priests sympathetic to Political Orthodoxy also lent their voices in favor of Russia's intervention in Ukraine. For example, Hegumen Luka (Stepanov) described the political change in Kiev in February 2014 as "a real threat of spiritual desecration of the lands which had been consecrated by the Orthodox Church." To prevent this desecration, military means are suitable — declared the priest.[44]

"The Russian Orthodox Army" in South-Eastern Ukraine

Let us now turn to the "metaphysical paradigm" presented in 2014 by I.V. Girkin (I.I. Strelkov), ex-Defense Minister of the Donetsk People's Republic (DPR). He frankly admitted to the following:

> From the very beginning of our "Slavic epic", in Sloviansk as well as in Donetsk, we have always felt the support of the clergy and the monks of the Russian Orthodox Church. First and foremost from the Sviatogorskaia Lavra. Despite possible repression, they openly came and blessed the militia ...

---

43 E. Kholmogorov, '*Russkaia Vesna*' [Russian Spring], in *Svobodnaia Pressa* [Free Press] (24 February 2014), http://svpressa.ru/politic/article/82769/ (accessed 21 December 2015).

44 L. Stepanov. '*Aeto ne bor'ba za zemli, a aeto bor'ba za Pravoslavie*' [It is not a fighting for lands, but for Orthodoxy], *Russkaia Narodnaia Linia* [Russian Popular Line] (10 March 2014), http://ruskline.ru/news_rl/2014/03/10/eto_ne_borba_za_zemli_a_eto_borba_za_pra voslavie/ (accessed 12 March 2014).

> Not many people know that the Sviatogorskaia Lavra closed its gates for president Poroshenko, who came there the day after his election and wanted the blessing of the Lavra priests. Lavra simply refused to let him onto its premises, and Poroshenko had to give an interview standing in front of the closed gates of the monastery.[45]

The majority of the militia started to think of themselves as warriors fighting under the banner of Orthodoxy. Among the generalizing self-designations of the troops were names such as "The Russian Orthodox Army", with different contextual variations like "The Orthodox Army of Novorossia," "The Orthodox army of Donetsk," and "The Orthodox Army of the South-Eastern Ukraine". There was also the appearance of specific songs, such as an unofficial military anthem of DPR, called "Donetsk Militia—Russian Orthodox" (song), with the following lyrics:

> He who stands with you till the very end, glorious and victorious,
> We'll never leave our own behind! The Russian Orthodox (Army)!
> For every fighter till the very end, glorious and victorious,
> On the battlefield—the Russian Orthodox![46]

Additionally, among the Novorossia militia, a veneration of the special version of The Tikhvin Icon of the Mother of God, taken from the Tikhvin monastery in Leningradskaya region, took place. The Icon has been called *"Opolchennaia"* (Military Icon). It was a genuinely popular initiative from the military people to bring it to Donetsk for veneration. However, it was against the will of the local Bishop—the Metropolitan of Donetsk and Mariupol, Hilarion (Shukalo), who would not give his blessing to the local clergy to

---

45 *"'Chelovek ne mozhet zhit' bez very,'—Igor' Strelkov rasskazal Russkoi Vesne o ego religioznykh ubezhdeniiakh"*, ['A man can't live without faith'—Igor Strelkov told 'The Russian Spring' about his religious convictions] *Russkaia vesna* [Russian Spring] (17 December 2014), http://rusvesna.su/news/1418820639 (accessed 16 February 2015).

46 *"Gimn dnr 'Russkaia praoslavnaia'"* [A hymn of Donetsk Popular Republic 'The Russian Orthodox'] *LiveJournal blog of Egor Kholmogorov* (2 December 2014), http://holmogor.livejournal.com/6694040.html (accessed 5 December 2014).

greet the icon and ordered that it not be brought into the Holy-Transfiguration Cathedral, the main Cathedral in Donetsk.[47]

The Novorossiia militaristic movement, while being influenced by some ideas of Political Orthodoxy, showed other bizarre forms of militaristic religiosity. For example, Alexander Kostin, commander of "The Battalion of the Blessed Virgin Mary of August, named after St. Alexander Nevsky" stated, that his mission was "the war for Holy Rus'".[48]

The concept of "Holy Rus'" in the context of the Novorossia movement became contextualized and deeply politicized and "Holy Rus'" was quickly embedded in the military-political context of the latest history of the Donbas. Seeing this war for Novorossiia as a battle for "Holy Rus'" was very much in accordance with the conceptions of Kholmogorov.

There were some Russian church centers who gave their support for the battle in the South-Eastern Ukraine. These included the Saint Michael Athos Hermitage of Zakubansk in the Republic of Adygea and the Holy Monastery of the Bogoliubov — a famous fundamentalist convent, headed by the Superior, Archimandrite Peter (Kucher), influential in the ecclesiastical milieu, not only of Russia but also of Ukraine. The Bogoliubov monastery even gave spiritual support to some of the Novorossia militia. During his rule of the militia in the Donetsk People's Republic, Igor' Strelkov (Girkin) was advised by Igor' Druz' and Margarita Zeidler, both spiritual "offsprings" of Archimandrite Peter (Kucher).[49]

To comprehend the situation it is necessary to point out that the Patriarch and authorities of the Russian Orthodox Church, in

---

47 *"V sobor Donetska ne pustili opolchentsev so starinnoi ikonoi, prinesennoi iz Rossii,"* [The militiamen were not allowed to bring an old icon from Russia into the Cathedral of Donetsk] *Interfax-religion* (30 September 2014), http://www.interfax-religion.ru/?act=news&div=56599 (accessed 23 January 2016).

48 *"My voiuem za Sviatuiu Rus"* [We are fighting for Holy Russia] *Russkaia Narodnaia Liniia* [Russian Popular Line] (6 November 2014), http://ruskline.ru/anali tika/2014/11/07/my_voyuem_za_svyatuyu_rus/ (accessed 10 November 2014).

49 K. Frolov, *'Tema Novorossii — faktor konsolidatsii pravoslavnykh patriotov'*, [The agenda of Novorossiia — a factor of consolidation of Orthodox patriots] *LiveJournal blog of Kirill Frolov* (15 December 2014), http://kirillfrolov.livejour nal.com/3381655.html (accessed 22 December 2015).

spite of their sympathies for the doctrine of "Russkii Mir" (Russian World), held a more moderate strategy for solving the conflict in Ukraine. Obviously there was an attitude that forbade any criticism of the Donetsk and Lugansk militia. For example, Nikolai Savchenko, a priest from the Church of Holy Transfiguration in Saint Petersburg who stood up for the Ukrainians, was dismissed from his parish and relocated to another one, more distant from the city center.[50] However, at the beginning of 2015, the Church authorities began to punish those clergymen who expressed their militaristic opinions more radically. At the end of the year, Patriarch Kirill dismissed the official speaker of ROC Moscow Patriarchate, the Archpriest Vsevolod Chaplin, from the post of Chairman of the Synodic Department for Church and Society Relations, because of Chaplin's radical stance on the situation in the Donbas.[51]

Consequences for the activists of "Russian Spring" and Donbas's fighters

The Ukrainian crisis and the militaristic methods of solving it had consequences not only for people in Donetsk and Lugansk areas but in all Ukraine. The Greek Catholic Church has also played a role in the militarization and politicization of religious life in Ukraine. For example, in the Church of Our Lady of Perpetual Help of the Ukrainian Greek Catholic Church (UGCC) in Lviv, a fresco depicting the Last Judgment was painted, featuring President Putin and Patriarch Kirill, the images of militiamen and "quilted jackets" (name given to the local residents of Donetsk and Lugansk regions, who supported the separatist resistance in Ukraine).[52] Another

---

50 *'Voina za mir v Peterburgskom khrame'*, [A war for peace in Saint-Petersburg church] *Fontanka* (27 May 2014) http://www.fontanka.ru/2014/05/27/039/ (accessed 6 June 2014).
51 *'Protoierei Chaplin ob"iasnil svoe uvol'nenie raznoglasiiami po Donbassu'*, [Archpriest Chaplin explained that his dismissal was caused by disagreements concerning Donbass] *rbk-daily* (24 December 2015) http://www.rbc.ru/politics/24/12/2015/567c3a6f9a79470e8c24b01b (accessed 25, December 2015).
52 *'Na stenakh l'vovskogo khrama poyavilis' izobrazheniya s voinami ATO i boyevikami "DNR"'* [The images of the ATO soldiers and the militants of the Donetsk People's Republic appeared on the walls of a church in Lviv], *Zerkalo Nedeli* (8 April 2015) https://zn.ua/CULTURE/na-stenah-lvovskogo-hrama-poyavilis-izobrazheniya-s-voinami-ato-i-boevikami-dnr-172346_.html (accessed 15 April 2019).

church of the UGCC, located in Chervonograd, Lviv region, depicted Vladimir Putin as a sinner in hell.[53] The process of politicization is also evident in the Ukrainian Orthodox Church of the Kiev Patriarchate led by Filaret (Denisenko), whose views may be regarded as a Ukrainian version of Political Orthodoxy.[54]

In 2018, when Ukraine's acquisition of its own Autocephalous Orthodox Church became an issue, some Ukrainian analysts, without denying its political significance, began to speak for "political Orthodoxy" as an inevitable development. For example, the Ukrainian journalist Ekaterina Shchetkina wrote that the politicization of Orthodoxy had taken place not only in Russia but also in Ukraine, stating that "this should not embarrass anyone." [55]

After the signing of the Minsk II Agreement in 2015, a breakup began to occur between the proponents of separatist sentiments in the Donbas. Moreover, there were disagreements on the strategies and the understanding of the situation among the participants of the combat action in Donbas. A rather weighty part of the ideologists and leaders of the "Russian Spring" in Donbas did not adopt the Kremlin position and condemned the signing of the Minsk II Agreement. Proponents of a military solution to the conflict constituted a prominent and conspicuously conservative revanchist force in opposition to the Kremlin. They started accusing the Russian government of cowardice, further insisting on the need to resume hostilities and to fight for the toppling of Poroshenko's regime. The leaders of this movement were the aforementioned Igor Girkin (Strelkov), Maxim Kalashnikov, Egor Prosvirnin, Konstantin Krylov, who played a key role in the creation of the public move-

---

53 '*Strashniy Sud: Putina uvideli goryashim v adu*'. [Last Judgment: Putin was seen burning in hell], *Politeka* (18 April 2017) https://politeka.net/news/428819-strashnyj-sud-putina-uvideli-goryashhim-v-adu-foto/ (accessed 15 April 2019).

54 In December 2018, it was integrated into the newly established Orthodox Church in Ukraine, to which official Tomos (a document, granting autocephaly) was granted by Ecumenical Patriarch Bartholomew.

55 E. Shetkina, "*Politicheskoie pravoslavie – prokliatie ili neizbezhnost'?*" [Political Orthodoxy — curse or inevitability?], in *RISU* (7 November 2018). https://risu.org.ua/ru/index/expert_thought/authors_columns/kshchotkina_column/73376/ (accessed 17 April 2019).

ment "Novorossiya" and the "Committee of January 25". Eventually, Strelkov set up the political organization "All-Russian National Movement under the leadership of Igor Strelkov" fully tailored "to his needs" in order to seize power from the current political regime.[56] It meant that Strelkov definitely opted for a role of an independent player in Russian politics, and can now be considered a leader of the so called "war party".

It should be noted that interpreting the conflict in a religious framework was characteristic for this group. Igor Strelkov, Maxim Kalashnikov, Igor Druz, and Egor Kholmogorov emphasized the religious apocalyptical background of the war, conceptualizing the war in the Donbas in eschatological millenarian terms as "the war for Holy Russia". Therefore, it is not so much religiosity in itself that is important, as the tendency towards eschatological and apocalyptical thinking.

Unlike these "hawks", as they were called in Russian media, other leaders of the "Russian Spring" refrained from interpreting the Donbas in an eschatological, mystical or conspiratorial framework. These individuals were able to reassess their political goals and strategies closer to the Kremlin's line, which, after 2015, had stakes on political, not military solutions. This group argues that the territory of Novorossia should not be separated from Ukraine and annexed to Russia but given a special status within Ukraine. The idea of this group is the following: Russia should have an opportunity to influence Ukraine politically and culturally through the Donbas, and to hinder the westernization of Ukraine and its accession to NATO. The writer Nikolai Starikov expressed this idea quite clearly during a dispute with Igor Strelkov.[57]

The organizations that abandoned the role of an independent player in Russian politics include the Union of Donbas Volunteers,

---

56 '*Ustav Vserossiiskogo Natsional'nogo dvizheniia pod rukovodstvom Igoria Strekova*', [Charter of All-Russian National Movement under the leadership of Igor Strelkov]. *Dvizheniye "Novorossiya" Igorya Strelkova*. (10 October 2016). http://novorossia.pro/25yanvarya/2522-29-sentyabrya-2016-ustav-prinyat.html (accessed 10 April 2019).
57 'I.Strelkov vs N.Starikov. "Tsentrsily/Silatsentra".' *YuoTube* (22 January 2015). https://www.youtube.com/watch?v=G04tXnvKx8Y (accessed 20 April 2019).

formed by field commanders who returned to Russia after participating in the combat actions led by Alexander Boroday. This organization declared as its task the social support for combatants in the region (representing the interests of war veterans in Ukraine, their social rehabilitation and material assistance), excluding any possibility for its members to make political statements and criticize the leadership of the self-proclaimed DPR and Luhansk People's Republic.[58] It is interesting that Konstantin Malofeev — an "Orthodox oligarch", one of the sponsors of the "Russian Spring" — refused the ideology of war and a military solution to the conflict. The latter organized "Tsargrad", a conservative TV-channel intended for an audience with an Orthodox-national slant, and in April 2019, he was appointed Chairman of the World Russian National Council, where the then Metropolitan Kirill (Gundyaev) presented in 2004 the doctrine of "Orthodox civilization" and his vision of the Russian World. As a postscript we can say that the persons who did not rely on the apocalyptical millenarian view in the interpretation of the Donbas war demonstrated a better negotiating capacity.

Conclusion

To summarize the above analysis, it should be restated that the main aim of the article was to analyze the forms of militaristic discourse and apologia of war that appeared alongside the development of Political Orthodoxy in Russia.

While analyzing this process, the author has tried to scrutinize the arguments of Political Orthodox activists who justify war from a religious point of view. These were arguments given by pro-Orthodox intellectual politicians, by the ordinary clergy and Church lay believers. When militaristic discourse made its appearance during the political crisis in Ukraine, the author focused more attention on the views of the clergy and Orthodox laymen who most arduously supported military methods for resolving the situation. The

---

58 Vendik Yuriy. "The Union of Donbas's volunteers" has been created in Moscow, Russian Service BBC (10 October 2015). https://www.bbc.com/russian/russia/2015/10/151010_donbass_volunteers_congress_moscow (accessed 20 April 2019).

political position of high ranked churchmen has also been analyzed.

After considering these groups' arguments and statements, it is reasonable to conclude:

1. A popularization of militaristic views within Post-Soviet Russian Orthodoxy in 2011 - 2015 seems not only the result of the political situation, but also of an earlier ongoing theoretical apologia of war, offered by Orthodox intellectuals and publically known priests. The consistency of argumentation does give us grounds to make an inference about the formation of a specific *"culture of war"* as one evident trend in Political Orthodoxy. It seems that this culture of war is a stable, self-standing tradition with its own peculiar theology, religious commitment, and a specific conservative spirituality that is protective of the military. With regard to the culture of war and using Huntington's concept of a "clash of civilizations", we can justifiably define Post-Soviet Political Orthodoxy as an ideological movement within Russian Orthodoxy that aims at promoting a religiously oriented homogeneous civilizational system through military-political means. Political Orthodoxy plays the role of a movement that legitimizes militaristic discourse, dictatorship, and actual practices of violence.[59]

2. As for the issue of the balance between politics and religion within Political Orthodoxy, we must admit that there are no grounds to deny the genuine religious nature and religious background of this movement. We are dealing here with a specific form of religion, and in part with a belief and sociocultural paradigm bound up with Orthodoxy. We have observed that it is the religious consideration that allows Orthodox zealots to demonize their opponents and regard war with them as "more than a mere war." Militaristic

---

59 For more details concerning the more wide-ranging problem of violence in Russian Orthodoxy, see A. Zygmont, 'The Problematics of Violence in Post-Soviet Russian Orthodox Discourse,' *State, Religion and Church*, 2 (2) (2014), pp. 29-53.

discourse in the interpretation of the "Novorossia campaign" and the new ideology of "Holy Rus'" confirms Juergensmeyer's description of "cosmic war," calling it one of the central images of the religious imagination, which also includes the idea of sacrifice. The discourse of war in contemporary Political Orthodoxy reflects a fairly clear picture of the struggle between the "sacred order" and its meaningfulness and the profane chaos and its meaninglessness: it is a projection of "cosmic war" on earth.[60] The image of the enemy is thus a projection of the "cosmic enemy" who enters this world, while religious identity is expressed as an identification of "us" with the sacred, and "the other one" (the enemy) with "the profane."[61] The opponent is demonized and vilified to the point where reconciliation is almost impossible. This "cosmic" dimension elevates the conflict beyond the level of human, political and rational solutions.

3. To a certain extent, Political Orthodoxy is an element of civil religion, as defined by Robert N. Bella and applied by Cyril Hovorun to Orthodoxy. It is indeed possible to agree with Hovorun's assertion that Political Orthodoxy "works like glue that through the Orthodox symbols and traditional values keeps together the irreligious people".[62] However, while taking into account the hopes of Chaplin and other Political Orthodox activists to change the state constitution, it is impossible to agree with Hovorun's assertion that such a version of civil religion secures legitimacy for regimes. In this case, we see that Political Orthodoxy cannot gain legitimacy for the current regime, but only for one that fits the system of values proper to an idealized "Orthodox civilization".

---

60 M. Juergensmeyer, *Terror in the mind of God: the global rise of religious violence* (California: University of California Press, 2003), p. 149.
61 See for more details Zygmont, 2014.
62 C. Hovorun. 'Political orthodoxy: an ideology? a civil religion? a heresy?' in *the International Conference on Political Orthodoxy and Totalitarianism in Post-Communist Era'* (Helsinki, 2015). The paper is available in *Academia.edu* https://www.academia.edu/12662544/Political_Orthodoxy_an_Ideology_a_Civil_Religion_a_Heresy (accessed 15 September 2015).

4. The concentration on the political means of dissemination of religion and its impact on society, described here as the trend in Russian Orthodoxy, can lead to a serious change in the culture of Orthodoxy, and the displacement of its ethical-behavioral and world outlook preferences. Thus while based on some Christian ethical norms in the first instance, Political Orthodoxy evidently will need to transform its original religious ethics and work out a new one, which legitimizes violence, a militaristic worldview and war as a positive value. Political Orthodoxy has a chance to be transformed into the new version of religion which crucially differs from standard notions of Christianity. Thus in the event of the social success of Political Orthodoxy, it will lead to an existence not only in circumstances of violence, but of consistent dictatorship.

Bibliography

Adamsky, D., *Russian Nuclear Orthodoxy. Religion, Politics and Strategy* (Palo Alto: Stanford University Press, 2019).

Bassin, M., *The Gumilev Mystique: Biopolitics, Eurasianism, and the Construction of Community in Modern Russia* (New York: Cornell University Press, 2016).

Chaplin, V., '*Istok konflikta – ne v iadernom oruzhii, no v grekhe vlastoliubiia*' [The source of the conflict – lies not in the nuclear weapon, but in the sin of ambition], *Index bezopasnosti* (Security index) 81 (1), v.13 (2007): 203-204.

Chaplin, V., '*Piat' postulatov pravoslavnoi tsivilizatsi*' [Five tenets of Orthodox civilization], *Politicheskii klass* (Political class) 12. (December 2006): 16-29.

'"*Chelovek ne mozhet zhit' bez very,*" – *Igor' Strelkov rasskazal Russkoi Vesne o ego religioznykh ubezhdeniiakh*' ['A man can't live without faith' – Igor Strelkov told 'The Russian Spring' about his religious convictions], *Russkaia vesna* (Russian Spring) (17, December 2014), http://rusvesna.su/news/1418820639 (accessed 16 February 2015).

Demin, V.N., *Lev Gumilev* (Moscow: Molodaia Gvardiia, 2007).

'Doklad predsedatelia Otdela vneshnikh tserkovnykh sviazey Moskovskogo Patriarkhata mitropolita Kirilla na viii Vsemirnom russkom narodnom sobore "Rossiia i pravoslavnii mir"' [Report of the Chairman of the Department for External Church Relations of the

Moscow Patriarchate Metropolitan Kirill at the viii World Russian People's Council, "Russia and the Orthodox world"], Russian Orthodox Church. Archive of the official website of the Moscow Patriarchate 1997–2009. (Moscow, 2004). https://mospat.ru/archive/page/church-and-society/30419.html (accessed 10 December 2015).

'*Doctrina-77 Ivana Okhlobystina*' [Doctrine-77 by Ivan Okhlobystin], Pravmir.Ru (13, September 2011), http://www.pravmir.ru/doktrina-77-ivana-oxlobystina-polnyj-tekst/ (accessed 11 December 2015).

Frolov, K., '*Tema Novorossii – faktor konsolidatsii pravoslavnykh patriotov*' [The agenda of Novorossiia – a factor of consolidation of Orthodox patriots], *LiveJournal blog of Kirill Frolov* (15 December 2014), http://kirillfrolov.livejournal.com/3381655.html (accessed 22 December 2015).

'*Gimn dnr "Russkaia pravoslavnaia"*' [A hymn of Donetsk Popular Republic 'The Russian Orthodox'], *LiveJournal blog of Egor Kholmogorov* (2 December 2014), http://holmogor.livejournal.com/6694040.html (accessed 5 December 2014).

'*Glava press-sluzhby upts mp prizval rossiian ne nazyvat' ukraintsev 'fashistami', 'banderovtsami', 'natsistami' i 'natsionalistami'* [A head of The Press-Service of the Ukrainian Orthodox Church of Moscow Patriarchate Archpriest Georgii Kovalenko requested Russians to stop calling Ukrainian people "fascists", "Banderovtsi", "Nazis" and "nationalists"], (24, February 2014), Portal-Credo.Ru (24 February 2014). http://www.portal-credo.ru/site/?act=news&id=106355 (accessed 25 February 2014).

Gumilev, L.N., Biografiia nauchnoi teorii ili avtonekrolog [Biography of a scientific theory or Auto-obituary (Necrology)], *Znamia* (Flag) 4. (1988): 202–216.

Gumilev, L.N., *Drevniaia Rus' i Velikaia step'* [Ancient Rus and the Great steppe] (Moscow: Mysl', 1989).

Haynes, J., *Religion in Global Politics*. (London, New-York: Longman, 1998).

Hovorun, C., 'Political Orthodoxy: an Ideology? a Civil Religion? a Heresy?', Paper presented in *the* International Conference 'Political Orthodoxy and Totalitarianism in Post-Communist Era' (Helsinki, 2015). The paper is available in Academia.edu https://www.academia.edu/12662544/Political_Orthodoxy_an_Ideology_a_Civil_Religion_a_Heresy (accessed 15 September 2015).

Huntington, S., The Clash of Civilizations and the Remaking of World Order (New York: Simon & Schuster, 1996).

Husain, M. Z., *Global Islamic Politics* (New York: Harper & Collins College Publishers, 1995).

I.Strelkov i "Komitet 25 Ianvaria" preduprezhdaiut [I. Strelkov and the "Committee of 25 January" warn]. Youtube (10 February 2016), https://www.youtube.com/watch?v=tqIybAe5ZCM (accessed 23 April 2019).

Ignatenko, A., *Islam i politika* [Islam and politics] (Moscow: Institute of Religion and Politics, 2004).

Juergensmeyer, M., 'Sacrifice and cosmic war'. In *Violence and the Sacred in the Modern World*, ed. M. Juergensmeyer (London: Frank Cass, 1992), 101–117.

Juergensmeyer, M., *Terror in the Mind of God: The Global Rise of Religious Violence*. (Berkeley, ca: University of California Press, 2003).

Khamidullina, K., '*Chelovecheskaia zhizn' radi territorial'noi tselostnosti!*' [Human life for the sake of territorial integrity!], Portal-Credo.Ru (14 June 2007), http://www.portal-credo.ru/site/index.php?act=fresh&id=623 (accessed 18 September 2015).

Kholmogorov, E., '*Atomnoe pravoslavie*' [Atomic Orthodoxy], *Russkii obozrevatel'* (Russian Observer) (31 August 2008), http://www.rus-obr.ru/idea/594 (accessed 4 March 2014).

Kholmogorov, E. '*Russkaia Vesna*' [Russian Spring], *Svobodnaia Pressa* (Free Press) (24 February 2014), http://svpressa.ru/politic/article/82769/ (accessed 21 December 2015).

Kholmogorov, E., '*Religii poslednego vremeni*' [End Time Religions], *Politicheskoe pravoslavie: strategicheskii zhurnal* [Political Orthodoxy: strategic magazine], 2 (Moscow: Institute of national strategy, Political news agency, 2006): 51–72.

Krasikov, A., 'Pravoslavie i Globalizatsiia' [Orthodoxy and Globalization], *Religiia i globalizatsiia na prostorakh Eurasii* [Religion and globalization across Eurasia] eds., A. Malashenko and S. Filatov (Moscow: ROSSPAeN, 2009) 28–90.

Makhnach, V., '*Uniia. Bor'ba za pravoslavie*' [Struggle for Orthodoxy], Predanie.Ru *(audio-lectures).* http://staroe.predanie.ru/audio/lekcii/mahnach/#istoriya-rossii (accessed 20 December 2015).

Malashenko, A., *Islamskie orientiry Severnogo Kavkaza* [Trends in Islam in the Northern Caucasus] (Moscow: Gendal'f, 2001).

Mirskii, G., '*Politicheskii islam' i zapadnoe obshestvo*' [Political Islam and Western Society], *Polis* 1 (2002): 78–86.

Mitrofanova, A., *Politizatsiia "pravoslavnogo mira"* [Politicization of the Orthodox world] (Moscow: Nauka, 2004).

Moiseev, E., *Kontseptsiia russkogo mira kak tsivilizatsionnyi proekt xxi veka* [The conception of the Russian World as a civilizational project of the xxi century], *Kurskaia pravoslavnaia dukhovnaia seminariia* [Kursk Orthodox Seminary] (2015), http://kurskpds.ru/articles/kontseptsiya-russkogo-mira-kak-tsivilizatsionnyy-proekt-khkhi-veka/ (accessed 29 September 2016).

'*My voiuem za Svyatuiu Rus'* [We are fighting for the Holy Russia] *Russkaia Narodnaia Liniia* [Russian Popular Line] (6 November 2014), http://ruskline.ru/analitika/2014/11/07/my_voyuem_za_svyatuyu_rus/ (accessed 10 November 2014).

'*Na stenakh l'vovskogo khrama poiavilis' izobrazheniia s voinami ATO i boievikami "DNR"'* [The images of the ATO soldiers and militants of the Donetsk People's Republic appeared on the walls of a church in Lviv], *Zerkalo Nedeli* (8 April 2015) https://zn.ua/CULTURE/na-stenah-lvovskogo-hrama-poyavilis-izobrazheniya-s-voinami-ato-i-boevikami-dnr-172346_.html (accessed 15 April 2019).

'Nereligioznii evrei protiv pravoslavnogo protoiereia. Protoierei Vsevolod Chaplin protiv politika Leonida Gozmana' [An irreligious Jew against an Orthodox archpriest. Archpriest Vsevolod Chaplin against politician Leonid Gozman], Portal-Credo.Ru (8 June 2007), http://www.portal-credo.ru/site/?act=news&id=54730 (accessed 19 September 2015).

'Obrashenie Sviateyshego Patriarkha Moskovskogo i vseia Rusi Kirilla k mestobliustiteliu Kievskoi mitropolich'ei kafedry mitropolitu Chernovitskomu i Bukovinskomu Onufriiu, arkhipastyriam, pastyriam i vsem vernym chadam Ukrainskoi Pravoslavnoi Tserkvi v sviazi s situatsiei na Ukraine' [Appeal of the Patriarch of Moscow and all Russia Kirill to the Deputy to the Locum Tenens of the Metropolitan Diocese of Kiev Metropolitan Onufrii of Chernivtsi and Bukovyna, archpastors, pastors and all faithful children of the Ukrainian Orthodox Church with respect to the situation in Ukraine], (2 March 2014), Patriarchia.Ru. http://www.patriarchia.ru/db/text/3588256.html (accessed 18 December 2015).

'Pochaevskaia lavra ne sdaetsia. Monakhi umrut za veru. Monakhi "poriut" za veru' [Pochayiv Lavra doesn't capitulate. Monks will die for the faith. Monks will 'tear anyone to pieces' for the faith], LiveJournal blog of Kirill Frolov (20 February 2014) (accessed 20 February 2014).

Politicheskaia Deklaratsiia Obsherusskogo natsional'nogo dvizheniia pod rukovodstvom Igoria Strelkova [Political Declaration of the All-Russian national movement under the leadership of Igor Strelkov], in: *Dvizhenie 'Novorossiia Igoria Strelkova'* [The Movement 'Novorossiia Igoria Strelkova']. (28 May 2016), http://novorossia.pro/25yanvarya/1942-politicheskaya-deklaraciya-obscherusskogo-nacionalnogo-dvizheniya-pod-rukovodstvom-igorya-strelkova.html (accessed 25 April 2019).

Politicheskoe pravoslavie: strategicheskii zhurnal [Political Orthodoxy: strategic magazine] 2 (Moscow: Institute of national strategy, Political news agency, 2006).

'Protoierei *Chaplin ob"iasnil svoie uvol'nenie raznoglaziiami po Donbassu'* [Archpriest Chaplin explained that his dismissal was caused by disagreements concerning Donbass], rbk-daily (24 December 2015). http://www.rbc.ru/politics/24/12/2015/567c3a6f9a79470e8c24b01b (accessed 25 December 2015).

'"Radonezh" organizoval diskussiiu o pravoslavii i pravakh cheloveka', [Radonezh organized a discussion on Orthodoxy and human rights], *SOVA.ru* (13 July 2004). http://www.sova-center.ru/religion/discussions/society/2004/07/d2499/ (accessed 24 January 2016).

'Rossiia dolzhna vmeshat'sia v dela Ukrainy i spasti eë, schitaiut v Russkoi tserkvi' [Russia must intervene in the Ukrainian affairs and save it—this is a position of the officials from the Russian Orthodox Church], *Interfax-religion* (28 January 2015). http://www.interfax-religion.ru/?act=news&div=54273 (accessed 19 December 2015).

Shetkina, E. *"Politicheskoie pravoslavie – prokliatie ili neizbezhnost'?"* [Political Orthodoxy—curse or inevitability?], *RISU* (7 November 2018). https://risu.org.ua/ru/index/expert_thought/authors_columns/kshchotkina_column/73376/ (accessed 17 April 2019).

Stepanov, L., *'Eto ne bor'ba za zemli, a eto bor'ba za Pravoslavie'*, [It is not a fighting for lands, but for Orthodoxy], *"Russkaia Narodnaia Liniia"* [Russian Popular Line] (10 March 2014), http://ruskline.ru/news_rl/2014/03/10/eto_ne_borba_za_zemli_a_eto_borba_za_pravoslavie/ (accessed 12 March 2014).

'Strashniy Sud: Putina uvideli goryashim v adu' [Last Judgment: Putin was seen burning in hell], *Politeka* (18 April 2017) https://politeka.net/news/428819-strashnyj-sud-putina-uvideli-goryashhim-v-adu-foto/

Suslov, M. 'The Russian Orthodox Church and the crisis in Ukraine,' in *Churches in the Ukrainian Crisis*, eds. A. Krawchuk and T. Brener (Basingstone: Palgrave Macmillan, 2016), 139–141.

Tibi, B., *The Challenge of Fundamentalism. Political Islam and the New World Disorder* (Berkeley: University of California Press, 1998).

'*Ustav Vserossiiskogo Natsional'nogo dvizheniia pod rukovodstvom Igoria Strekova*' [Charter of All-Russian National Movement under the leadership of Igor Strelkov]. Dvizheniye "Novorossiya" Igorya Strelkova. (10 October 2016). http://novorossia.pro/25yanvarya/2522-29-sent yabrya-2016-ustav-prinyat.html (accessed 10 April 2019).

'*V sobor Donetska ne pustili opolchentsev so starinnoi ikonoi, prinesennoi iz Rossii*' [The militiamen were not allowed to bring an old icon from Russia into the Cathedral of Donetsk], *Interfax-religion* (30 September 2014), http://www.interfax-religion.ru/?act=news&div=56599 (accessed 23 January 2016).

Vendik Yuriy. 'The Union of Donbas's volunteers has been created in Moscow', Russian Service BBC (10 October 2015). https://www.bbc.com/russian/russia/2015/10/151010_donbass_volunteers_congres s_moscow (accessed 15 April 2019).

Verkhovsky, A., *Politicheskoe pravoslavie: Russkie pravoslavnye natsionalisty i fundamentalisty, 1995–2001* [Political Orthodoxy: the Russian Orthodox nationalists and fundamentalists, 1995–2001] (Moscow: Panorama, 2003).

Verkhovsky, A., 'Politicheskoe pravoslavie v rossiiskoi publichnoi politike. Pod"em antisekuliarnogo natsionalizma' [Political Orthodoxy in Russian public policy. The rise of anti-secular nationalism], *SOVA.ru* (21 May 2005) http://www.sova-center.ru/religion/publications/ 2005/05/d4678 (accessed 25 January 2016).

Verkhovsky, A., Mikhailovskaia, Evgeniia & Pribylovsky, Vladimir, '*Politicheskaia Ksenofobiia. Radikal'nye gruppy. Predstavleniia politikov. Rol' Tserkvi*' [Political xenophobia. Radical groups. Views of politicians. The Role of the Church] (Moscow: Panorama, 1999).

'*Voina za mir v Peterburgskom khrame*' [A war for peace in Saint-Petersburg church], *Fontanka* (27 May 2014) http://www.fontanka.ru/2014/05/ 27/039/ (accessed 6 June 2014).

Volodikhin, D., "*Novii narod*" [The new nation] *Politicheskoe pravoslvie: strategicheskii zhurnal* [Political Orthodoxy: strategic magazine], 2 (Moscow: Institute of National Strategy, Political News Agency, 2006): 39–50.

Wojnar, M., 'The west and the great steppe in the history of Rus and Russia' *Studies into the History of Russia and Central-Eastern Europe*. XVII (2012): 5–30.

Zygmont, A., 'The problematics of violence in post-Soviet Russian Orthodox discourse', *State, Religion and Church*, 2 (2) (2014): 29–53.

'*Ia ne byl odinok'. Interv'iu L'va Gumileva "Leningradskoi pravde*" ['I was not alone'. Interview of Lev Gumilev to "Leningradskaya Pravda"], *Leningradskaia Pravda* (30 December 1990), Retrieved from: http://baznica.info/article /lev-gumilev-ya-ne-byl-odinok/ (accessed 29 September 2016).

The Russian Orthodox Church in Search of the Cultural Canon

*Mikhail Suslov**
University of Copenhagen

This paper documents and analyzes the building blocks of the Orthodox cultural canon and cultural policy. The author argues that in spite of the Church's attempts to renegotiate its status in (post-) secular society, the Orthodox cultural products have restricted access to the nation-wide market, partially due to the lack of theoretical reflection on culture, and partially because of the Church's unsettled accounts with Russian history of the 20th century. This produces an effect of increased reliance on the state's restrictive measures in the cultural sphere.

Keywords: Russian Orthodox Church, post-secularism, religious fundamentalism, Russian culture

Introduction

The Russian Orthodox Church (thereafter ROC) has become a powerful shaper of public discourse in contemporary Russia, whose voice resonates in political ideologies of the elites and everyday conversations of the grassroots. During the Soviet era, the ROC was excluded from the public sphere, and quite successfully ousted from the private lives of the millions of Soviet citizens. Believers were ridiculed, ostracized, and sometimes openly prosecuted or sent to psychiatric asylums. In the post-Soviet period, attempts of the ROC to reconnect with the pre-revolutionary past gave it moral ascendancy and the low start-up effect, which has won it the largest constituency in the country, counting circa 70% of people who call

---

*   The author would like to acknowledge comments made by Elena Namli and anonymous reviewers to the earlier version of the article.

themselves Orthodox believers.[1] At the same time, the actual number of regular church-goers is only between 2% and 4% of the population.[2] Recent sociological surveys show that only 2% of the respondents strictly observe the Great Lent, whereas 78% keep the usual diet. Only 5% of respondents plan to attend the Easter liturgy – the main religious service in the Orthodox Church.[3] To whatever the explanation of the gap between religious identity and religious practice might be adduced,[4] the important fact is that the Church possesses a huge reserve of people who *culturally* identify with Orthodoxy. Capitalizing on this, Patriarch Kirill (Gundiaev), the head of the Moscow Patriarchate, claims that even if they are not ardent believers, they are nevertheless "our flock".[5] However questionable this assumption might be,[6] it has two corollaries for the way in

---

1 'Rossiiane o religii' (2013) http://www.levada.ru/2013/12/24/rossiyane-o-religii/. The ROC'S clerics usually speak about some 80% of believers (accessed 1 November 2015).
2 Statistics says that only 2% to 4% of Russians keep the fast during Lent, or take communion. The Ministry of the Interior (which since the Soviet times traditionally monitors church attendance on the most important dates) reported 2.3 million participants at the Christmas service in 2008 (i.e. 3.3% of the population). See 'Rossiiane o religii' (2013); 'Dannye o posetivshikh rozhdestvenskie bogosluzheniia' (2008) http://www.sova-center.ru/religion/discussions/how-many/2008/01/d12353/ (accessed 1 January 2016).
3 'Velikii post i Paskha' (2018) https://www.levada.ru/2018/04/02/velikij-post-i-pasha-4/ (accessed 22 May 2019).
4 Cf., G. Davie, 'Vicarious Religion: A Methodological Challenge', in *Everyday Religion: Observing Modern Religious Lives*. ed. N. Ammerman, (Oxford: Oxford University Press, 2006), pp. 21–37.
5 Kirill (Gundiaev), Patriarch, 'Otritsaia Bozhiiu pravdu, my razrushaem mir.' Patriarchia.ru 10 March 2015) http://www.patriarchia.ru/db/print/4010650.html (accessed 1 January 2016).
6 A tangible proportion of Russians opposes the Church's ascendance in society and politics. Nearly 70% are against active participation of the ROC in political life. Between 1991 and 2013, the share of those who oppose teaching religion in schools increased from 10 to 17%. See: 'Religiia i tserkov' v obshchestvennoi zhizni' (2013) https://www.levada.ru/2013/04/18/religiya-i-tserkov-v-obshh estvennoj-zhizni/ (accessed 27 May 2019). Probably, it is high time to speak about an anti-ROC backlash or at least about a certain fatigue, when people, exasperated by the ROC's assertiveness, sumptuous lifestyle of the clerics and their servility vis-à-vis the state, and to raise their voices against new incursions of the Church into the public sphere. One of the signs of this new development are the May 2019 protests in Yekaterinburg against building a new church in one of the city's centrally located parks. See: Semen Novoprudnyi, 'Skvernyi khram: Pochemu protest v Yekaterinburge pokazal istinnoe otnoshenie rossiian

which the ROC positions itself in Russian society: first, the majority of the Russian population constitutes the natural missionary target of the Church and the market for its "goods" and "services". Second, the ROC's leaders argue that the Church is the living embodiment and the central "identifier" of the Russian nation, because Russia's state forms, societal shapes, dominant ideologies, even territories have changed drastically throughout the 20th century, whereas the Church has remained the same.

With those issues at stake, the Church logically claims that the state would prioritize the ROC's interests. The third and fourth terms of Vladimir Putin in power (since May 2012) have been very opportune for the ROC, since the Church's supply of traditional values has met with increasing demand from a conservative majority from below, as well as from the conservative elite from above.[7] In spite of the anti-ROC's campaign and a number of scandals, connected with the "Pussy Riot" affair and the luxurious lifestyle of Patriarch Kirill, the ROC has slightly gained in popular trust during the period between 2013 and 2015 (48 and 54% respectively), but it nevertheless lags behind the President (80%) and the army (64%).[8] Indeed, even if not altogether unclouded,[9] the relations between the Church and the state are generally very friendly and supportive — also in the sphere of culture. In the last two decades the Church has increased its cultural outreach and developed its infrastructural muscles, featuring, among others, the film festivals *Golden Knight* (1992) and *Radonezh* (1995), the Orthodox tv channel *Soiuz* (2005), the Patriarchal Literary Prize (2009), the Patriarchal Council for Culture (2010), Orthodox music radio channel *MuzSoiuz* (2015) and

---

k "dukhovnym skrepam'" (2019) https://spektr.press/skvernyj-hram-pochemu-protest-v-ekaterinburge-pokazal-istinnoe-otnoshenie-rossiyan-k-duhovnym-skrepam/ (accessed 27 May 2019).

7 On conservatism in contemporary Russia see: M. Suslov and D. Uzlaner (eds.), *Contemporary Russian Conservatism: Problems, Paradoxes and Dangers* (Leiden: Brill, forthcoming 2019).

8 'Rossiiane stali bol'she doveriat' armii' (2015) http://www.levada.ru/2015/10/07/rossiyane-stali-bolshe-doveryat-armii/ (accessed 1 November 2015).

9 For the controversy over the annexation of Crimea and the war in Eastern Ukraine, see M. Suslov, 'Russian Orthodox Church and the Crisis in Ukraine', in *The Churches in the Ukrainian Crisis*. eds. T. Bremer and A. Krawchuk (Bern: Palgrave Macmillan, 2016).

so on. But the single most important incursion of the Church into the life of the Russians is the incorporation of the obligatory course "Bases of Orthodox Culture" in secondary school curricula.[10]

In other words, the ROC has enough resources and ambitions to rise to a position of the ultimate authority in both ethics and aesthetics in today's production of culture in Russia. However, the ROC's attempts to shape the cultural agenda are not unproblematic, mostly because its claims are not met with an adequate positive vision of what culture should be. It lacks a clearly defined cultural canon, but not the wish to have one. In a sense, this position could be called "dominance without hegemony".[11]

This paper analyses how the ROC is refining its cultural policy and defining its cultural canon, documenting and interpreting the Church's insufficient and contradictory theorization of culture. The timeframe of this research applies the magnifying glass to the most recent events, from roughly 2009, when Patriarch Kirill (Gundiaev) was elected as the head of the ROC, to the present. Yet, the paper cursorily observes most general cultural developments back into the past as well. Culture became an object of theological inquiry from the Orthodox viewpoint relatively recently, with the end of the Russian *ancien régime* in 1917, when religion ceased to be a "by default" yardstick for cultural production. Today's traditionalism in politics as well as in culture cannot but become an ideological choice of rational deliberation and post-secular "re-branding" of traditional values—religious ones included. The post-secular model maintains that religion can play an important role in the public sphere but it must not attack the bases of the liberal consensus, including ideas of the priority of human rights, inalienable human dignity, and freedom of expression. As Peter Berger remarked, "the

---

10 See, for example, J. Willems, 'Religiöse Bildung in Russlands Schulen. Orthodoxie, nationale Identität und die Positionalität des Faches,' in: *Grundlagen orthodoxer Kultur (opk)* (Münster: lit, 2006); K. Richters, *The Post-Soviet Russian Orthodox Church: Politics, Culture and Greater Russia* (London: Routledge, 2013), p. 36 et seq.

11 To be sure, the source of inspiration for this conceptualization came from R. Guha, *Dominance without Hegemony: History and Power in Colonial India* (Cambridge, Mass.: Harvard University Press, 1997).

religious tradition, which previously could be authoritatively imposed, now has to be marketed".[12]

In the early 1990s, when the Church possessed the moral advantage of being prosecuted, and the atmosphere of novelty and dissidence, any Orthodox cultural product could find a broad audience under the brand "recollection of the forgotten legacy" or "restoration of the lost tradition". These times have gone, the ROC has assumed an authoritative role in society and cultural life, but today this role has to be rationally and theoretically substantiated, and masterfully marketed. However, there is no theoretical bedrock on which the Church can rest in this area, and it has to collect bits and pieces of theological and ideological traditions. The Church also has to compete with secular cultural products in "selling out" its produce, but it does not possess enough skills and resources to do so. Thus, the post-secular environment is not comfortable for the ROC while the Church is striving to carve out a different understanding of its role in secular culture, which is far removed from a post-secular consensus. The paper will discuss the ROC's claims that culture in general and Russian culture in particular was formed by religion and therefore there can be no "neutral ground" on which the religious and the secular can meet for a constructive dialogue. Instead, the ROC maintains that the meeting ground for dialogue with secular culture should already be religious, whereas secular artists — understandably — fear that in this case, it would not be a dialogue at all.

The paper is grounded on the analysis of the theoretical discourses on culture, produced by the ROC's clerics and intellectuals. This angle of study exempts me from the necessity to theoretically qualify the notoriously fuzzy term "culture". Instead, I will be following the methodological path, outlined by the Cambridge school

---

12 P. Berger, 'Social Sources of Secularization', in *Culture and Society: Contemporary Debates*. eds. J. Alexander and S. Seidmanz (Cambridge: Cambridge University Press, 1990), p. 244. Cf.: H.-G. Ziebertz, U. Riegel, 'Europe: A Post-secular Society?', *International Journal of Practical Theology* 13(2) (2010): 293–308; A. Kyrlezhev, 'Postsekuliarnaia epokha', *Kontinent*, 120 (2004) from http://magazines.russ.ru/continent/2004/120/kyr16.html (accessed 1 January 2016).

of intellectual history, and focus on the uses of the term in their historically specific contexts:[13] the term in point here is "Orthodox culture" and the concomitant host of notions, deployed in public speech to designate the Church's relation to "creativity", "arts", "literature", "music", "cinema", and so forth. I am trying to understand what Church leaders, intellectuals, and grassroots mean when they say "Orthodox culture", and how they incorporated this term into a broader debate on the role of the Church in society. The focus of the research is, then, not only "highbrow" artistic production, cultural institutions, or cultural industry, but also everyday life discourses about culture and grassroots' cultural practices.

Likewise, there is no cast-iron understanding of whose voice is to be counted, or whom we shall consider as, for example, an "Orthodox writer", for the simple reason that the ROC has no clear view of this. Still, we can grasp the gist of this debate by analyzing the use of this term in the instances when the Patriarchal Literary Prize was awarded to various writers with different distances from the Church. Some of them were Orthodox priests, some were lay people writing predominantly on Church themes, and some addressed religious questions only obliquely but identify as Orthodox. As a useful start for an academic discussion, I drew on three pools of sources. The first pertains to the cultural producers and public intellectuals with a pronounced connection to the ROC, e.g. clerics and lay Orthodox theologians. The second embraces those, who openly call themselves Orthodox and who are recognized by the ROC as such. The third group of sources puts together public opinions on the cultural products, defined as Orthodox. To give an example, the animation film *Incredible Travelling of Serafima* was included into the analysis, because it was branded as "Orthodox" and recognized as such by Patriarch Kirill, who gave it his blessing. I am equally interested in the discourses around this film, whether

---

13 E.g. Q. Skinner, *Visions of Politics. Regarding Method* (Cambridge: Cambridge University Press, 2002); K. Palonen, 'Quentin Skinner's Rhetoric of Conceptual Change', *History of the Human Sciences* 10(2) (1997), pp. 61–80.

commented by Vladimir Legoida, the head of the Information Department of the ROC, or by anonymous Internet commentators, who watched this film and thereby were impelled to define their position in relation to the Orthodox cultural product.

Conceptualization of Culture

In Russian Orthodoxy, there is a line of thought, which professes extreme compartmentalization of faith and sees secular culture as incorrigibly corrupt, completely out of touch with religion, and thereby irrelevant to religious culture. For this group of believers, the Russian word *iskusstvo* (arts) originates from *iskus* (temptation), i.e. the idea that the arts have a demonic provenience.[14] This position echoes some aspects of the iconoclastic debates of the 8th and 9th centuries, namely, the radicalization of Platonic philosophy and the idea that artificially created images of God would only distract believers from purely intellectual comprehension of and communication with God.[15] Time and again, followers of this line of thought voice discontent over the depiction of deities outside the context of a canonical icon, resist the idea of representing religious themes by means of acting on a scene, masks and histrionics,[16] and feel uncomfortable when confronted with instrumental music in churches.

This theological background was reinforced by the Soviet-era expulsion of religion from everyday life,[17] which resulted in the consolidation of the subcultural esoteric group of the few "chosen" people — the believers. Believers, according to this worldview, are separated from the apostatized masses with their apostatized culture. Compartmentalization of religious culture is reminiscent of

---

14 E.g. 'Iskusstvo i iskus' (2006) http://ruskline.ru/analitika/2006/06/07/isku sstvo_i_iskus (accessed 1 January 2016).
15 The literature on iconoclasm is vast; for this study I consulted with J. Meyendorff, *Byzantine Theology: Historical Trends and Doctrinal Themes*. 2nd ed. (New York: Fordham University Press, 1979).
16 Cf. father Sergei Bulgakov's assessment of acting: "... the mask eats away the heart, the 'role' [eats away] the soul, which comes loose on its axis and loses its integrity and solidity." S. Bulgakov, *Filosofiia imeni* (Paris: YMCA-Press, 1953), p. 173 et seq.
17 A. Shishkov, 'Nekotorye aspekty desekuliarizatsii v postsovetskoi Rossii', *Gosudarstvo, religiia, tserkov' v Rossii i za rubezhom* 30(2) (2012).

secularism "inside out", with its claim that the secular and the religious do not mix with each other. Moreover, contemporary Russian Orthodoxy, with its tight connections with ideological traditionalism, has developed a pronounced anthropological pessimism,[18] associated with the discourses on guilt and repentance,[19] whose logical consequence is the negation of the Promethean spirit of artistic creativity and assertion of the priority of religion over culture. In this vein, Olesia Nikolaeva, a popular Orthodox writer, castigates iconic émigré philosopher of religion Nikolai Berdiaev, who put creativity above salvation. She argues that creativity is contingent upon the human being's relations to God. Understood in this way, creativity is a work of penance (*poslushanie*) of sorts, which cannot exist separately from the Christian striving for salvation. This means that there could be only one culture—Christian culture, and there is no culture outside of Christianity.[20]

This vision offers a "high-barrier" interpretation of religious culture, which does not allow the ROC to reach out to the whole of the Russian population and to reclaim the most recognizable accomplishments of Russian culture as a part of Orthodox culture. By contrast, some religious figures toy with the "low-barrier" interpretation of culture, according to which even secular arts could be understood religiously. The theological tradition catering to this idea is the Hesychastic concept that human creativity is a collaboration

---

18   Cf. N. O'Sullivan, 'Conservative Ideology: The Philosophy of Imperfection' in *Conservatism*, ed. N. O'Sullivan (London: Dent, 1976).
19   Cf. B. Knorre, 'Kategorii viny v sisteme tsennostei tserkovno-prikhodskoi subkul'tury', in *Prokhod i obshchina v sovremennom pravoslavii: kornevaia sistema rossiiskoi religioznosti*. eds. A. Agadzhanian and K. Russele [Rousselet]. (Moscow, 2011), pp. 318–335. Knorre reasonably highlights that the "kenotic" (self-belittling) sensibility represents the good as an essentially fragile and rare occurrence and the bad as a "by default" option of human existence. Hence, any manifestation of creativity is seen as a priori sinful, unless its unconditional leaning on religion is well proved.
20   O. Nikolaeva, *Pravoslavie i tvorchestvo* (Moscow: Nikeia, 2012), pp. 26, 62, 72, 227. By so arguing, Nikolaeva repeats the interpretation of émigré religious thinker Ivan Il'in, very popular in contemporary Orthodox literature (Ivan Il'in, *Krizis bezbozhiia* (Moscow: 'Dar', 2005 [1935]), 42). Cf. E. Meshcherina, *Dukhovnye osnovy tvorchestva: Stat'i o russkoi kul'ture* (Moscow: 'Kanon+', 2015), p. 22. Nikolaeva is the wife of priest Vladimir Vigilianskii who served as the Head of the Press Department of the Moscow Patriarchate in 2005–2012.

with God.[21] This way of reasoning was explored by Nikolai Berdiaev, who insisted that human creativity is "theurgical" in the sense that people become like God (*upodobliat'sia Bogu*) in the process of artistic creation, in which they continue God's work in this world. Grounded on the existentialist philosophy, Berdiaev's theory of culture emphasized the importance of individual freedom for artistic creativity.[22]

In the late 1990s, when the ROC's key document defining its relation to society, state and culture, i.e. the "Bases of the Social Doctrine", was debated, Hegumen Ioann Ekonomtsev openly supported this interpretation. He argued that the only criterion, which can be used to define whether a cultural object is "from God", is talent (talent here *is* partaking in God's energy): a talented work of art is always from God; a mediocre work of art is never from God. Ekonomtsev warned against the reductionist judging of cultural products, which reminded him of the Soviet-era prosecution of dissident artists, who were judged by the conformity to abstract ideological dogmas. Now, he argues, the ROC tends to profess, which work of art is "from God" and which is not, but this is a conceited blasphemy because only God knows it.[23] At the other end of the spectrum, one of the Orthodox intellectuals has gone so far as to claim that bad taste in art and literature is sinning against God and the most blasphemous work of art is a talentless one.[24]

This view outsources the judgment on secular arts to the art critics and extolls the artistic creativity and freedom of expression.

---

21 Hesychasm is a mystic tradition in Orthodoxy, associated mostly with St Gregory Palamas of the 14th century. In brief, the idea is that God is unintelligible in essence but intelligible in energies, which is another name for God's blessing. With the help of ascetic practices (or for this matter, artistic creativity), people can reunite with God. For a contemporary Russian interpretation of Hesychasm see: S. Khoruzhii, *O starom i novom* (St Petersburg: Aleteiia, 2000).

22 N. Berdiaev, *Smysl tvorchestva: Opyt opravdaniia cheloveka* (Moscow, 1994 [1916]). For an overview on Berdiaev's theory of culture see: Chen' Zhen'-Khen', *N.A. Berdiaev o russkoi kul'ture*. Candidate of science thesis (St Petersburg, 2002).

23 A. Zubov, 'Khristianstvo i kul'tura', Znamia, 10 (1999) http://magazines.russ.ru/znamia/1999/10/konfer.html (accessed 1 January 2016).

24 S. Mazaev, 'Grekh protiv vkusa', in *Politicheskoe pravoslavie: Strategicheskii zhurnal №2*. eds. P. Sviatenkov, B. Mezhuev and M. Remizov (Moscow: APN, 2006), pp. 286–287.

For this reason, the "low-barrier" interpretation could not suit the intellectual core of the Orthodox Church either. The Orthodox intellectuals agree with Hesychasm that religion and culture are inseparably linked, but they need a theory, which proves religion's upper hand in this alliance. In order to substantiate the ascendance of religion over secular culture, philosopher Pavel Florensky's theory was unearthed and propagated. Leaning on Oswald Spengler's cultural criticism, Florensky argues that culture was born from a religious cult and essentially retains this connection. When culture severs its ties to ritual — as did happen during the European Renaissance and especially Enlightenment — it is disconnected from the spring of creativity and becomes fruitless, spiritless, and void of talent. We can observe this, he argued, by the example of contemporary Western culture.[25] His theory of culture elevates the Church to a position of cultural authority, possessing rights to judge and rectify apostatized secular arts, measured by the yardstick of its relation to God. He opined that, "if, in the field of culture, we are not with Christ, than we are against Christ".[26]

Professor Andrei Zubov, one of the authors of the "Bases of the Social Doctrine", and Nikita Struve, the editor of YMCA-Press since 1978, continued this theoretical path, stating that historically inseparable, in today's world art and religion may or may not be in communion. A good work of art is one, which reminds us about the tie with God, and it is thereby a truly Christian work of art, whereas a bad one further separates culture from religion, and people from God.[27]

This "medium-barrier" interpretation is the arterial line of theorizing "culture" in the ROC, which sees Orthodoxy at the heart of

---

25 P. Florenskii, 'Avtoreferat', *Voprosy filosofii*, 12 (1988), p. 114; Florenskii, 'Iz bogoslovskogo naslediia', *Bogoslovskii sbornik 17* (1977), pp. 119–230; P. Florenskii, 'Zapiska o khristianstve i kul'ture (1923)', in P. Florenskii, *Sochineniia: V 4-kh tomakh* (Moscow: Mysl', 1994–1999) vol. 2, pp. 547–559.
26 Florenskii, 'Zapiska o khristianstve i kul'ture', p. 550.
27 'Khristianstvo i kul'tura', *Znamia* 10 (1999). http://magazines.russ.ru/znamia/1999/10/konfer.html (accessed 1 January 2016). Cf. E. Barabanov, 'Sud'ba khristianskoi kul'tury', *Kontinent*, 151 (2012 [1976]) http://magazines.russ.ru/continent/2012/151/b46.html (accessed 1 January 2016).

Russian culture. It was supported by Metropolitan Kirill, now Patriarch, and entered into chapter 14, part 2 of the "Bases". It says that secular culture, although not necessarily anti-Christian in essence, can either elevate people to the heights of religious spirituality or unleash their most base instincts and thereby destroy them and the world around them — both God's creations in the religious understanding. This negative culture is defined as "anti-religious" or "anti-human", which sets people in opposition to God. Having stated this, the Church reserves the exclusive right for itself to identify "negative culture" and fight with its manifestations.[28] This is because, as Patriarch Kirill explains, works of arts exert influence on human souls and hearts, and hence the Church cannot be neutral to it.[29]

Ethno-National Interpretation of Culture

ROC's 'medium barrier' interpretation of culture acquires concretization in the ethno-national approach, according to which, roots of the Russian culture lie in Orthodoxy. This official theory of culture capitalizes on the more general debates on the place of the ROC in secular life in Russia, where religion has become a salient marker of national identity.[30] Such an understanding has two implications, elucidated in this section; the first is the ROC's unquestioned right to judge which cultural object is genuinely Russian and which is not; the second is securitization of Russian culture and the vocal call

---

28 Osnovy Sotsial'noi Kontseptsii rpts, xiv, 2.
29 Kirill (Gundiaev), Patriarch, 'Neobkhodima postoiannaia ploshchadka dlia dialoga Tserkvi i mira iskusstva' http://tass.ru/obschestvo/2517401 (accessed 1 January 2016). See also: Kirill (Gundiaev), Patriarch. *Patriarkh i molodezh': Razgovor bez diplomatii* (Moscow: Danilovskii blagovestnik, 2009). Cf. Hilarion (Alfeev), Metropolitan. *Tserkov' otkryta dlia kazhdogo* (Minsk: Belorusskaia Pravoslavnaia Tserkov', 2011).
30 E.g. J. Garrard and C. Garrard, *Russian Orthodoxy Resurgent: Faith and Power in the New Russia* (Princeton: Princeton University Press, 2009). Cf. A. Agadjanian, 'Revisiting Pandora's Gifts: Religious and National Identity in the Post-Soviet Societal Fabric', *Europe-Asia Studies* 53(3) (2001), p. 473 et seq; S. Ryzhova, 'Tolerance and Extremism: Russian Ethnicity in the Orthodox Discourse of the 1990s', in *Religion and Identity in Modern Russia: The Revival of Orthodoxy and Islam*. eds. J. Johnson, M. Stepaniants and B. Forest (Aldershot: Ashgate, 2005), p. 65 et seq.

for protection from the alien and hostile cultural implants on the Russian soil.

As scholar of religion Sergei Filatov puts it, the ROC is trying to take away the monopoly of preserving and interpreting the Russian cultural tradition from art critics, scholars and museum workers.[31] Ethno-national theory of culture lays the foundation on which today's ROC's propagation of the continuity of Russian history and reconciliation with the Soviet past could be built. As Patriarch Kirill professes, under the godless communist regime the Russian culture continued the mission of the persecuted Church because it taught people essentially the same Orthodox values.[32]

The theoretical grounds of this claim were developed in the early 2000s, around the year 2002, when the ROC elaborated its concept of the "canonical territory"[33] and launched the state-sponsored campaign against what it called "Catholic proselytism in Russia". The chief ideologue was again Metropolitan Kirill of Smolensk, who promoted the concept of "ethnic religiosity", i.e. the idea that Russian culture is first and foremost Orthodox culture, which has become widely accepted even in lay discourses. Later, as Patriarch, he offered three interrelated concepts: "basic culture", "cultural filters" and "cultural sovereignty".

The term "basic culture" (*bazisnaia kul'tura*) means a common cultural denominator, capable of uniting different sub-cultures into a single nation. Today, Kirill maintains, the only common cultural denominator in Russia is Orthodox faith, which laid the national

---

[31] E.g. S. Filatov, 'Patriarkh Kirill – dva goda planov, mechtanii i neudobnoi real'nosti', in *Pravoslavnaia tserkov' pri novom patriarkhe*. eds. A. Malashenko and Filatov (Moscow, 2012), p. 50.
See also: Filatov, 'Orthodoxy in Russia: Post-atheist Faith', *Studies in World Christianity* 14(3) (2008), pp. 187–202.

[32] Kirill (Gundiaev), Patriarch, 'Vystuplenie Predstoiatelia Russkoi Tserkvi na tseremonii vrucheniia Patriarshei literaturnoi premii' (2015) http://www.patriarchia.ru/db/text/4100606.html (accessed 1 January 2016). Cf. Hilarion (Alfeev), Metropolitan, 'Russkaia poeziia xx veka sokhranila v sebe moshchnoe religioznoe i khristianskoe nachalo' (2015) http://www.patriarchia.ru/db/print/4099271.html (accessed 1 January 2016).

[33] E.g. D. Payne, 'Spiritual Security, the Russian Orthodox Church, and the Russian Foreign Ministry: Collaboration or Cooptation?' *Journal of Church and State* 52(4) (2010), pp. 1–16.

cultural foundation in 988 when ancient Rus' was baptized by Prince Vladimir.[34] Parallel with the "basic culture" concept, Patriarch Kirill spoke of the "cultural or information filters". In today's postmodern world, he argues, all cultures have been uprooted, mixed up and hybridized, so that information freely floats from country to country. This destroys the hierarchy of values in a way that an icon by Andrei Rublev becomes the same consumable piece of information as the music clip by pop singer Madonna. In order to restore the hierarchy of values, people have to have internal information filters, calibrated according to the "basic culture", which would privilege Russian cum Orthodox traditional culture.[35] The idea of "spiritual or cultural sovereignty" echoes the notorious "sovereign democracy" theory of Vladislav Surkov. It was advanced by Patriarch Kirill at the All-Russian People's Assembly in November 2013, powerfully incorporating the ROC's cultural policy into the Russian state's geopolitical style of thinking.[36] "Spiritual sovereignty" means securitization of Russia's "basic culture", supposedly threatened by alien values and lifestyles.[37] The concept of 'spiritual sovereignty' has inspired much of the recent legislation. For example, the Strategy of the State Cultural Policy (2016) speaks of the 'washing out [*razmyvanie*] of the traditional Russian spiritual and moral values' as a threat to Russia's national security.[38]

Figure 1 shows that interconnected mentioning of culture, church and Orthodoxy in the central and religious press surged

---

34 E.g. Kirill, Patriarch, *Propovedi 2009–2010* (Sergiev Posad: Izd. Sviato-Troitskoi Sergievoi Lavry, 2010), p. 52.
35 Kirill (Gundiaev), Patriarch. *Patriarkh i molodezh': Razgovor bez diplomatii* (Moscow: Danilovskii blagovestnik, 2009), p. 99; Kirill, *Sviatoi kniaz' Vladimir: Tsivilizatsionnyi vybor Rusi* (Moscow: Izd-vo Moskovskoi Patriarkhii, 2015).
36 Cf. M. Suslov, "'Holy Rus": The Geopolitical Imagination in the Contemporary Russian Orthodox Church', *Russian Politics and Law* 52(3) (2014), pp. 67–86.
37 E.g. Kirill (Gundiaev), Patriarch, *Preodolenie smuty* (Moscow: Izd-vo Moskovskoi patriarkhii, 2013), 41; 'Patriarkh v otvet na sanktsii prizval zashchishchat' dukhovnyi suverenitet strany' (2018) https://tass.ru/obschestvo/5455523?utm_source=twitter.com&utm_medium=social&utm_campaign=smm_social_share&utm_content=21865722 (accessed 23 May 2019).
38 'Strategiia gosudarstvennoi kul'turnoi politiki na period do 2030 goda' (2016). http://docs.cntd.ru/document/420340006 (accessed 27 May 2019).

spectacularly from 2002 to 2008, reflecting the process of nationalization of the ROC and its rise to a position of the key shaper of the official Russian ideological agenda.

Figure 1   Absolute number of mentioning the word "culture" in the Church press — 8 titles (green), "Church and culture" in the central press — 476 titles (blue), and "Orthodoxy and culture" in the central press (red).

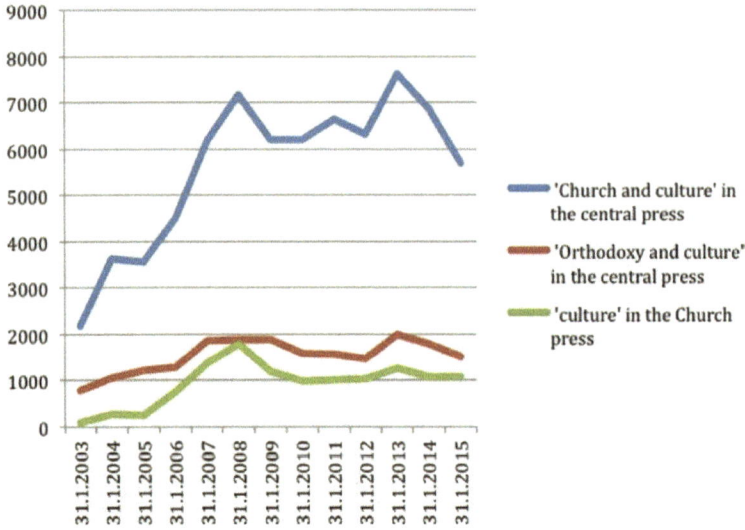

Source: Integrum Profi. Created by author on 30 May 2015.

Today, the master-narrative of the ROC is that "all Russian culture grows from the seeds of Orthodoxy".[39] For example, Alla Borodina's textbook *Bases of Orthodox Culture* for secondary schools calls Orthodoxy a "cultural organizer" in Russia and tends to mix together Russian national identity and Orthodox confessional identity.[40] The argument about the Orthodox roots of Russian culture automatically elevates the ROC to the position of the most important

---

39 Kliment (Kapalin), Metropolitan, 'Vsia russkaia kul'tura proizrastaet iz semian pravoslaviia' (2014). http://rusk.ru/newsdata.php?idar=66137. (accessed 1 January 2016).
40 A. Borodina, Osnovy pravoslavnoi kul'tury. Uchebnoe posobie dlia osnovnoi I starshei stupenei obshcheobrazovatel'nykh shkol, litseev, gimnazii. 2nd ed. (Moscow: Prosveshshchenie, 2003).

agency, defining cultural policy for the whole of the Russian people.[41] In 2012, Vladimir Medinskii, the newly appointed Minister of Culture, known for his nationalist and traditionalist views, initiated a speedy rapprochement between the state cultural policy and the ROC's cultural policy. The final showdown came with the public debates (2014) on the "Fundamentals of the Russian Cultural Policy", when the Church's representatives, most notably the influential Archimandrite Tikhon Shevkunov, came up with proposals to include the statement about Orthodoxy as the central and key element of Russian culture.[42] However, the version adopted on 24 December 2014 contained no reference to Orthodoxy in its Preamble.[43]

This failure to institutionalize the ROC's upper hand in Russian culture mirrors the internal predicament, in which the Church has trapped itself with its vision of Orthodox culture. It wants to lower the entry barrier for cultural production to be considered as religious in order to claim that all Russian culture is essentially Orthodox, but by so doing, the Church has to admit that the best accomplishments of the Russian culture gravitate away from religion.

Let us consider the confessional literary scholar Aleksei Liubomudrov's statement that an Orthodox work of literature is one in whose worldview God and the idea of salvation in the Church are the central values.[44] This view manifestly excludes the vast majority of the most venerated Russian writers and artists, whose works do not center on the Eucharist or the idea of salvation in the Church, and implicitly marginalizes the ROC, representing its contribution to the Russian culture as a sectarian "niche product".

---

41 A. Soldatov, 'Russkaia pravoslavnaia tserkov' na puti k monopolizatsii 'dukhovnogo prostranstva Rossii", *Otechestvennye zapiski*, 1(2003).
42 Tikhon (Shevkunov), archimandrite, '"Svetskost" gosudarstva ne podrazumevaet iskliucheniia religii iz obshchestvennoi zhizni' (2014) http://rusk line.ru/news_rl/2014/09/23/arhimandrit_tihon_shevkunov_svetskost_gosuda rstva_ne_podrazumevaet_isklyucheniya_religii_iz_obwestvennoj_zhizni (accessed 1 January 2016).
43 It mentioned, however, that "Orthodoxy played the special role in the formation of Russia's system of values" in Introduction. See: 'Osnovy gosudarstvennoi kul'turnoi politiki (24 December 2014).' http://static.kremlin.ru/me dia/events/files/41d526a877638a8730eb.pdf. (accessed 1 January 2016).
44 Aleksei Liubomudrov, Dukhovnyi realism v literature russkogo zarubezh'ia: B.K. Zaitsev, I.S. Shmelev. Doctor of science thesis (St Petersburg, 2001), 8.

It might well be that writers Boris Zaitsev and Ivan Shmelev meet these criteria of "Orthodox-ness", but what about Pushkin or Tolstoy? Although an incessant religious thinker, Tolstoy was also an outspoken critic of the Church as a result of which he was excommunicated in 1901.

One more example is the voluminous work of another confessional specialist in Russian literature, Professor Mikhail Dunaev, entitled *Orthodoxy and the Russian Literature* (1996–2004). Here the author puts forward the hypothesis that Russian literature, although not necessarily focused on subjects of Biblical history, nevertheless pictures the world in Orthodox categories.[45] In contradiction to this hypothesis, the rest of his study is a castigation of Russian writers from a dogmatic viewpoint. To pick up just a few of his statements: "By the end of his life, Leskov became obsessed with hatred of Orthodoxy"; "the goal of Leonid Andreev is to abase Christ and the Apostles;" "Blok was insensitive to authentic religious life"; "Gorky was serving the demon", and so on.[46] Contrary to Dunaev's intention, his reconstruction of Russian literature portrays it as anti-Christian *par excellence*.

More topical debates about culture revolve around the popularity of the non-mainstream youth music culture such as hip-hop songs. Existing on the margins of the official, state-controlled and TV-dominated culture, Russian rap dominates the digital cultural space, providing a handy medium for the youth to talk about politics and to express their discontent.

---

45   M. Dunaev, *Pravoslavnye osnovy russkoi literatury xix v.* Doctor of science thesis (Moscow, 1999), 3. Cf. with the statement by Vitalii Kaplan, the editor of the cultural branch in the ROC'S youth journal *Foma:* "If we look at the ... Russian classic literature ... we will see that the vast majority of these works has deep Christian nature" (Vitalii Kaplan, 'Nastoiashchaia literatura fal'shivit' ne mozhet' (2015) http://foma.ru/nastoyashhaya-literatura-falshivit-ne-mozhet. html (accessed 1 January 2016).

46   Quoted from: O. Zolotukhina, 'Problema "khristianstvo i russkaia literatura" v sovremennoi filologii', *Vestnik Tomskogo gosudarstvennogo universiteta,* 313 (2008): 14.

Understandably, there have been attempts to 'domesticate' rap by the propagators of the current regime,⁴⁷ as well as to instrumentalize it for the purposes of the Church mission.⁴⁸ For example, the music band 'Komba BAKKh' stages its radical political Orthodox agenda by drawing on the religious Messianism in the following rap verses:

> Moscow the Capital [is] our Third Rome —
> These are not empty words of the doctrines.
> [This is] the central theme of the Russian culture,
> The powerful response to the dictatorship of lawlessness.⁴⁹

At the same time, Orthodox clerics express much apprehension of rap music's negative impact on youth morality. Metropolitan Hilarion, for example, was horrified by one of the rap songs with dozens of millions of views on Youtube. This song, in his opinion, was propagating drugs, debauchery, homosexual relations and suicide – all staples of the present-day moral panics, initiated by the ROC.⁵⁰ Little wonder, that many Orthodox activists share concerns about the popularity of hip-hop; they see moral perils and foreign instigation there. One of the documents of this kind refers to the infamous 'Dulles's plan', arguing that the music hits by Monetochka and other popular singers are actually puppets of the ominous external forces, who intentionally propagate Satanism and morally

---

47 E.g. 'Kiselev zachital rep po itogam goda' (2019) https://lenta.ru/news/2019/01/03/kiselev_rap/ (accessed 23 May 2019).
48 M. Bokov, 'Batiushka v stile hip-hop' (2013) https://www.pravmir.ru/batyushka-v-stile-xip-xop/; Anton Skripunov, 'Zachityvai i kaisia: Zachem pravoslavnye vzialis' za hip-hop' (2017) https://ria.ru/20170909/1502115206.html (accessed 23 May 2019).
49 Stolitsa Moskva, nash Tretii Rim // — Eto ne pustye slova ocherednykh doktrin. // Tsentral'naia tema russkoi kul'tury, // Moshchnyi otvet diktature beschinstva. (It is worth noting that the lyrics are rendered in the Old Russian script). 'Tretii Rim' (n.d.) https://teksty-pesenok.ru/rus-komba-bakh/tekst-pesni-tretij-rim/1826201/ (accessed 27 May 2019).
50 Hilarion (Alfeev), Metropolitan, 'Vsiakaia popytka Tserkvi voiti v prostranstvo molodezhnoi subkul'tury zasluzhivaet podderzhki i priznaniia' (2017) http://www.patriarchia.ru/db/text/5039540.html (accessed 27 May 2019).

corrupt the Russian youth in order to destroy Russia's cultural tradition.[51] A popular media figure Father Georgi Maksimov unequivocally calls rap battles 'the flagrant symbol of the moral degradation of humanity' and a 'sin, which spoils and destroys life'.[52]

As we can gather from the controversy around the Russian rap music, the ROC is framing it according to the 'medium-barrier' ethno-national interpretation of culture. The ROC reserves the right for itself to pronounce on and judge the secular culture, to castigate its 'negative tendencies' from the religious viewpoint, and to work out (more or less successfully) models of appropriation of the secular cultural forms for the Church's purposes. The central method of engaging with the secular culture is securitization. The ROC eagerly aligns morally unacceptable forms of culture with the threat to the Russian state and 'civilization'.

Shaping the Orthodox Cultural Canon in Literature

While there is no unanimity in the theoretical understanding of what Orthodox culture is, the question can still be posed: what can be teased out empirically from the ongoing cultural production under the aegis of the Moscow Patriarchate? In literature, at first glance, Orthodox works occupy a very modest place, targeting mostly the internal Church audience of the "churchisized" population. For example, in 2013 the top 10 fiction books in Russia by print runs did not include any Orthodox authors.[53] And yet some books managed to make their way to a broader readership, such as father

---

51 V. Filimonov and L. Kudriashova, 'Satanizm "nevinnym" golosom: Monetochka, Grechka i prochie soblazny molodezhi ot masterov rastleniia' (n.d.). http://www.inform-relig.ru/news/detail.php?ID=16879. (accessed 27 May 2019) See also: V. Filimonov and L. Kudriashova, 'Kurs Monetochki vzletel do nebes' (2018) http://ruskline.ru/analitika/2018/09/2018-09-11/kurs_mon etochki_vzletel_do_nebes/ (accessed 27 May 2019).
52 'Sviashchennik o rep-battlakh' (2017) https://www.youtube.com/watch?time _continue=136&v=Z5fKEA9c408 (accessed May 27 2019). Nikita Mikhalkov, one of the key cultural figures in Russia and a proponent of the current regime, struck the same note when he criticized music band IC3PEAK for forgetting the concepts of sin and shame. See: N. Mikhalkov, 'Rebiata, a vy ne a.u.e.li?'(2018) https://www.youtube.com/watch?v=4gwjWMx6Euk (accessed 27 May 2019).
53 Knizhnyi rynok Rossii: *Sostoianie, tendentsii i perspektivy razvitiia* (Moscow, 2014), p. 15.

Tikhon Shevkunov's bestselling collection of short stories *Nesviatye sviatye* (2011), which has been published in some 2 million copies and downloaded 10,000 times from the Internet.[54] The Patriarchal Literary Prize, awarded annually since 2011, has cherry-picked the iconostasis of contemporary authors whose works give an impression of how "Orthodox literature" should look like. Importantly, among 12 winners, only one—Archpriest Nikolai Agafonov—is from the clergy, whereas others represent various degrees of the broader outreach, including heavyweights of the nationally-oriented flank of Soviet and Russian literature—Vladimir Krupin, Valerii Ganichev, Stanislav Kuniaev, and Iurii Bondarev.[55] This selection corroborates the firm will of the ROC to establish an ethno-national, broad understanding of Orthodox culture with relatively low entry barriers. The secretary of the Prize's board of trustees, Metropolitan Kliment (Kapalin) emphasizes that winners should not necessarily be Orthodox, but they have to "belong to Russian culture".[56] As we can judge from this, for Kliment 'belonging to Russian culture' is the litmus test for being Orthodox.

Curiously, writers of science fiction (sf) were nominated for this prize as well: Iulia Voznesenskaia, the author who wrote in the genre of Orthodox fantasy, Dmitrii Volodikhin, the author of Orthodox space operas,[57] and the controversial National-Bolshevik Aleksandr Prokhanov, known for his political (anti-)utopias. One of the experts presiding over the Prize is Father Vsevolod Chaplin, former Head of the Public Relations Department of the Moscow Patriarchate, who is also known as the author of anti-utopias written

---

54   V. Vigilianskii, '"Nesviatye sviatye" dostoiny knigi Ginnesa' (2015) http://ria.ru/poltava/20150313/1052261023.html (accessed 1 January 2016).
55   This literary prize has a webpage, available at http://patlitpremia.ru/persons/.
56   Kliment (Kapalin), Metropolitan, 'Tserkov' ishchet edinomyshlennikov' (2015). http://www.patriarchia.ru/db/print/1168112.html (accessed 1 January 2016). Cf.: D. Volodikhin, '"Den" pravoslavnogo pisatelia' (2015) http://foma.ru/den-pravoslavnogo-pisatelya.html (accessed January 1, 2016).
57   Another popular writer in this genre is Aleksandr Zorich. Cf. his novel *Zavtra voina*. 4th ed. (Moscow: Astrel', 2012). The main tenet of this strand in sf is the image of would-be Russia as an Orthodox empire, so powerful and advanced that it is conquering and colonizing the outer space (D. Volodikhin, 'Khram i kosmodrom: Futuristicheskie obrazy v russkoi imperskoi fantastike', *Politicheskii zhurnal*, 3 (2008)).

under the pseudonym of Aron Shemaier. The latter recently received a literary prize, conferred by the already mentioned Dmitrii Volodikhin,[58] the organizer of the sf convention "Bastion". Orthodoxy and sf overlap in the books of Georgii Letitskii (whose real name is Father Georgii Belodurov), and the aforementioned Vitalii Kaplan.

Evidently, Orthodox sf is becoming one of the mainstream genres for expressing the Orthodox cultural canon. Together with the flirtations with rock music, the sf extension of the Orthodox literature manifests the Church's attempts to reach out to the youth audience by representing Orthodoxy as a marketable "brand" on a par with such franchises as "Middle-earth" or "Narnia".[59] Science fiction and fantasy are also convenient for describing and testing different sociopolitical models. Indeed, for many of the Orthodox fictions the driving force of the narrative is not a moral problem but rather a cultural difference. The plotline focuses on contrasting the good "us"-community to the bad "them" community, much like the plot structure of the cult novel *The Young Guard* (1946) by Aleksandr Fadeev, which belongs to the socialist realist canon. Here the moral problem is reduced to the tension between an already integral and harmonious personage and the hostile environment. Another possible collision could be centered on the cultural relocation of the protagonist from the wrong side of the barricade to the right one. Importantly, the heroes in this fiction are already predisposed towards religion, so their move does not initiate a moral drama. For example, the protagonist of *The Way of Cassandra* (2002) by Iulia Voznesenskaia is getting gradually acculturated to the monastic life, and is forgetting the sinful ways of the laypeople. Thus, fictitious personages surrender their agency to a community of believers, and the core problematic focuses not a personal moral choice,

---

[58] Volodikhin defined his credo in writing as "preserving cultural sovereignty, maintaining Russian language, literature, history and Orthodoxy" (D. Volodikhin, *Intellektual'naia fantastika* (Moscow: Istoriko-prosvetitel'skoe obshchestvo, 2007), p. 159.

[59] In parallel, the sub-genre of sacral sf has developed in today's Russian literature, featuring such authors as Dalia Truskinovskaia, Gleb Eliseev, Elena Khaetskaia, Elena Chudinova (I. Moskvin, "'Nabliudatel'. Proekt. Sakral'naia fantastika,' *Znamia*, 1 (2005): 225–228; Volodikhin, "Domoi!", *Moskva*, 2 (2007)).

but on belonging and faithfulness. Following Mark Lipovetskii's interpretation of contemporary Russian literature as a mixture of post-modernism and socialist realism ("post-sots"), one can observe that Orthodox literature is markedly post-socialist, whose protagonist "is modeled after an epic hero … He appears as already psychologically mature; the hero does not develop but in the best cases merely 'unfolds' [his properties] … [This literature] almost always combines two opposite strategies: it registers the collapse of collective identities and weaves it into a transfixing nostalgia for "we".[60]

It is suggestive that confessional literary studies have advanced the copycat term "spiritual realism", intended to grasp the orientation of Orthodox fiction towards depiction of religious phenomena as real facts of everyday life, and not merely as symbols. Introduced by such critics as Mikhail Dunaev and Aleksei Liubomudrov,[61] the term "spiritual realism" translates the iconodulic theology into the language of literary fiction. By showing the presence of God in people's lives, Orthodox literature not only depicts but also glorifies God, thereby morphing into a prayer or sorts. Thus, Olesia Nikolaeva prefaces her book with an explanation that her intention is to document the miraculous presence of the deity in her life. She warns, however, that this verges on a sinful temptation because miracles of God's interventions are manifestations of God's glory, inexpressible in human language.[62] A literary narrative in this sense is not literature in a strict sense but rather a practice of communication with God. The artistic method of this lit-

---

60 M. Lipovetskii, Paralogii: Transformatsii (post)modernistskogo diskursa v russkoi kul'ture 1920–2000-kh godov (Moscow: nlo, 2008), pp. 732, 741.
61 See, e.g.: Liubomudrov, 'Dukhovnyi realizm kak otrazhenie religioznoi kul'tury v khudozhestvennoi literature,' Vestnik slavianskikh kul'tur 9, 1–2 (2008). Today, the term is used by the home-made Church literary scholars, see: I. Avanesian, 'Problemy izucheniia dukhovnogo realizma kak khudozhestvennogo metoda v sovremennom literaturovedenii', Filologicheskie nauki: Voprosy teorii i praktiki 20(2) (2013): 13–15; I. Kazantseva, 'Traditsii dukhovnogo realizma v proze V.N. Krupnina', Vestnik Viatskogo gosudarstvennogo gumanitarnogo universiteta, 1 (2009), pp. 150–154.
62 Nikolaeva, 'Nebesnyi ogon" i drugie rasskazy. 8th ed. (Moscow: izd-vo Sretenskogo monastyria, 2012), pp. 5–6.

erature could truly be called "spiritual realism" because it reconstructs a utopian world which looks realistic yet in which Orthodox postulates can not be questioned.[63] Similarly to how the socialist culture appropriated and metamorphosed various aspects of the Orthodox culture, today's Orthodoxy cannot separate itself from the idea of societally conscious, utopian and state-controlled cultural forms.

Orthodox Animation Film Incredible Travelling of Serafima

In order to better integrate the discussion of the discourses about culture and cultural practices with the grassroots reception of Orthodox cultural products, I will discuss the animation film *The Extraordinary Travelling of Serafima* (director Sergei Antonov), released in August 2015. This film became a meeting ground, on which the elite's attempt to recycle the assumption of synonymy between the Russian and Orthodox cultures, faced the actual popular attitudes of the Russian audience to such attempts. The film was partially financed by the Ministry of Culture of Russia and partially by the Foundation of St Seraphim of Sarov. We can assume that the film reflects visions and ideas of the highest clerics of the ROC; it contains a very pronounced interpretation of Russian history, which goes beyond the confines of our present research. The plotline is about Serafima, a small girl whose father was a priest killed by the Bolsheviks. She lives in an orphanage, and the story is set in the period of the Great Patriotic War of 1941–45. She believes in God and wears her lost mother's cross. The cruel Communist teacher tries to take away the cross and compels Serafima to say that God does not exist. She refuses and in punishment she is to be sent to a penal colony. She falls ill and in feverish ravings she meets her celestial

---

63 Cf. with the socialist realist canon, as expressed at the 1st All-Union Convention of Soviet Writers: "... [the task of] historical precision [*konkretnost'*] of the artistic representation should be combined with the task of intellectual remaking and educating of the Soviet people" (*Pervyi vsesoiuznyi s'ezd sovetskikh pisatelei, 1934. Stenograficheskii otchet* (Moscow, 1934), 4). The utopian propensity of socialist realism was explored in the famous article Abram Terts [Siniavskii], "Chto takoe sotsrealizm?" in *S raznykh tochek zreniia. Izbavlenie ot mirazhei. Sotsrealizm segodnia* (Moscow, 1990), pp. 54–80.

protector St Seraphim, who shows her Heaven and introduces her to God (figure 2). When the car comes to take her to the colony, she miraculously runs to her lost mother.

Figure 2   A snapshot from the trailer of the animation film Neobyknovennoe puteshestvie Serafimy (2015), representing the scene of Serafima's visionary travelling to heaven, guided by St Serafim of Sarov.

Source: http://www.kinopoisk.ru/film/893199/video/123448/ (accessed 1 February 2016).

In spite of the film's abundant discrepancies in the plotline, dubious rendition of the historical moment, and hopelessly bad graphics, *Serafima* was designed as a flagship of the Orthodox cultural production, as the first full-length Orthodox animation film ever. It was accompanied by massive advertising, including a special word of commendation from Patriarch Kirill. *Serafima* was released in the best possible time for animation movies — the last weekend of August — just before the start of the school year, and it was shown in 895 copies (cf. the Oscar-nominated European animation film of 2014 *The Song of the Sea* was released in Russia in 22 copies only). And still, it would be a stretch to call it a success; many commentators, even favourably disposed towards Orthodoxy or staunchly Orthodox, noted that they were sitting alone in the cinema hall; others noted that this was a "niche" product, fine-tuned for the already "churchisized" public, but utterly uninteresting for the broader audience. The film with a budget of 2 million dollars has returned less than 1.5 million so far. The average rate of the film on kinopoisk.ru (this is a Russian analogue of the IMDb) is remarkably low—4,67 (out of 10), grounded on 1,843 votes.[64] A few positive reviews point at the fact that *Serafima* is an antidote to vulgarity and bad taste, and more specifically—an alternative and opposition to American-style popular culture products.[65] Opposing *Serafima* to the Hollywood standard is probably the most common argument of the commentators.[66] In general, however, *Serafima* triggered much controversy even among the Orthodox believers. Two main discontents with the film were focused on its vision of the history of the Great Patriotic War, and on the theological appropriateness of the artistic interpretation of religious themes.

First, conservative critics highlighted the thoroughly negative image of the communist and atheistic authorities. They maintain that *Serafima* represents views of the liberal flank of the ROC. As historian Elena Seniavskaia argues, the film insidiously implies that if the regime is godless, violently oppressing the Orthodox protagonist, then in its fight with Nazi Germany the truth is on the side of the latter. Thus, in spite of the film's self-proclaimed glorification of Orthodoxy, it, in fact, creates an evil slander against Russia and the Russian (read: Orthodox) culture.[67]

Second, *Serafima* aroused suspicion with its non-canonical interpretation of Church dogmas. Commentators criticize the visualization of heaven, its inhabitants and God (cf. figure 2). Some critics argue that this visualization is akin to the devil's temptation, or that it is sacrilegious because saints are shown as common people or as

---

64 http://www.kinopoisk.ru/film/893199/votes/ (accessed 1 January 2016).
65 F. Ermoshin. 'Strannaia "Serafima"' (2015) http://www.taday.ru/text/2145118.html (accessed 1 January 2016).
66 Aleksandr. Comment on 3 September 2015 from http://azbyka.ru/ fiction/neobyknovennoe-puteshestvie-serafimy/; (accessed January 1, 2016). Dmitrii Rusin, 'Besstrashnoe puteshestvie Serafimy' (2015) http://pravchelny.ru/all_publications/ publications/?ID=12857 (accessed 1 January 2016).
67 E. Seniavskaia. '"Dobryi mul'tik" pro devochku Serafimu, pravoslavnyi krestik i stalinskie repressii.' https://gazeta.eot.su/article/dobryy-multik-pro-devochku-serafimu-pravoslavnyy-krestik-i-stalinskie-repressii (accessed 1 January 2016).

fairy-tail heroes.[68] Avid spectators harnessed the argument of sacrilege, pointing at the film's too detailed depiction of St Seraphim and archangels as common people. They say that the very notion of an "Orthodox (animation) film" is an oxymoron, similarly to how "it would be delusional to speak of Orthodox dancing, Orthodox theater and so on".[69] As one of the commentators noted, "this is a pure sacrilege to show St Seraphim as a fairytale hero."[70] Another argument pointed at Serfima's visionary experience as a "state of temptation" [*prélestnoe sostoianie*], damaging to the soul's purity.[71] For many Orthodox believers, artistic depiction of key events and characters of the New Testament is sacrilegious, when Apostles or saints are represented as "normal" people, even if an artist is absolutely well-intentioned. The novel by Timofei Veronin (2009), which provided the basis for the animation film, received negative reviews from the conservatives, who accused the author of blasphemy.[72] Following this line of argumentation, some commentators deplored the very idea of relocating religious artifacts and events (e.g. icons, censers, churches, prayers, fasting, services, etc.) from the religious context to the sphere of popular culture.[73] Hence, *Serafima* is castigated for reducing Orthodoxy to the status of the marketable glamorous brand.[74]

---

68 D. Targonskii. 'Neobyknovennye prikliucheniia Serafimy – "rozy" Russkogo mira.' http://www.religion.in.ua/main/30502-neobyknovennye-priklyuchen iya-serafimy-rozy-russkogo-mira.html (accessed 1 January 2016).
69 A. Matsnev. Comment on 13 October 2015 at 12:49. http://www.blagogon .ru/digest/644/. (accessed 1 January 2016).
70 Lina. Comment on 14 October 2015 at 17:29. Cf. Nina V. Comment on 21 October 2015 at 11: 32. http://www.blagogon.ru/digest/644/ (accessed 1 January 2016).
71 A. Tat'iana. Comment on 19 October 2015 at 14:32. http:// www.blagogon.ru/digest/644/ (accessed 1 January 2016).
72 A. Korolev. 'Gor'ko priznavat'sia, chto otrok slabovat umom ...' (2009) http://rusk.ru/st.php?idar=105733 (accessed 1 January 2016).
73 Igor' P. Comment on 4 November 2015 at 14:24. http://www.blagogon.ru/di gest/644/ (accessed 1 January 2016).
74 Cf. "[we shall] boycott this pseudo-Orthodox glamour product" (Natalia, M. Comment on 13 October 2015 at 16:12. http://www.blagogon.ru/ digest/644/.) (accessed 1 January 2016).

The public, critically disposed towards Orthodoxy, assessed *Serafima* almost unanimously in negative terms. Here are a few quotations from the comments on kinopoisk.ru: "this disgusting animation film has a disgusting idea that Orthodox believers are always the best";[75] "this is not an animation film, but badly made cheap propaganda";[76] "this is a sermon for 200 roubles"[77] (meaning the cost of the ticket to the movie); "The main protagonist, who is supposed to evoke positive emotions, in fact exasperates me; she is disagreeable, arrogant and emotionless. Why is she a good hero in the film? Only because she believes in God and wears a cross — and that's enough? Well, I am not convinced ..."[78]

To sum this up, *Serafima* was a trial balloon to brand an Orthodox cultural product as a popular franchise for mass consumption nationwide; it was an attempt to destabilize the border between the churchisized minority and the vicariously believing majority of people, who associate themselves with Orthodoxy and thereby constitute the target audience for Orthodox cultural products. Now we know that it is not so. 500,000 spectators and 1.5 million US dollars is way short of the success of, for example, the Disney animation movie *Frozen*, which collected 34 million US dollars in Russia with an audience of 5 million spectators.

Conclusions

Very moderate resonance of *Incredible Travelling of Serafima* shows that the ROC has to fight on two cultural fronts. On the one hand, the ROC wants to overcome the inertia of the high-barrier understanding of Orthodox culture among its own flock in order to get rid of the sectarian self-positioning as a "chosen minority" and to promote an alternative vision of Orthodoxy as the core of Russian

---

75 Boggrot. Review on 10 September 2015 http://www.kinopoisk.ru/user/636 0808/comments/ (accessed 1 January 2016).
76 IvanHoe159. Review on 6 September 2015 http://www.kinopoisk.ru/user/ 4728524/comment/2289894/ (accessed 1 January 2016).
77 Berik_ts. Review on 31 August 2015 http://www.kinopoisk.ru/user/633 6687/comments/ (accessed 1 January 2016).
78 Innodzhen_DS. Review on 24 September 2015 http://www.kinopoisk.ru/user /5186034/comment/2297713/ (accessed 1 January 2016).

national culture. On the other, the ROC has yet to learn how to produce competitive cultural products for the market, which appears to be out and out secular. Religious cultural products can well be demanded on broader, largely secular markets,[79] but the ROC's case is different. In spite of the recent conservative turn and preponderance of the religious marker for the identity of the Russians, the Church's aspirations to represent Orthodoxy as Russia's "basic culture" were not met by actual grassroots habits of cultural consumption: the theory hangs in the air. Of course, the Church's intellectuals were not blind to the fact that Orthodox cultural identity is not directly translatable into real believing and belonging. Father Vsevolod Chaplin, then still the speaker of the ROC, quite in tune with the Iranian revolution of 1979, called for the "moral revolution" in Russia.[80] This statement echoes more cautious ideas, voiced by Patriarch Kirill, who wanted to "re-format" the whole of Russian society in accordance with the Church's precepts.[81] But where to find the pivot for this transformation, given that the ROC is navigating in a culturally pluralist society?[82]

It seems that the ROC is increasingly seeing this pivot in the state's administrative power. The logic of the moral panics initiated by the Church in relation to some recent cultural events, such as the production of the opera *Tannhäuser* in Novosibirsk (premiered in December 2014),[83] demonstrates the proclivity of the Orthodox activists to reinstitute a kind of preliminary censorship *à la* Soviet-era *Glavrepertkom* in the form of public councils, which would check if taxpayers' money supports cultural production agreeable to the

---

79 Cf. B. Turner, 'Religion in a Post-Secular Society', in The New Blackwell Companion to the Sociology of Religion. B. Turner, ed. (Chichester : Wiley-Blackwell, 2010), p. 651.
80 V. Chaplin, 'Obshchestvu nuzhna nravstvennaia revolutsiia' (2011) http://www.pravoslavie.ru/49038.html (accessed 1 January 2016).
81 E.g.: 'Patriarkh Kirill prizval veruiushchikh sovershit' vnutrenniuiu revoliutsiiu' (2014) http://ria/ru/religion/20140828/1021757945.html. (accessed 1 January 2016).
82 Cf. with the statement of Peter Berger that Modernity does not necessarily secularize but it necessarily produces pluralism (P. Berger, 'Secularization Falsified', *First Things*, 180 (2008), pp. 23–27.
83 See Irina Kotkina's contribution to this special issue.

majority of the Russian population.[84] To reiterate, the ROC's striving to go beyond the post-secular pluralistic society and "restore a context in which religious values are the objects of social consensus"[85] prodded the Church to embrace the ethno-national theory of culture. In a way, as Elena Namli has expressed, Russian Orthodoxy, once again, has ceded to the "temptation of power".[86] Coupled with the lack of theological reflection on culture and with the ascendance of the socialist cultural standards, it has created the situation of "dominance without hegemony", which, in turn, can only augment the Church's reliance on the state which leads to disconnectedness from the centers of cultural production.

Bibliography

Abram Terts [Siniavskii], 'Chto takoe sotsrealizm?' In *S raznykh tochek zreniia. Izbavlenie ot mirazhei. Sotsrealizm segodnia* (Moscow, 1990) 54–80.

Agadjanian, A., 'Revisiting Pandora's Gifts: Religious and National Identity in the PostSoviet Societal Fabric', *Europe-Asia Studies* 53(3) (2001): 473–488.

Aleksandr. Comment on 3 September 2015, http://azbyka.ru/fiction/ne obyknovennoeputeshestvie-serafimy/ (accessed 1 January 2016).

Andreeva, T., Comment on 19 October 2015, http://www.blagogon.ru/di gest/644/ (accessed 1 January 2016).

Avanesian, I., 'Problemy izucheniia dukhovnogo realizma kak khudozhestvennogo metoda v sovremennom literaturovedenii', *Filologicheskie nauki: Voprosy teorii i praktiki* 20(2) (2013): 13–15.

Barabanov, E., 'Sud'ba khristianskoi kul'tury', *Kontinent*, 151 (2012 [1976]), http://magazines.russ.ru/continent/2012/151/b46.html (accessed 1 January 2016).

Berdiaev, N., *Smysl tvorchestva: Opyt opravdaniia cheloveka* (Moscow, 1994 [1916]).

Berger, P., 'Secularization Falsified', *First Things*, 180 (2008): 23–27.

---

84 'Stenogramma obshchestvennogo obsuzhdeniia' (2015) http://mkrf.ru/ministerstvo/departament/detail.php?ID=623062. (accessed 1 January 2016).
85 S. Saha, *Religious Fundamentalism in the Contemporary World* (Langham, Md: Lexington Books, 2004), p. 33.
86 E. Namli, 'Pravoslavnoe bogoslovie i iskushenie vlast'iu,' *Gosudarstvo, religiia, tserkov' v Rossii i za rubezhom* 32(3) (2014), pp. 12–41.

Berger, P., 'Social Sources of Secularization'. In *Culture and Society: Contemporary Debates*. ed. J. Alexander and S. Seidman (Cambridge: Cambridge University Press, 1990) 239–49.

Berik_ts. Review on 31 August 2015, http://www.kinopoisk.ru/user/6336687/comments/ (accessed 1 January 2016).

Boggrot. Review on 10 September 2015, http://www.kinopoisk.ru/user/6360808/comments/ (accessed 1 January 2016).

Bokov, M. 'Batiushka v stile hip-hop', Pravmir.ru 26 November 2013, https://www.pravmir.ru/batyushka-v-stile-xip-xop/ (accessed 28 May 2019).

Borodina, A., *Osnovy pravoslavnoi kul'tury. Uchebnoe posobie dlia osnovnoi i starshei stupenei obshcheobrazovatel'nykh shkol, litseev, gimnazii*. 2nd ed. (Moscow: Prosveshchenie, 2003).

Bulgakov, S., *Filosofiia imeni* (Paris: YMCA-Press, 1953).

Chaplin, V., 'Obshchestvu nuzhna nravstvennaia revolutsiia', *Pravoslavie.ru* 4 October 2011, http://www.pravoslavie.ru/49038.html (accessed 1 January 2016).

'Dannye o posetivshikh rozhdestvenskie bogosluzheniia', Sova-Center 9 January 2008, http://www.sova-center.ru/religion/discussions/how-many/2008/01/d12353/ (accessed 1 January 2016).

Davie, G., 'Vicarious Religion: A Methodological Challenge'. In *Everyday Religion: Observing Modern Religious Lives*. ed. N. Ammerman (Oxford: Oxford University Press, 2006) 21–36.

Dunaev, M. *Pravoslavnye osnovy russkoi literatury xix v.*, Doctor of Science Thesis, Moscow Pedagogic University, Moscow (1999).

Ermoshin, F., 'Strannaia "Serafima"', *Tat'ianin den'* 23 September 2015, http://www.taday.ru/text/2145118.html (accessed 1 January 2016).

Filatov, S., 'Orthodoxy in Russia: Post-atheist Faith', *Studies in World Christianity* 14(3) (2008), 187–202.

Filatov, S., 'Patriarkh Kirill—Dva goda planov, mechtanii i neudobnoi real'nosti'. In *Pravoslavnaia tserkov' pri novom patriarkhe*. Eds. A. Malashenko and S. Filatov (Moscow: ROSSPEN, 2012).

Filimonov, V., and Kudriashova, L., 'Satanizm "nevinnym" golosom: Monetochka, Grechka i prochie soblazny molodezhi ot masterov rastleniia', *Inform-Religiia* n.d., http://www.inform-relig.ru/news/detail.php?ID=16879 (accessed 28 May 2019).

Filimonov, V., Larisa Kudriashova, 'Kurs Monetochki vzletel do nebes', *Russlaia narodnaia liniia* 11 September 2018, http://ruskline.ru/analitika/2018/09/2018-09-11/kurs_monetochki_vzletel_do_nebes/ (accessed 28 May 2019).

Florenskii, P., 'Avtoreferat', *Voprosy filosofii* 12 (1988): 113–116.

Florenskii, P., 'Iz bogoslovskogo naslediia'. *Bogoslovskii sbornik* 17 (1977): 119–230.

Florenskii, P., 'Zapiska o khristianstve i kul'ture (1923)'. In *Florenskii, Sochineniia v 4-kh tomakh*, vol. 2 (Moscow: Mysl', 1996) 547–559.

Garrard J. and Garrard, C., *Russian Orthodoxy Resurgent: Faith and Power in the New Russia* (Princeton: Princeton University Press, 2009).

Guha, R., *Dominance without Hegemony: History and Power in Colonial India* (Cambridge, Mass.: Harvard University Press, 1997).

Hilarion (Alfeev), Metropolitan, 'Russkaia poeziia xx veka sokhranila v sebe moshchnoe religioznoe i khristianskoe nachalo', *Patriarchia.ru* 27 May 2015, http://www.patriarchia.ru/db/print/4099271.html (accessed 1 January 2016).

Hilarion (Alfeev), Metropolitan. *Tserkov' otkryta dlia kazhdogo* (Minsk: Belorusskaia Pravoslavnaia Tserkov', 2011).

Hilarion (Alfeev), Metropolitan, 'Vsiakaia popytka Tserkvi voiti v prostranstvo molodezhnoi subkul'tury zasluzhivaet podderzhki i priznaniia', *Patriarchia.ru* 18 October 2017, http://www.patriarchia.ru/db/text/5039540.html (accessed 28 May 2019).

Igor' P. Comment on 4 November 2015 at 14:24, http://www.blagogon.ru/digest/644/ (accessed 1 January 2016).

Il'in, I., *Krizis bezbozhiia* (Moscow: "Dar", 2005 [1935]).

Innodzhen_DS. Review on 24 September 2015, http://www.kinopoisk.ru/user/5186034/comment/2297713/ (accessed 1 January 2016).

'Iskusstvo i iskus', *Russkaia narodnaia Liniia* 7 June 2006, http://ruskline.ru/analitika/2006/06/07/iskusstvo_i_iskus (accessed 1 January 2016).

IvanHoe159. Review on 6 September 2015, http://www.kinopoisk.ru/user/4728524/comment/2289894/ (accessed 1 January 2016).

Kaplan, V., 'Nastoiashchaia literatura fal'shivit' ne mozhet', *Foma* 5 (145) May 2015, http://foma.ru/nastoyashhaya-literatura-falshivit-ne-mozhet.html (accessed 1 January 2016).

Kazantseva, I., 'Traditsii dukhovnogo realizma v proze V.N. Krupnina', *Vestnik Viatskogo gosudarstvennogo gumanitarnogo universiteta*, 1 (2009): 150–154.

Khoruzhii, S., *O starom i novom* (St Petersburg: Aleteiia, 2000).

Kilill (Gudniaev), Patriarch, 'Vystuplenie Predstoiatelia Russkoi Tserkvi na tseremonii vrucheniia Patriarshei literaturnoi premii', *Patriarchia.ru* 28 May 2015, http://www.patriarchia.ru/db/text/4100626.html (accessed 1 January 2016).

Kirill (Gundiaev), Patriarch, *Sviatoi kniaz' Vladimir: Tsivilizatsionnyi vybor Rusi* (Moscow: Izd-vo Moskovskoi Patriarkhii, 2015).

Kirill (Gundiaev), Patriarch, 'Neobkhodima postoiannaia ploshchadka dlia dialoga Tserkvi i mira iskusstva', *Tass* 11 December 2015, http://tass.ru/obschestvo/2517401 (accessed 1 January 2016).

Kirill (Gundiaev), Patriarch, 'Otritsaia Bozhiiu pravdu, my razrushaem mir.' Patriarchia. ru 10 March 2015c, http://www.patriarchia.ru/db/print/4010650.html (accessed 1 January 2016).

Kirill (Gundiaev), Patriarch, *Preodolenie smuty* (Moscow: Izdatel'stvo Moskovskoi Patriarkhii, 2013).

Kirill (Gundiaev), Patriarch, *Propovedi 2009–2010* (Sergiev Posad: Izd. Sviato-Troitskoi Sergievoi Lavry, 2010).

Kirill (Gundiaev), Patriarch. *Patriarkh i molodezh': Razgovor bez diplomatii* (Moscow: Danilovskii blagovestnik, 2009).

'Kiselev zachital rep po itogam goda', Lenta.ru 3 January 2019, https://lenta.ru/news/2019/01/03/kiselev_rap/ (accessed 28 May 2019).

Kliment (Kapalin), Metropolitan, 'Tserkov' ishchet edinomyshlennikov', Patriarchia.ru 30 March 2015, http://www.patriarchia.ru/db/print/1168112.html (accessed 1 January 2016).

Kliment (Kapalin), Metropolitan, 'Vsia russkaia kul'tura proizrastaet iz semian pravoslaviia', *Russkaia liniia* 20 May 2014, http://rusk.ru/newsdata.php?idar=66137 (accessed 1 January 2016).

Knizhnyi rynok Rossii: Sostoianie, tendentsii i perspektivy razvitiia: Otraslevoi doklad. Ed. V. Grigor'ev (Moscow: Federal'noe agentstvo po pechati i massovym kommunikatsiiam, 2014).

Knorre, B., 'Kategorii viny v sisteme tsennostei tserkovno-prikhodskoi subkul'tury'. In *Prokhod i obshchina v sovremennom pravoslavii: kornevaia sistema rossiiskoi religioznosti*. ed. A. Agadzhanian and K. Russele [Rousselet] (Moscow: Ves' mir, 2011) 318–35.

Korolev, A., 'Gor'ko priznavat'sia, chto otrok slabovat umom ...', *Russkaia liniia* 7 May 2009, http://rusk.ru/st.php?idar=105733 (accessed 1 January 2016).

Kyrlezhev, A., 'Postsekuliarnaia epokha', *Kontinent*, 120 (2004), http://magazines.russ.ru/continent/2004/120/kyr16.html (accessed 1 January 2016).

Lina. Comment on 14 October 2015, http://www.blagogon.ru/digest/644/ (accessed 1 January 2016).

Lipovetskii, M., *Paralogii: Transformatsii (post)modernistskogo diskursa v russkoi kul'ture 1920–2000-kh godov* (Moscow: NLO, 2008).

Liubomudrov, A., 'Dukhovnyi realizm kak otrazhenie religioznoi kul'tury v khudozhestvennoi literature,' *Vestnik slavianskikh kul'tur* 9(1-2) (2008): 113-120.

Liubomudrov, A. *Dukhovnyi realism v literature russkogo zarubezh'ia: B.K. Zaitsev, I.S. Shmelev*, Doctor of Science Thesis, Institute for Russian Literature/Russian Academy of Science, St Petersburg (2001).

Matsnev, A., Comment on 13 October 2015, http://www.blagogon.ru/digest/644/ (accessed 1 January 2016).

Mazaev, S., 'Grekh protiv vkusa'. In *Politicheskoe pravoslavie: Strategicheskii zhurnal 2*. ed. P. Sviatenkov, B. Mezhuev, and M. Remizov (Moscow: APN, 2006) 286-87.

Meshcherina, E., *Dukhovnye osnovy tvorchestva: Stat'i o russkoi kul'ture* (Moscow: "Kanon+", 2015).

Meyendorff, J., *Byzantine Theology: Historical Trends and Doctrinal Themes*. 2nd ed. (New York: Fordham University Press, 1979).

Mikhalkov, N. 'Rebiata, a vy ne a.u.e.li?', Besogon TV Youtube channel, 14 December 2018, https://www.youtube.com/watch?v=4gwjWMx6Euk (accessed 28 May 2019).

Moskvin, I., 'Nabliudatel'. Proekt. Sakral'naia fantastika', *Znamia* 1 (2005): 225-228.

Namli, E., 'Pravoslavnoe bogoslovie i iskushenie vlast'iu', *Gosudarstvo, religiia, tserkov' v Rossii i za rubezhom* 32(3) (2014): 12-41.

Natalia. Comment on 13 October 2015, http://www.blagogon.ru/digest/644/ (accessed 1 January 2016).

Nikolaeva, O., *"Nebesnyi ogon'" i drugie rasskazy*. 8th ed. (Moscow: Izd-vo Sretenskogo monastyria, 2012).

Nikolaeva, O., *Pravoslavie i tvorchestvo* (Moscow: Nikeia, 2012).

Nina V., Comment on 21 October 2015, http://www.blagogon.ru/digest/644/ (accessed 1 January 2016).

O'Sullivan, N. *Conservatism* (London: Dent, 1976).

Novoprudnyi, S. 'Skvernyi khram: Pochemu protest v Yekaterinburge pokazal istinnoe otnoshenie rossiian k "dukhovnym skrepam"', *Spektr* 15 May 2019, https://spektr.press/skvernyj-hram-pochemu-protest-v-ekaterinburge-pokazal-istinnoe-otnoshenie-rossiyan-k-duhovnym-skrepam/ (accessed 28 May 2019).

Palonen, K., 'Quentin Skinner's Rhetoric of Conceptual Change', *History of the Human Sciences* 10(2) (1997): 61-80.

'Patriarkh Kirill prizval veruiushchikh sovershit' vnutrenniuiu revoliutsiiu', Patriarchia.ru 10 March 2015, http://www.patriarchia.ru/db/print/4010650.html (accessed 1 January 2016).

'Patriarkh v otvet na sanktsii prizval zashchishchat' dukhovnyi suverenitet strany', *TASS* 14 August 2018, https://tass.ru/obschestvo/5455523 ?utm_source=twitter.com&utm_medium=social&utm_campaign=s mm_social_share&utm_content=21865722 (accessed 28 May 2019).

Payne, D., 'Spiritual Security, the Russian Orthodox Church, and the Russian Foreign Ministry: Collaboration or Cooptation?' *Journal of Church and State* 52(4) (2010): 1-16.

Pervyi vsesoiuznyi s'ezd sovetskikh pisatelei, 1934. Stenograficheskii otchet (Moscow: Khudozhestvennaia literatura, 1934).

'Religiia i tserkov' v obshchestvennoi zhizni', Levada-Center 18 April 2013, https://www.levada.ru/2013/04/18/religiya-i-tserkov-v-obshhest vennoj-zhizni/ (accessed 28 May 2019).

Richters, K., *The Post-Soviet Russian Orthodox Church: Politics, Culture and Greater Russia* (London: Routledge, 2013).

'Rossiiane o religii', *Levada-Center* 24 December 2013, http://www.levada. ru/2013/12/24/rossiyane-o-religii/ (accessed 1 November 2015).

'Rossiiane stali bol'she doveriat' armii', *Levada-Center* 7 October 2015, http://www.levada.ru/2015/10/07/rossiyane-stali-bolshe-dovery at-armii/ (accessed 1 November 2015).

Rusin, D., 'Besstrashnoe puteshestvie Serafimy', *Pravoslavnoe Zakam'e* 19 September 2015, http://pravchelny.ru/all_publications/publication s/?ID=12857 (accessed 1 January 2016).

Ryzhova, S., 'Tolerance and Extremism: Russian Ethnicity in the Orthodox Discourse of the 1990s'. In *Religion and Identity in Modern Russia: The Revival of Orthodoxy and Islam.* ed. J. Johnson, M. Stepaniants, and B. Forest (Aldershot: Ashgate, 2005), 65-90.

Saha, S., *Religious Fundamentalism in the Contemporary World* (Langham, Md: Lexington Books, 2004).

Seniavskaia, E., "Dobryi mul'tik' pro devochku Serafimu, pravoslavnyi krestik i stalinskie repressii', *Sut' vremeni* 148 7 October 2015, https://gazeta.eot.su/node/1805/draft (accessed 1 January 2016).

Shishkov, A., 'Nekotorye aspekty desekuliarizatsii v postsovetskoi Rossii', *Gosudarstvo, religiia, tserkov' v Rossii i za rubezhom* 30(2) (2012): 165-177.

Skinner, Q., *Visions of Politics. Regarding Method* (Cambridge: Cambridge University Press, 2002).

Skripunov, A. 'Zachityvai i kaisia: Zachem pravoslavnye vzialis' za hip-hop', *RIA Novosti* 9 September 2017, https://ria.ru/20170909/150211 5206.html (accessed 28 May 2019).

Soldatov, A., 'Russkaia pravoslavnaia tserkov' na puti k monopolizatsii 'dukhovnogo prostranstva Rossii', *Otechestvennye zapiski*, (2003), http://www.strana-oz.ru/2003/1/russkaya-pravoslavnaya-cerkovna-puti-k-monopolizacii-duhovnogo-prostranstva-rossii (accessed 1 January 2016).

'Stenogramma obshchestvennogo obsuzhdeniia', *Minister of Culture of the Russian Federation* 19 March 2015, http://mkrf.ru/ministerstvo/departament/detail.php?ID=623062 (accessed 1 January 2016).

'Strategiia gosudarstvennoi kul'turnoi politiki na period do 2030 goda', *Konsortsium Kodeks* 29 February 2016, http://docs.cntd.ru/document/420340006 (accessed 28 May 2019).

Suslov, M., '"Holy Rus": The Geopolitical Imagination in the Contemporary Russian Orthodox Church', *Russian Politics and Law* 52(3) (2014): 67–86.

Suslov, M., 'Russian Orthodox Church and the Crisis in Ukraine'. In *The Churches in the Ukrainian Crisis*. ed. T. Bremer and A. Krawchuk (Bern: Palgrave Macmillan, 2016).

Suslov, M. and Uzlaner, D., (eds.), *Contemporary Russian Conservatism: Problems, Paradoxes and Dangers* (Leiden: Brill, forthcoming 2019).

'Sviashchennik o rep-battlakh', *Ierei Georgii Maksimov Youtube channel* 3 September 2017 https://www.youtube.com/watch?time_continue=136&v=Z5fKEA9c408 (accessed 28 May 2019).

Targonskii, D., 'Neobyknovennye prikliucheniia Serafimy—"rozy" Russkogo mira', *Religiia v Ukraini* 28 2015, http://www.religion.in.ua/main/30502-neobyknovennye-priklyucheniya-serafimy-rozy-russkogo-mira.html (accessed 1 January 2016).

Tikhon (Shevkunov), archimandrite, 'Svetskost' gosudarstva ne podrazumevaet iskliucheniia religii iz obshchestvennoi zhizni', *Russkaia narodnaia liniia* 23 September 2014, http://ruskline.ru/news_rl/2014/09/23/arhimandrit_tihon_shevkunov_svetskost_gosudarstva_ne_podrazumevaet_isklyucheniya_religii_iz_obwestvennoj_zhizni (accessed 1 January 2016).

Turner, B., 'Religion in a Post-Secular Society'. In *The New Blackwell Companion to the Sociology of Religion*. Ed. B. Turner (Chichester : Wiley-Blackwell, 2010) 649–667.

'Velikii post i Paskha', *Levada-Center* 2 April 2018, https://www.levada.ru/2018/04/02/velikij-post-i-pasha-4/ (accessed 28 May 2019).

Vigilianskii, V., '"Nesviatye sviatye" dostoiny knigi Ginnesa', *Ria-Novosti* 13 March 2015, http://ria.ru/poltava/20150313/1052261023.html (accessed 1 January 2016).

Volodikhin, D., 'Den' pravoslavnogo pisatelia', *Foma* 31 May 2015, http://foma.ru/den-pravoslavnogo-pisatelya.html (accessed 1 January 2016).

Volodikhin, D., 'Domoi!' *Moskva* 2 (2007): 178–189.

Volodikhin, D., 'Khram i kosmodrom: Futuristicheskie obrazy v russkoi imperskoi fantastike', *Politicheskii zhurnal*, (2008), http://www.inter fax-religion.ru/?act=print&div=7785 (accessed 1 January 2016).

Volodikhin, D., *Intellektual'naia fantastika* (Moscow: ipo, 2007).

Willems, J., *Religiöse Bildung in Russlands Schulen. Orthodoxie, nationale Identität und die Positionalität des Faches "Grundlagen orthodoxer Kultur"* (opk) (Münster: lit, 2006).

Zhen'-Khen', Ch. N.A. *Berdiaev o russkoi kul'ture*, Candidate of Science Thesis, St Petersburg University, St Petersburg (2002).

Ziebertz, H.-G. and Riegel, U., 'Europe: A Post-secular Society?' *International Journal of Practical Theology* 13(2) (2010): 293–308.

Zolotukhina, O., 'Problema "khristianstvo i russkaia literatura" v sovremennoi filologii', *Vestnik Tomskogo gosudarstvennogo universiteta*, 313 (2008): 13–16.

Zorich, A., *Zavtra voina*. 4th ed. (Moscow: Astrel', 2012).

Zubov, A., 'Khristianstvo i kul'tura', *Znamia*, 10 (1999), http://magazines.russ.ru/znamia/ 1999/10/konfer.html (accessed 1 January 2016).

We Will ROC You!
'Tannhäuser' Opera Scandal and the Freedom of Artistic Expression in Putin's Russia

Irina Kotkina
Independent Scholar

This paper analyses developments of the new cultural policy of the Russian government and the role of the Russian Orthodox Church (ROC) in the implementation of this cultural policy. This question is embedded into a broader research problem of the status of the ROC in today's Russian society, and its relation to the phenomena of secularization and post-secularization. This paper argues that although the ROC has no clear-cut cultural policy and is under the influence of the government, it recently made significant steps towards embracing a hegemonic vision of Orthodox cultural policy with the help of a series of legal litigations about secular cultural products. Wagner's Tannhäuser *opera production in Novosibirsk and the scandal initiated by the ROC is under scrutiny as a case study in this paper.*

Keywords: opera, contemporary Russian cultural politics, blasphemy, religion

Overture

This paper analyses developments of the new cultural policy of the Russian government and the role of the Russian Orthodox Church (ROC) in the implementation of this cultural policy. During the post-Soviet period, and especially since the enthronization of Kirill (Vladimir Gundiaev) as the Patriarch of the Moscow Patriarchate, the ROC has developed an authoritative position vis-à-vis secular Russian society, trying to represent itself as a "state-organizing" (*gosudarstvoobrazuiushchii*), nation-shaping, and culture- structuring institution of *all* Russians. However, Russia is a thoroughly secularized and confessionally heterogeneous society and, consequently, there is great resistance to the ROC's attempts to "re-Christianize" it, as the Church prefers to frame this strategy.[1] Indeed, in spite of the large proportion of the population, which identifies itself culturally and historically with Orthodox Christianity, the actual number of church-goers is small. According to Levada survey of 2013, only 22% support the idea of compulsory religious education in secondary schools.[2] The number of "culturally Orthodox Christians" has stabilized around the year 2009 at the level of 70%,[3] showing that resources to spread Orthodoxy extensively among Soviet-era non-believers have been exhausted. Instead, the Church has to find ways of transforming this 70% into a real flock, which regularly attends services and — importantly — gives generous offerings. So far, the Church's attempts to improve the situation in this regard, have failed. The same Levada survey exposes, at best, a lack of progress, or, at worse, an opposite tendency towards decline in the community of believers, among whom only 2% kept Lent in 2015 (cf. 4% in 1998), whereas the number of people who do not observe Lent is 77% (79% in 1998). Only 6% *planned* to go to the Easter service (to be noted: in Eastern Christianity this is *the* main Church festivity), compared to 11% in 1998.[4]

With such statistics, we can see that the ROC's ambitions of becoming a cultural headliner and leader of public opinion cannot be sustained. The ROC continues to need the helping hand of the state more than the other way round.[5]

---

1 The ideas of re-Christianization were expressed, for example, in: 'Pervye itogi ob'edinenia RPTS I RPTSZ, Online Konferentsiia, Mitropolit Kirill' (14 August 2007), http://ria.ru/online/20070814/71442391.html (accessed 17 April 2016); 'Vtoroe kreschenie Rusi — fil'm mitropolita Volokolamskogo Illariona', (27 July 2014), http://www.pravmir.ru/vtoroe-kreshhenie-rusi-film-mitropolita-volokolamskogo-ilariona-video/ (accessed 17 April 2016).
2 'Rossiiane vyskazalis' protiv prepodavaniia religii v shkole' (2013), http://www.levada.ru/2013/03/01/rossiyane-vyskazalis-protiv-prepodavaniya-rel igii-v-shkole/ (accessed 12 March 2016).
3 'Religioznaia vera v Rossii' (2012), http://www.levada.ru/2011/09/26/religi oznaya-vera-v-rossii/ (accessed 12 March 2016).
4 'Velikii post i Paskha' (10 April 2015), http://www.levada.ru/2015/04/10/ve likij-post-i-pasha/ (accessed 12 March 2016).
5 On the relations between the ROC and the state, see T. Bremer, *Cross and Kremlin: A Brief History of the Orthodox Church in Russia* (Grand Rapids, Michigan: William B. Eerdmans Publishing Company, 2013); I. Papkova, *The Orthodox Church and Russian Politics* (Washington, DC: Woodrow Wilson Center Press, 2011); K.

This dependency should not be taken too literally, but it is more common than not that the state instrumentalizes the Church in exchange for some *ad hoc* benefits, while the reverse is less common, i.e. the Church making the state its mouthpiece for a religious cause. I will argue in this paper that the state stands behind many of the restrictions that the ROC has been trying to impose on secular society in the cultural sphere in recent years. The focus of this paper is the scandal, which followed the production of the opera *Tannhäuser* in Novosibirsk in December 2014. This case demonstrates how the interaction between the state and the Church may serve as an attempt to re-introduce ideological censorship.

My discussion of the *Tannhäuser* scandal is designed to be an introduction to the broader analysis of post-secularity and freedom of expression in post-Soviet Russia. I will specifically draw upon the concept of a "moral panic",[6] which helps me to describe how social construction of various "threats" securitizes certain aspects of culture and thereby imposes some forms of censorship. My understanding of censorship here is broad; it is any kind of external suppression of ideas or cultural forms, deemed objectionable or inappropriate by the external agency. In today's Russia, unlike the Soviet Union, there is no ruling ideology, which could serve as a guide for a censor; instead, the present hallmark of censorship is a "security threat". This makes censorship pervasive and the borderline between legality and arbitrariness blurry, because anything could be considered as a "threat" to certain aspects of security.[7]

For that matter, during the last decade the state and the ROC alike have been at pains to securitize Russian culture. In order to do

---

Richters, *The Post-Soviet Russian Orthodox Church : Politics, Culture and Greater Russia* (London: Routledge, 2012); G. Simons and D. Westerlund, *Religion, Politics and Nation-building in Post-communist Countries* (Farnham: Ashgate Publishing, 2015); C. Wanner, *State Secularism and Lived Religion in Soviet Russia and Ukraine* (New York: Oxford University Press, 2012).

6   C. Krinsky, *The Ashgate Research Companion to Moral Panics* (Farnham, Surrey: Ashgate, 2013).
7   See on the problems of censorship: M. Dewhirst, 'Censorship in Russia, 1991 and 2001', *Journal of Communist Studies and Transition Politics*, 18(1) (2002): 21–34; G. Simons and D. Strovsky, 'Censorship in contemporary Russian journalism in the age of the War Against Terrorism; historical perspective', *European Journal of Communication* 21(2) (2006), pp. 189–211.

so, culture was reinterpreted in two ways. Firstly it was represented as Russia's key national asset, and a major bargaining chip in geopolitical games, on a par with the natural resources like oil and gas,[8] advanced military, or advantageous territorial location. Secondly, culture was reimagined along the lines, characteristic of, for example, American cultural conservatism,[9] where culture is seen not as fluid and contingent on everyday life practices, but rather as a fixed canon. This canon is understood as fixed once and for all in the past, continuing to resonate in today's life, and precisely this *resonance* defines the nation, and warrants its resilience and integrity. In Patriarch Kirill's jargon, this cultural canon is termed "basic culture" (*bazisnaia kul'tura*).[10] According to this vision, any perceived encroachment on culture comes down to an attack on the nation itself. "Guidelines of the State Cultural Policy", elaborated by the Ministry of Culture, which is headed by the controversial political figure Vladimir Medinskii, and signed by President Putin in December 2014, gives us a model of how culture could be securitized. In the Introduction it says that the state makes culture one of the national priorities, and considers it one of the most important factors of the "growth of the quality of life, harmonization of social relations, ... dynamic socio-economic development, and ... preservation of the single cultural space and territorial integrity of Russia".[11] Basically, this means that any cultural heterodoxy or deviation—whoever is in a position to define it as such—could be seen as an infringement on Russia's sovereignty, economy or territory.

---

8   'Osnovy gosudarstvennoi kul'turnoi politiki' (2014). Chapter i, paragraph 7. http://static.kremlin.ru/media/events/files/41d526a877638a8730eb.pdf (accessed 20 April 2016). For culture as natural resource in Russian political discourse, see I. Kalinin, 'Carbon and cultural heritage: the politics of history and the economics of rent', *Baltic Worlds* 2-3: 65–74 http://balticworlds.com/wp-content/uploads/2014/10/BW-2-3-2014-TEMA-uppslag.pdf.
9   A. Brinkley, 'The problem of American conservatism', *The American Historical Review* 99(2) (1994): 409–429. I. Kristol, *Reflections of a neoconservative: Looking back, looking ahead* (New York: Basic Books, 1983).
10 See Mikhail Suslov's discussion of the term in this issue.
11 'Osnovy gosudarstvennoi kul'turnoi politiki' (2014). Chapter i, paragraph 11. http://static.kremlin.ru/media/events/files/41d526a877638a8730eb.pdf (accessed 20 April 2016).

This article is based on the close reading of the press and social media discourses about the *Tannhäuser* affair. I used keyword searches in Yandex.ru and Blogs.yandex.ru search engines, which provided me with a panoply of materials. This pool of data was used to minutely reconstruct the whole story and identify the key figures and discursive frames, used in the debates. The study has a pronounced empirical tendency and deals with the cultural processes, which are still unfolding; consequently, my conclusions have a provisional character.

My other caveat is that the analysis focuses on the discourses about and around the moral panic, caused by the *Tannhäuser* performance. This means that I do not probe into the structural and institutional underpinnings of the scandal, such as various factions inside the ROC with different moral and political agendas. To be sure, the ROC is not a monolith, and a voice of a single cleric or even a bishop does not necessarily represent the whole Church. Moreover, the converse also applies: contemporary Russian opera is not altogether iconoclastic and dissenting; many significant opera figures have found a comfortable symbiosis with the official course towards traditionalism and religiosity. What is important for this research is that on the level of discourses, a particular group of producers of *Tannhäuser* was seen as an epitome of the blasphemous secular art, while the producers of this art perceived criticism from the Church and the state as an undifferentiated oppressing force.

According to "Fundaments of the State Cultural Policy", the Russian government will support cultural production which corresponds to the "national traditional values". There is no clear explanation of what "national traditional values" means, but the implementation of the selective approach to the support of the arts conforming to an ideological agenda speaks very much to the attempts to elaborate a certain cultural canon and to impose some mechanisms of control. According to Gunther Berghaus, the establishment of a cultural canon slows down the independent development of the arts if it does not stop it altogether. Stalinist cultural policy considered "classics" to be the yardstick by which the cultural canon was established. The Ministry of Culture in a sense followed the same pattern, trying to instill certain norms in the artistic process in order to weaken if not to invalidate the mechanism of aesthetic innovation, whenever the artistic process deviated from what the ROC tries to define as "classic" and "moral".[12] The article argues that any attempt to establish a cultural canon — be it the socialist realist or today's conservative and religious one — requires a series of moral panics for its elaboration and implementation. The ROC, however, is not authoritative and hegemonic enough to sustain those moral panics without leaning on the state. Unlike the affair with the exhibition in the Sakharov Center,[13] today, the state is willing to play first violin and to operationalize the ROC's moral agenda for its own purposes.

However, unlike the period of the developed socialist realism, today the state is (still) not able to offer a consistent cultural canon, but is actively trying to formulate such a canon and to extend this project onto to the whole cultural field with as much rigor as possible. The ROC supports the state in this endeavor, trying to colonize the field of secular culture and reinterpret it in religious terms.[14] This new religious activity manifests itself primarily in the court trials supported by the legislation on the "insults of religious feelings".[15] Quite a few scandals and litigations were initiated by those who call themselves believers and who try to legally defend their feelings from what they consider an insult.

Further, I attempt to inquire into what stands behind these litigations.

The ground for these trials was created in 2011 when the Archbishops Council of the ROC adopted the document "The Attitude of

---

12 G. Berghaus and E. Dobrenko (eds.), *Sotsrealisticheskii kanon* (St. Petersburg: Akademicheskii Proekt, 2000).
13 The art exhibition 'Prohibited Art—2006' took place from the 7 to 31 March 2007, in the Museum and Public Centre named after A. Sakharov. The curator of the exhibition was Andrei Erofeev and the museum director Yurii Samodurov. The religious and nationalists activists harshly criticized the exhibition, and the criminal conviction of the exhibition organizers for the inciting religious hatred followed. See also M.N. Ryklin, *Svastik, krest, zvezda. proizvedenie iskusstva v epohu upravliaemoi demokratii* (Moscow: Logos, 2006).
14 See Mikhail Suslov's article in the same issue.
15 Article 148 of the Criminal Code of the Russian Federation.

the Russian Orthodox Church to Public and Intended Blasphemy and Slander against the Church". The document states: "in cases when Holiness of God is offended in the public sphere ... [the Church] has to give qualified evaluation of this act and identify measures to counter blasphemy [...]".[16] This document serves not only internal church policy, but also aims at the media. By this document, the ROC attempted to prevent publication of materials, which could potentially be dangerous to its image. As time passed, the concept of the "insult of religious feelings" has become widespread in public discourse, with its most notable milestones in 2012, when the Pussy Riot affair flared up,[17] and in August 2015, when Vadim Sidur's exhibition in the Manezh in Moscow was plundered by Orthodox fundamentalists. To this list can be added — as a crowning moment — the *Tannhäuser* affair in Novosibirsk, from December 2014–June 2015, which serves as a case history for this study.

Act 1: Moral Panics

Wagner has not been staged often in Novosibirsk; moreover, his operas are rarely performed in Russia. Mariinskii Theater, with its chief conductor Valerii Gergiev, made a breakthrough with a production of Wagner's entire *Ring* cycle in the early 2000s. Before this, there had been no continuous Soviet tradition of staging Wagner, apart from pre-revolutionary productions. Thus, the premiere in Novosibirsk became an event not only for Siberia, but also for the whole country. The premiere took place on December 20, 2014 and was positively received in the leading Russian media. Theater reviews of the opera premiere were enthusiastic and found the interpretation of the opera thought provoking. Anna Gordeeva, the Moscow cultural critic, wrote: "I do not remember any other director [Timofey Kuliabin] who challenged opera in Russia so radically

---

16 Published 4 February 2011: patriarchia.ru›db/text/1401898.html (accessed 11 February 2016).
17 J. Willems, *Pussy Riots Punk-Gebet: Religion, Recht und Politik in Russland* (Berlin: Berlin University Press, 2013).

before".[18] In the blogosphere, in the opera and ballet discussion group on Vkontakte.com, one of the most popular online platforms in Russia, *Tannhäuser* also received wide appraisal in December. The comments were as follows: "to listen to this opera is a heavenly pleasure, I stress—heavenly",[19] "I liked this opera—the vocal part and also the idea of the cinema festival, where the director (the main character) participates."[20] "It is a very serious production, though a radical one, but it is worth seeing one more time, and I will go see it once more for sure."[21] So, the audience and critics considered the production of *Tannhäuser* to be one of the most significant opera productions in 2014. It was reported in the press that the entire team of artists and the director of the opera were nominated for the "Golden Mask 2015", one of the major Russian theater awards. The expert council of the "Golden Mask", which consisted of well-known critics and theater activists from the whole of Russia, visited the first production of *Tannhäuser* and found it a great accomplishment. Many opera connoisseurs travelled to Novosibirsk from Moscow, St. Petersburg and other Russian cities in order to see the production.

Timofey Kuliabin, the director of the production, is a successful and nonconventional opera director, although he works full-time as the director of the Novosibirsk drama theater "Red Torch". His 2014 production *Onegin* received the special "Golden Mask" award as an outstanding drama, which made him a well-known director in the Russian theatre world. The practice of engaging drama directors in opera productions, popular for some time, has recently

---

18 A. Gordeeva, 'Sibir', opera, kino i nemtsy. V Novosibirskoi opera pokazali vagnerovskogo *Tannhäuser*', *Gazeta.ru*, 24 December 2014: http://www.gazeta.ru/culture/2014/12/24/a_6357137.shtml (accessed 16 December 2015).
19 O. Serova, 'Richard Wagner, *Tannhäuser*. Prem'era 20.12.14, ngatoib—obsuzhdaem spektakl'', Discussion group on vk.com, post 23 December 2014, https://vk.com/topic-30300472_31535545 (accessed 22 January 2016).
20 R. Kadachigov, 'Richard Wagner, *Tannhäuser*. Prem'era 20.12.14, ngatoib—obsuzhdaem spektakl'', Discussion group on vk.com, post 26 March 2015, https://vk.com/topic-30300472_31535545 (accessed 22 January 2016).
21 A. Tsevan, 'Richard Wagner, *Tannhäuser*. Prem'era 20.12.14, NGTOiB—obsuzhdaem spektakl'', post 25 February 2015, discussion group on vk.com, https://vk.com/topic-30300472_31535545 (accessed 22 January 2016).

gained popularity in Russia, too, specifically in Moscow, St. Petersburg, and Perm. Drama directors, free from the clichés of the opera genre, often have fresher views and tend to apply modern techniques to the productions. However, engaging a drama director in the opera production was a novelty for the Novosibirsk Opera Theater, and the audience had not been previously exposed to the unconventional interpretations of opera texts, which Kuliabin offered.

Kuliabin challenged the plot of Wagner's opera in order to highlight the drama of true religiosity as opposed to hypocrisy. The legendary *Minnesänger* and poet Tannhäuser is represented in the opera as a film director, who makes a film featuring an unconventional history of Jesus Christ's life set in this world. Tannhäuser presents this film at a cinema festival but the self-righteous jury members fail Tannhäuser's film. In the end, however Tannhäuser triumphs due to his true talent and authentic religiosity.

This production uses provocative stage techniques such as topless female characters. They also appear in the poster of the film, which was the key object of criticism from the Church. This poster features the cross on a female bosom and it also appears in the performance for several seconds. Opera critics argued that these features could not detract from the very important moral problems raised in this opera. As Anna Gordeeva pointed out before the scandal was initiated: "The inner meaning of the opera, staged in Novosibirsk, is about the struggle between external and internal, between depth and superficiality. The external and superficial is the official world, the official rules. The inside and depth are the main character's reflections about Christ and about love. It is clear that Kuliabin sees the main conflict of the opera not in the opposition of earthly love to heavenly love, but in the clash of genuine religious belief and ostentatious religiosity."[22]

The moral panic has not started until Metropolitan Tikhon (Emel'ianov) of Berdsk and Novosibirsk wrote a letter to the public prosecutor's office in Novosibirsk oblast, in which he condemned the production as insult to the religious feelings of his flock. In his letter, dated 27 February 2015, he criticized the production using

---

22   Anna Gordeeva, ibid.

the familiar arguments of "offending religious feelings", giving them some new twists: "By insulting the feelings of the believers the theater incites religious enmity (think about recent events in Paris [*Charlie Hebdo*]). They insulted the feelings of not only believers, but of all the responsible citizens of the Russian Federation (because the Cross, which was represented in a disgraceful way, is the symbol of the state, and not only of Christianity). 80 per cent of the citizens of Russia consider themselves to be true believers, (and 100 per cent sympathize with Orthodoxy). Therefore, the insult is very grave. Not only this disgraceful production, but also other productions of Novosibirsk theaters are insulting, yet they were all financed by the state budget. Why should the money of the true believers be spent on such immoral activity?"[23] Similarly, another cleric, Archpriest Dmitry Smirnov, stated that *Tannhäuser* is the continuation of the "Punk-Mass" (meaning the Pussy-Riot performance in the Cathedral of Christ the Savior in 2012).[24]

By analyzing the statements of Tikhon, we can infer from these passages that the main aim of the clerics was not primarily a struggle with the alleged insult, but the striving to gain the upper hand in the field of culture, which enjoyed relative freedom before. Tikhon's criticism attacks the director as an offender of the Russian state and its symbols. Drawing a parallel with the terrorist attacks on *Charlie Hebdo*, Tikhon represents the director as a major threat to Russian nationhood; he is especially aggravated by the supposed embezzlement of public money. Construing this claim, Tikhon draws a big picture in which he stands side by side with the state and the Church's constituency, whereas the director is depicted in the camp of the enemies of the state. Archpriest Dmitrii Smirnov added an even darker stroke, comparing the director with Pussy Riot members, thereby giving the production a pronounced political coloration.

---

23 'Tikhon: *Tannhäuser* napravlen na razzhiganie religioznoi vrazhdy', 27 February 2015, http://sibkray.ru/news/4/873250 (accessed 22 January 2016).
24 'O. Dmitrii Smirnov o spektakle *Tannhäuser:* eto prodolzhenie pank-molebna', 8 March 2015, http://www.pravoslavie.ru/77752.html (accessed 22 January 2016).

This is how the moral panic widely covered in the blogosphere began, whose participants displayed a huge variety of positions, ranging from complete support of the Church's position to its total negation. However, the pivot of the contestation was the question about the public control over the budget, spent on the opera production. Importantly, many critics who participated actively in the court trial had not even seen this opera; their judgment was based on video clips, which feature the scandalous poster.

Act 2: Crime and Punishment

In the paragraphs below, I will show in detail the development of the scandal. This will allow us to clearly see the position of the ROC before and after the legal hearing, and to fix upon the moment when the governmental officials stepped into the *Tannhäuser* affair.

On February 24, 2015 the prosecutor's office of Novosibirsk city administration filed a case against the chief manager of the Novosibirsk Opera Boris Mezdrich, and the director of *Tannhäuser*, Timofey Kuliabin, based on the appeal made by the Metropolitan of Novosibirsk and Berdsk, Tikhon. On February 25, 2015 Boris Mezdrich replied that he disagrees with the claims of the Prosecutor's office and is willing to defend his position in court. He also insisted that the *Tannhäuser* production is going to be on show in March 2015, as it was planned beforehand. On February 26, 2015 Novosibirsk Archdiocese of the Russian Orthodox Church published the text of the appeal to the Prosecutor of the Novosibirsk region, Evgenii Ovchinnikov, with the request to check the production for the violation of the rights of believers. The case was sent to the magistrate of the corresponding judicial district, the Central District of Novosibirsk. In the case of a conviction, Boris Mezdrich faced a fine of up to 200 thousand rubles. Director Kuliabin — up to 50 thousand rubles, or up to 120 hours of compulsory work. In addition, the investigative committee began the preliminary inquiry based upon Article 148 of the Criminal Code ("Violation of the right of freedom of conscience and religion").

On March 10, 2015 the Justice Court of the Central District of Novosibirsk initiated the two trials: one against Timofey Kuliabin, the other against Boris Mezdich. The charges were built on Part 2 of Article 5.26 of the Administrative Code, namely: "Deliberate public desecration of religious or theological literature, objects of religious veneration, signs or emblems filled with ideological symbolism and paraphernalia, or their damage or destruction" in the opera *Tannhäuser* carried out on the stage of the Novosibirsk opera". The court relied on the expert opinion of the three witnesses for the defense.

The first expert was Dr. Boris Z. Falikov, historian of religion and publicist, associate professor of the Religious Studies Center of the Russian State University for the Humanities, one of the most prominent Russian experts in theology. The second expert was Dr. Vladimir V. Vinokurov, associate professor and author of more than 30 academic papers, professor emeritus of the Moscow State University, and prominent specialist in theology. The third expert was Roman P. Dolzhansky, a leading theater critic, columnist of the newspaper *"Kommersant"*, art director of the festival *"New European Theatre"*, and deputy artistic director of the Theater of the Nations.

All three experts gave negative answers to the question about the deliberate insult of the religious feelings. Vladimir V. Vinokurov noted: "The production does not contain the image of Christ of the Gospel, because Christ as presented in the Gospel is the only truth for believers, but Christ as presented on the stage is just a fiction". The second expert, Boris Falikov, noted that religious symbols and attributes are not original and are presented in the production as other theatre props, and therefore are not sacred.[25] On 10 March 2015, the court acquitted the both defendants. According to the Court of Justice, the "offensive actions" were not found in the actions of either defendant.

Already on March 5, 2015 the head of the ROC Synodal Information Department, Vladimir Legoida, issued the conciliatory appeal on behalf of the ROC: "He stressed that, in his opinion, the Metropolitan of Novosibirsk and Berdsk, Tikhon, acted in accordance

---

25 'Eksperty ne nashli oskorblenia khristianskih simvolov v opere "Tangeizer"', 10 March 2015, http://www.vz.ru/news/2015/3/10/733512.html (accessed 4 February 2016).

with the law, given the exceptional nature of the situation. But this does not give the right to every believer or priest to apply to the court every time he perceives something as "blasphemy". We are supposed to peacefully find a common ground and understanding with creative people and with the journalists."[26]

Act 3: Enter the Ministry of Culture

After the court decision was publicly announced, it was not the Church representative, but the representative of the government, the Head of the Duma Committee for Public Associations and Religious Organizations, Iaroslav Nilov, who made the statement in the press that according to him the creators of *Tannhäuser* "still ought to be punished one way or another".[27] In his address, he eventually called for the court-decision to be ignored and regarded as nonexistent. Moreover, he expressed the fear that the Church was too passive in defending its point of view, and "if under the pressure of the liberal public figures and the theater goers, and passive position of the believers, the creators of the *Tannhäuser* production would remain unpunished, the performance will go on tour to St. Petersburg, Moscow — and the story will be continued."[28]

Thus, the politician understood perfectly that the production enjoyed strong support from many artists and public figures, who expressed their disagreement with the actions of the ROC[29], but he insisted on the necessity of the appeal against a court decision. Jaroslav Nilov (b. 1982) belongs to a young generation of politicians, and has already made himself known as the creator of the so-called Law of "the black list". He is the initiator of the Federal Law № 139-fz dated 28 July 2012 "On protection of children from information

---

26 'RPTs prizvala oskorblennykh v chuvstvakh veruiushih ne bezhat' srazu v prokuraturu', 5 March 2015, http://vz.ru/news/2015/3/5/732984.html (accessed 5 February 2016).
27 'Net slava bogu ser'eznykh sotsial'nyh posledstvii', 10 March 2015, http://vz.ru/culture/ 2015/3/10/733547.html (accessed 5 February 2016).
28 Ibid.
29 Among many public figures who supported Novosibirsk Opera were prominent actors Evgenii Mironov, Chulpan Hamatova, Oleg Tobakov, director Kirill Serebriannikov to name just a few.

harmful to their health and development" and some other legislative acts on the issue of "restricting access to illegal information on the Internet." This law involves filtering of Internet sites on the blacklist system and blocking prohibited Internet resources. Most experts expressed concern that the law opens the possibility of censorship of the Internet.[30] The *Tannhäuser* affair thus opened the possibility to further promoting the idea of censorship. Nilov, who was previously responsible for censorship issues in the government, did not miss this chance.

On March 13, 2015 the Deputy Prosecutor of Novosibirsk, Igor Stasiulis, informed the news agency Ria-Novosty that the Novosibirsk Prosecutor's Office will appeal against the decision of the Court of Justice. The Court of Justice did not find the insulting religious sanctities in *Tannhäuser*.[31]

Now the ROC also sensed strong state support and changed its position from the conciliatory stance of the underdog to an active position of the aggressor. The Metropolitan of Novosibirsk and Berdsk, Tikhon, appealed to the Governor of the Novosibirsk Region, Vladimir Gorodetsky, with a letter in which he stated an ultimatum that societal dialogue on the *Tannhäuser* production is possible only after it is removed in its present form from the repertoire.[32]

Finally, the Ministry of Culture in its turn took its part in the governmental campaign and announced the so-called "public hearing" dedicated to the "conflict with the *Tannhäuser* production". The "public hearing" in the Ministry of Culture on March 13, 2015 was attended by the representatives of the ROC, and the two working groups of the Public Council at the Ministry of Culture of Russia (first — on the theater and second — on the public policy in the

---

30 'Netsenzurnoe Lobbi', 11 July 2012, http://lenta.ru/articles/2012/07/10/stop censorship/ (accessed 5 February 2016).
31 'Prokuratura obzhaluet reshenie suda, zakryvshego delo po "Tangeizeru"', 13 March 2015, http://ria.ru/culture/20150313/1052332917.html#ixzz3zI3oGMgX (accessed 5 February 2016).
32 'Mitropolit trebuet sniat' "Tangeizer" s repertuara', 13 March 2015, http://www.colta.ru/news/6637?page=70 (accessed 5 February 2016).

sphere of culture), and also by the experts and heads of cultural institutions. There were present: Boris Mezdrich, Minister of Culture, Vladimir Medinskii, representatives of the ROC, including Legoida and Vsevolod Chaplin, and many conservative intellectuals and artists, such as Kapitolina Koksheneva,[33] Stanislav Rybas, and Nikolai Burliaev.

Following the "public hearings", the Ministry of Culture issued a resolution, which, in spite of the judgment of the Court of Justice which found no *corpus delicti* in the actions of the theater manager and the director, accused Mezdrich of "lack of control over the institution he heads."[34] Moreover, after representatives the ROC initiated and government officials escalated the scandal, the Ministry of Culture blamed the theater for what had happened: "Unfortunately, the administration of the theater ignored the first public protests. This led to an escalation of the conflict, its transition from the public space to the court litigation, which seemed to us unnecessary and unconstructive."[35] Summing-up the resolution, the Ministry of Culture claimed inadmissibility of censorship, but simultaneously threatened punitive measures against the theater and the production, if Mezdrich did not offer public penance, and the opera production was not radically changed. "The Ministry of Culture considers it appropriate to make radical changes to the production, as well as to bring a public apology to all those whose religious feelings were hurt. Considering censorship inappropriate, we are still mindful of our right, more—of our duty, based on the "Fundamentals of Cultural Policy", to take in the extreme cases, ad-

---

33 K. Koksheneva is a literary and theatre critic well known for her ultra-conservative and nationalist views. S. Rybas is a political pro-Kremlin activist and writer glorifying Stalinism and 'strong power' in general. N. Burliaev is a movie and theatre actor, Orthodox activist and open homophobe, ardent supporter of Putin's politics in the Crimea.
34 'Stenogramma obshchestvennogo obsuzhdenia postanovki opery "Tangeizer" v ngatobe. 13.03.2015', http://mkrf.ru/ministerstvo/departament/detail.php?ID=623062&print=Y (accessed 6 February 2016.).
35 Ibid.

ministrative and financial measures, including the denial of funding for inappropriate productions made on the stages of the state cultural institutions."[36]

The general manager of the Novosibirsk Opera refused to take any of the measures, suggested by the Ministry of Culture. The only one he did take was the removal of the poster, which illustrated the movie screened by the chief character of the production, and which appeared on the stage for a very short period. Mezdrich refused to change the production further, because he considered that it would distort its meaning completely. He also refused to make public excuses, because he did not consider himself guilty and had the court decision to prove his innocence.

Act 4: Forces Behind the Scene

It is possible to argue that by the means of public scandals and legal claims, which the Orthodox Church has initiated so far, there stand political forces that are aspiring to control the cultural field and to set the rules of the game in the sphere of creative activity, which was previously insulated from ideology. It appears that the complaints of Father Tikhon, who never saw the production in the Novosibirsk Opera, planted a seed into a very fertile soil of governmental support and desire to set boundaries for the artists. The Russian Orthodox Church, which in the recent years acquired more and more state support, now unexpectedly touched upon a theme, which was very much on the agenda of the Ministry of Culture. At the same time, it is hard to judge to what extent the success of the "Anti-*Tannhäuser*" campaign was accidental. Nevertheless, there is plenty of evidence that after the initiation of the legal processes, although not successful *de jure*, the ROC insisted on the dismissal of the chief management of Novosibirsk Opera, and cancellation of the *Tannhäuser* production after only four performances. *De facto*, this case is particularly important because it serves as an example of the re-introduction of artistic censorship in Russia, not present in Rus-

---

36   Ibid.

sian public life since the Soviet times. Moreover, it is censorship imposed after the fact: the production was banned and artistic personnel were prosecuted after the opera was staged.

In recent years, the Orthodox Church has been testing the boundaries of permissible intrusion into secular life. In the *Tannhäuser* affair, their main claims were in fact broader than disapproval of just one theatrical production. In the public discussion dedicated to *Tannhäuser,* Father Leonid Kalinin voiced the opinion primarily circulated in a letter by Archimandrite Tikhon (Shevkunov), who discovered two chief societal phenomena, which needed to be subjected to negative criticism by the Orthodox Church. "Firstly, it became clear that blasphemy—from overt to covert, directed primarily against Orthodoxy, has now become a significant component of the cultural life of modern society [...] The second huge problem, to which I would like to draw attention, is that there is no mechanism for the protection of the classics from the creative vivisection in today's Russia."[37] Significantly, Father Tikhon had previously been a vocal supporter of the re-establishment of censorship in Russia, arguing that it would be beneficial for people's morality and artistic creativity, because, according to his vision, artists needed some kind of external pressure as an incentive for perfection.[38]

Thus, the Church has issued a call for the introduction of a moral police, though the Church spokesmen are negating this. According to Tikhon, "the Church does not interfere with the freedom of creativity. Moreover, the Church does not want and does not intend to take on oversight functions. But when you try to take away even the right to protest against blasphemy, which offends us, that is, the right to a simple feeling, saying that what is happening in the public space is not our business—it is too much, even for the Liberals, gentlemen."[39] Not only does the conservative majority among the ROC's clerics have the feeling that it can take a more active part in public life, but also that it can reinstate its active conservative

---

37 'Stenogramma'.
38 Tikhon (Shevkunov), Archimandrite, *S Bozh'ei pomoshch'iu vozmozhno vse: O vere i otechestve* (Moscow: Knizhnyi mir, 2014), pp. 98, 184–185.
39 Ibid.

political program. This will not be possible without the sentiment that the state supports Church aspirations and political program.

The role of the Church in all the events leading to the removal of *Tannhäuser* from the Novosibirsk stage was significant but not crucial. Though the Russian Orthodox Church had an interest in this scandal (in order to re-instate its cultural influence and importance), the Ministry of Culture co-opted the Church's initiative. It is possible to argue that the Orthodox Church is an institute, whose actions are beneficial to the central authorities, because the Church voices the authorities' ideas.

To fully understand the change in the Church/state relations as these have developed since the 1990s, it is useful to compare the *Tannhäuser* event with the screening of Martin Scorsese's controversial film *The Last Temptation of Christ* on Russian television in 1997. This controversial film represents Jesus Christ simultaneously as God and as a human being. Its showing was planned for NTV, one of the national channels, on November 9, 1997. Patriarch of Moscow and All Russia, Alexii II, and the Holy Synod of the Russian Orthodox Church were against showing the film, because, according to the Russian Church, the film violates Russian law and public morality. They acknowledged this on November 5, 1997. Nevertheless, the film was put on air the date it was scheduled. The Russian Orthodox Church Archdeacon, Andrei Kuraev, called the television broadcast of the film an insult to the feelings of believers and "blasphemy". His arguments were very much the same as those voiced against the *Tannhäuser* premiere in 2015: "This movie is blasphemous not only from the point of view of believers. Obviously, a broad and powerful anti-cultural movement now gives support to the underestimating of the Gospel. Present-day philistinism thirsts to debase, to defile all that is pure and elevated. Pushkin is no longer interesting for his poetry, but for his "Don Juan's list"; Tchaikovsky is often recollected in connection with the problems of sexual minorities [...] So philistines are eager to drag Christ into their bed — in order just to show that He is "the same as we are"."[40]

Notwithstanding the ardent opposition of the Church to the freedom of artistic expression, this incident at that moment in time had no further legal consequences. Patriarch Alexii II considered the conflict resolved already in 1998, though he did not change his opinion regarding the issue. The Interfax news agency cited his words in this regard: "Alexii II believes that his conflict with NTV, which was caused by the 1997 broadcasting of Martin Scorsese's film *The Last Temptation of Christ*, has already been exhausted. In this regard, the Patriarch said that he had received a letter from Vladimir Gusinskii, the owner of the NTV, in which the latter expressed his regret and apology. "He thought that the broadcast of this film is the manifestation of freedom. But I told him that the insult to the feelings of one part of the population made by another part of it is not freedom" — said the Patriarch."[41]

Between 1997 and 2015, the legal status of the Orthodox Church in Russia did not change, but its role as an instrument of influencing public opinion increased significantly. At the same time, the ROC's traditionalist agenda began to resonate with the general conservative turn in Russian society and among the political elite.

Act 5: Guilty without Guilt

On March 29, 2015 Boris Mezdrich was fired from the position of chief manager of the Novosibirsk Opera. The Ministry of Culture provided an explanation, which was published on its web page in bold letters: "What is most important — we do not see [him] understanding a simple thing: federal academic theater — is primarily the

---

40 A. Kuraev, (Deacon), 'Fil'm *Poslednee iskushenie Khrista* pokazan. Kakie uroki?', http://halkidon2006.narod.ru/do/bogoslovie_1/841_Kuraev.htm (accessed 3 February 2016).
41 'Patriarh Aleksii schitaet, chto v nyneshnem godu ego vstrecha s papoi rimskim nevozmozhna', 16 July 1998 http://www.interfax-religion.ru/cis.php?act=archive&div=1469 (accessed 3 February 2016).

institute suitable for education, rather than an institution for the shocking and provocative self-promotion at public expense. Stubborn arrogance, unwillingness to engage in dialogue and unwillingness to explain his plans are unacceptable for the head of the federal academic institution."[42]

Vladimir Kekhman, the businessman in the middle of a procedure for bankruptcy, was appointed the general manager of the Novosibirsk Opera the same day. Kekhman was previously the general manager of the Mikhailovskii Opera Theatre in St. Petersburg (2007-2015), investing his money into this enterprise. He had no professional qualifications for this position before 2007. On the contrary, he was well known as an exporter of bananas and other fruit to the Russian markets. Nevertheless, in 2009 the businessman got the diploma in theatre production from the St. Petersburg State Theatre Academy. Kekhman openly voiced his position in the Ministry of Culture: "What has been done in the Novosibirsk Opera House—is sacrilege. I, as an Orthodox baptized believer, as a Jew, take it as an insult. This is a demonstration of the internal wickedness in the style and spirit of the Union of Militant Atheists. Frankly, I was talking today with Mezdrich, and he told me that he is not going to give up the production and will struggle for it till the very end. I think that he is obliged to resign, and it is necessary to remove the production from the repertoire."[43] Making such statements, and removing the production from the stage immediately after his appointment, Kekhman showed his loyalty to the Ministry of Culture and to the cultural policy of the present government in general.

On the same day, March 29, 2015, a meeting took place in the central square of Novosibirsk, showing support for the actions of the Ministry of Culture. According to the BBC reporter, there were

---

42 'Novosti ministerstva', 1 April 2015, http://mkrf.ru/press-center/news/mini sterstvo/kommentariy-minkultury-rossii-po-kadrovym-izmeneniyam-v-novo sibirskom-akademiche? sphrase_id=3809299 (accessed 6 February 2016).
43 'Novosti ministerstva', 18 March 2015, http://mkrf.ru/press-center/news/mi nisterstvo/pozitsiya-minkultury-po-itogam-obshchestvennykh-slushaniy-po-povodu-konflikta-vo (accessed 6 February 2016).

about 1,500 people present, but the official press mentioned 2,000.[44] The meeting was headed by the Novosibirsk Archpriest Alexander Novopashin, who proclaimed the main slogan of the campaign: "Protect the shrines — save Russia". In his speech, Alexander Novopashin called on Vladimir Putin personally "to protect" the believers whose feelings were being insulted. The Metropolitan Tikhon, who called the people not attending the meeting "Christ co-crucifiers", for some reason did not attend the meeting himself. Instead, there were many other figures from the political establishment. For example, the head of the faction "United Russia" in the Novosibirsk Legislative Assembly, Andrei Panferov, denounced the creators of *Tannhäuser*, comparing them to the "Ukrainian fascists": "The names of these people are scabrous blasphemers (*skabrezniki*) and heathens, there is no other name for them. They think that what is happening in Ukraine, where the killing of our compatriots takes place, will bypass them and they will not be punished. But they will be the first who will hang on lamp posts [...]"[45]

On Monday, March 30, 2015 the Ministry of Culture in a statement on its website called on the Novosibirsk diocese to withdraw the appeal at the Prosecutor's office and to continue the discussion as a mutually respectful dialogue, not as a mass meeting or court litigation.

This statement clearly shows that it was not the ROC but the government, who played the leading role in the company. Moreover, having received instructions from the Ministry of Culture, the ROC not only withdrew the petition to the Prosecutor, but also dissociated itself from any statement on the operatic repertoire.

On the official site of the Novosibirsk archdiocese, the ROC reported: "Novosibirsk diocese did not submit to the authorities any appeals for the initiation of administrative or criminal proceedings concerning the controversial staging of the opera *Tannhäuser*. The legal situation surrounding the performance is outside the jurisdic-

---

44 M. Loginova, 'Na mitinge protiv 'Tangeizera' poprosili pomoshchi u Putina', 29 March 2015, http://www.bbc.com/russian/russia/2015/03/150329_novo sibirsk_tannhauser_pro test_rally (accessed 6 February 2016).
45 Ibid.

tion of the Russian Orthodox Church. The entire legal situation surrounding *Tannhäuser* and personnel decisions in the system of the Ministry of Culture of the Russian Federation are outside the jurisdiction of the ROC, and the church does not restrict creative freedom and does not impose censorship."[46]

It seems that now, before the introduction of direct censorship regulations, the government is trying to probe to what extent the creative intelligentsia is willing to collaborate and to submit to censorship regulations. It was not the *Tannhäuser* production, which was blamed for the cleavage of Russian society, it was the policy of the Ministry of Culture, which made a clear split in the creative intelligentsia. In fact, many who make up this intelligentsia, perceived the signal from the Ministry of Culture and even proposed to introduce censorship or some institute of control themselves.

Encore

On April 1, 2015 a round table took place in the Public Chamber of the Russian Federation.[47] At this round table, the first Deputy Chairman of the Union of Theater Activists, Gennady Smirnov, reminded the audience of the famous "Hays Code", which regulated the production of films in Hollywood from the 1930s until the 1960s, as an example of a compromise between the creative community and society. He said: "I think it's a perfectly sensible idea, because if we do not set the limits for ourselves, it would be the state that does it". Smirnov also announced the readiness of the Union of Theater Activists to work on a code of conduct. To accelerate this process, in his opinion, a direct request from the Ministry of Culture was necessary. The discussion repeatedly turned on the topic of the return of censorship in the form of "artistic councils"

---

46 'Novosibirskaia eparkhia—situatsiia s 'Tangeizerom' ne v iurisdiktsii rpts', 1 April 2015, http://ria.ru/religion/20150401/1055871853.html#ixzz3zI4yf05Y (accessed 6 February 2016).
47 The Public Chamber is elected every three years and is responsible for interaction of citizens with the state and local authorities in order to take into account the needs and interests of citizens, protection of their rights and freedoms in the formation and implementation of public policies, as well as for the implementation of public control over the authorities' activities.

(*khudozhestvennye sovety*). This analogy was brought up by Elena Yampolskaia, the chief editor of the newspaper *Kul'tura* ("Culture"). The writer Yuri Polyakov proposed a similar solution: "I would like to propose a temporary solution—a motion for "artistic councils", which act in conflict situations, wherever they occur. They should unite respected people of different ethical, political and artistic views. Until we solve the censorship problem at the macro-level, we can easily solve specific local problems already now."[48]

Moreover, on March 30 2015, the Deputy Head of the Presidential Administration, Magomedsalam Magomedov, expressed the wish that the repertoire of state theaters needs to be viewed by the governmental officials before productions are put on stage in order to avoid the *Tannhäuser* scandal. In his interview, published on April 1, 2015, Legoida expressed his general agreement with Magomedov and noted that it is quite possible to institutionalize such a governmental body, which would preview the productions before the premiere.[49]

On April 2, 2015 the Novosibirsk Court of the Central District website reported that the Prosecutor's Office has withdrawn its protests against decisions of the Court of Justice about the closure of administrative proceedings against the chief manager of the theater and the director of the opera *Tannhäuser*.[50]

The same day, Vladimir Solov'ev, a well-known TV and media personality, famous for voicing the most conservative pro-Kremlin views, made the *Tannhäuser* affair the topic of his evening show "Evening with Vladimir Solov'ev". Solov'ev made the scandal known to broad TV audiences on a prime time television show.

---

48 'V op predlozhili sozdat' vyezdnye khudozhestvennye sovety i eticheskii kodeks deiatelei iskusstv', 1 April 2015, http://www.vz.ru/news/2015/4/1/737635.print.html (accessed 7 February 2016).

49 V. Legoida: Svoboda tvorchestva ne iavliaetsia indul'gentsiei, 1 April 2015, http://ria.ru/interview/20150401/1055897768.html#ixzz3zI5lF0Qj (accessed 7 February 2016).

50 'Prokuror otozval protesty na reshenie suda po delu Opery "Tangeizer"', 2 April 2015, http://ria.ru/culture/20150402/1056126344.html#ixzz3zI6RrkR4 (accessed 9 February 2016).

The positions his guests (among whom were the new general manager of the Novosibirsk Opera, priests, conservative and liberal theatre activists) expressed were familiar from the debate in the press. Solov'ev's comments, which he made as the moderator and discussant of the talk show, were, however, an addition to the debate. He asked whether "the state can intervene in the creative process that it sponsors." He depicted the *Tannhäuser* affair as "the conflict between the Orthodox public and creative intelligentsia." Moreover, he saw the resolution of the scandal "in the compromise between what the public and the Ministry of Culture want and what the creative intelligentsia are insisting upon."[51] Thus, in his arguments he unquestionably equalized the state interest with the interest of the "Orthodox public", not the intelligentsia. By opining about the state sponsoring artistic productions, from which follows that the creators of art must be obedient to state officials, Solov'ev expressed one of the favorite arguments of the Ministry of Culture and of all other opponents of artistic freedom. It became clear that the state would now introduce financial censorship, based on the new "Fundamentals of Cultural Policy", the aims of which is to support only art that is "national in its character and based on the traditional values".[52] Without clearly formulating what these "traditional values" are, this document opens the doors for artistic constraint based on ideological grounds. Moreover, continuing this line of argument, the "producers" of art are considered to be "accountable to the taxpayers".[53] The "taxpayers" according to this logic are equated with the "Orthodox public" (notwithstanding the fact that the ROC in Russia is freed from taxes). The opinions of the "creative intelligentsia", though paying their taxes, are not heard, if they express dissenting views.

Stimulating this campaign, the state showed its willingness and desire to introduce censorship. Moreover, if ideological censorship has not yet been officially introduced, the financial censorship

---

51 'Tangeizer. Tsenzura. Vecher s Vladimirom Solov'evym', 2 April 2015, http://www.videofan.in.ua/online/tangejzer-tsenzura-vecher-s-vladimirom-solovv im-02042015mp4/171131165 -216644514/ (accessed 10 February 2016).
52 Ibid.
53 Ibid.

is already present. *Tannhäuser* was the first production, which was removed from the stage after several successful performances on purely ideological grounds, and notwithstanding the supportive decision of the Court of Justice. Caring about the "taxpayers money", nobody cared about the budget of 12.5 million Russian roubles, which was invested into this opera, and the invited conductor of *Tannhäuser,* who was not even paid for his last appearance at the Novosibirsk Opera.

At the same time, there were rumors that the Ministry of Culture and the Minister Medinskii himself went too far with this scandal and that he would be dismissed from his post.[54] On April 4, 2015 a meeting "against Church radicalism" took place in Novosibirsk, which attracted about 2,500 people. This meeting, although approved by the authorities, was not covered by the national official media, but only by the opposition media. Information could be found only on the internet sources, which are now blocked in Russia, such as for example on grani.ru.[55] Medinskii, however, remained in his position. In April, the information appeared in the press that Novosibirsk Archpriest Alexander Novopashin, one of the anti-opera activists in Novosibirsk, was awarded the medal for "labor achievements and many years of diligent work and public activities" by the President in March 2015.[56]

The Curtain Drops

The analysis of the *Tannhäuser* scandal makes transparent the state's attempt to establish control over the field of artistic production, to throw a testing ball towards the possibility of revitalizing preliminary censorship in the form of public artistic councils, and to rein-

---

54 "Tangeizer" mstit Kekhmanu i Medinskomu', 3 April 2015, http://riafan.ru/233415-tangeyzer-mstit-Kekhmanu-i-medinskomu (accessed 10 February 2016).
55 'Miting protiv tserkovnogo radikalizma v Novosibirske sobral neskol'ko tysiach uchastnikov', 5 April 2015, http://grani.ru/Politics/Russia/m.239810.html (accessed 10 February 2016).
56 'Putin nagradil ordenom raskritikovavshego 'Tangeizer' sviashchennika', 27 March 2015, http://altervision.org/putin-nagradil-ordenom-raskritikovavshego-tangejzer-svyashhen nika-iz-novosibirska/ (accessed 10 February 2016).

force the state's claim to represent Russia as the fortress of traditional values. In this context, the ROC was used as a powerful leverage to raise the moral panic and to capitalize on the discourses of the insult to religious feelings, already tested in the previous scandals. The ROC has its own rationale in fighting against heterodoxic interpretations of religiosity outside and beyond the official ROC. Besides, it has its own stake in the battle for the cultural hegemony, being at pains to prove that Russian culture is essentially religious Orthodox culture.

However, if one follows closely the events around the *Tannhäuser* production, it is hard to get rid of the impression that the ROC has played the role of the wingman of the state, which snatched the initiative after the first trial was lost. The undeniable fact is that in spite of the decision of the court, the theatre circles have lost their cause, and more than that, they displayed a pronounced lack of resistance to the idea of preliminary censorship, which is now disguised by the business-like discourses about the just distribution of public funds. Today, when the ruling elite still has a fairly nebulous official ideology (although it is rapidly progressing towards having one), the ROC serves as the main supplier of the positive agenda for censorship.

Figure 1   Posters for the Film "Tannhäuser"

Figure 2   Poster for the Film "Tannhäuser"

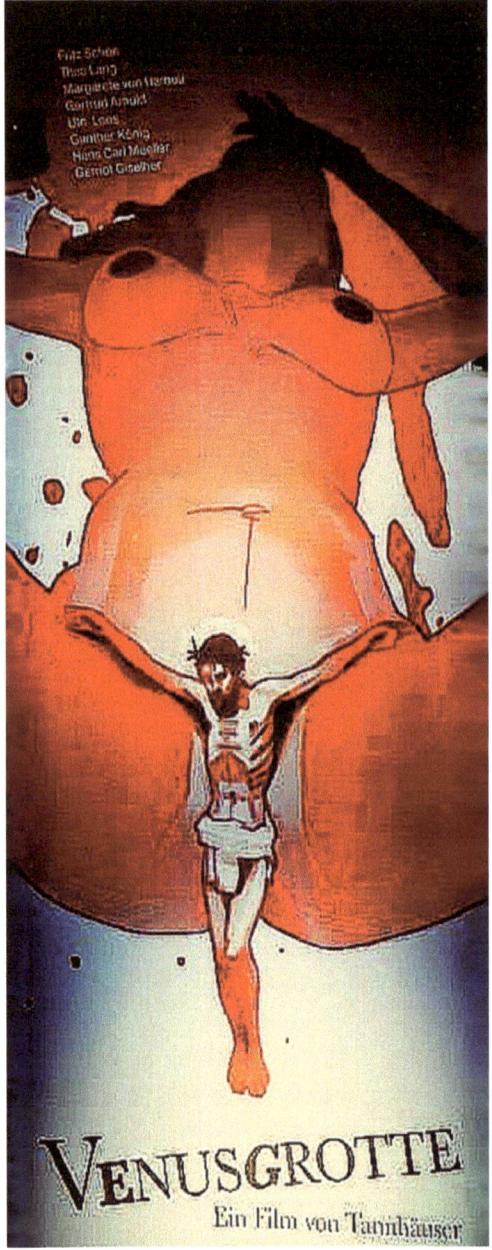

Bibliography

Berghaus, G. and Dobrenko, E. (eds.), *Sotsrealisticheskii kanon* (St. Petersburg: Akademicheskii Proekt, 2000).

Bremer, T., *Cross and Kremlin: A Brief History of the Orthodox Church in Russia* (Grand Rapids, Michigan: William B. Eerdmans Publishing Company, 2013).

Brinkley, A., 'The problem of American conservatism', *The American Historical Review*, 99(2) (1994): 409-429.

'Eksperty ne nashli oskorblenia khristianskih simvolov v opere "Tangeizer', *Vzgliad* 10 March 2015, http://www.vz.ru/news/2015/3/10/733512.html (accessed 4 February 2016).

Gordeeva, A., 'Sibir', opera, kino i nemtsy. V Novosibirskoi opera pokazali vagnerovskogo Tangeizera', *Gazeta.ru*, 24 December 2014, http://www.gazeta.ru/culture/2014/12/ 24/a_6357137.shtml (accessed 16 December 2015).

Dewhirst, M., 'Censorship in Russia, 1991 and 2001', *Journal of Communist Studies and Transition Politics* 18(1) (2002): 21-34.

Kadachigov, R., 'Richard Wagner, *Tannhäuser*. Prem'era 20.12.14, NGATOiB - obsuzhdaem spektakl", Discussion group on vk.com, post 26 March 2015, https://vk.com/topic-30300472_31535545 (accessed 22 January 2016).

Kalinin, I., 'Carbon and cultural heritage: the politics of history and the economics of rent', *Baltic Worlds* 2-3: 65-74 http://balticworlds.com/wp-content/uploads/2014/10/BW-2-3-2014-TEMA-uppslag.pdf (accessed 17 April 2016).

Krinsky, C., *The Ashgate Research Companion to Moral Panics* (Farnham, Surrey: Ashgate, 2013).

Kristol, I. *Reflections of a neoconservative: Looking back, looking ahead* (New York: Basic Books, 1983).

Kuraev, A. (Deacon), 'Fil'm *Poslednee Iskushenie Khrista* Pokazan. Kakie Uroki?', http://halkidon2006.narod.ru/do/bogoslovie_1/841_Kuraev.htm (accessed 3 February 2016).

Loginova, M., 'Na mitinge protiv 'Tangeizera' poprosili pomoshi u Putina', 29 March 2015, http://www.bbc.com/russian/russia/2015/03/150329_novosibirsk_tannhauser_protest_rally (accessed 6 February 2016).

'Miting protiv tserkovnogo radikalizma v Novosibirske sobral neskol'ko tysiach uchastnikov', 5 April 2015, http://grani.ru/Politics/Russia/m.239810.html (accessed 10 February 2016).

'Mitropolit trebuet sniat' "Tangeizer" s repertuara', 13 March 2015, http://www.colta.ru/news/6637?page=70 (accessed 5 February 2016).

'Netsenzurnoe lobbi', 11 July 2012, http://lenta.ru/articles/2012/07/10/stopcensorship/ (accessed 5 February 2016).

'Net slava bogu ser'eznykh sotsial'nyh posledstvii', 10 March 2015, http://vz.ru/culture/2015/3/10/733547.html (accessed 5 February 2016).

'Novosibirskaia eparkhia – situatsia s 'Tangeizerom' ne v iurisdiktsii rpts', 1 April 2015, http://ria.ru/religion/20150401/1055871853.html#ixz z3zI4yf05Y (accessed 6 February 2016).

'Novosti ministerstva', 1 April 2015, http://mkrf.ru/press-center/news/ministerstvo/kommentariy-minkultury-rossii-po-kadrovym-izmen eniyam-v-novosibirskom-akademiche?sphrase_id=3809299 (accessed 6 February 2016).

'O. Dmitrii Smirnov o spektakle *Tannhäuser:* eto prodolzhenie pank-molebna', 8 March 2015, http://www.pravoslavie.ru/77752.html (accessed 22 January 2016).

'Osnovy gosudarstvennoi kul'turnoi politiki' (2014) http://static.kremlin .ru/media/events/files/41d526a877638a8730eb.pdf (accessed 17 April 2016).

Papkova, I., *The Orthodox Church and Russian Politics* (Washington, DC: Woodrow Wilson Center Press, 2011).

'Patriarkh Aleksii chitaet, chto v nyneshnem gody ego vstrecha s papoi rimskim nevozmozhna', 16 July 1998 http://www.interfax-religion .ru/cis.php?act=archive&div=1469 (accessed 3 February 2016).

'Pervye itogi ob'edinenia RPTs i RPTsZ, online konferentsiia, mitropolit Kirill', 14 August 2007, http://ria.ru/online/20070814/71442391.html (accessed 17 April 2016).

'Prokuratura obzhaluet reshenie suda, zakryvshego delo po "Tangeizeru"', 13 March 2015, http://ria.ru/culture/20150313/1052332917.html#ix zz3zI3oGMgX (accessed 5 February 2016).

'Prokuror otozval protesty na reshenie suda po delu opery "Tangeizer', 2 April 2015, http://ria.ru/culture/20150402/1056126344.html#ixzz3 zI6RrkR4 (accessed 9 February 2016).

'Putin nagradil ordenom raskritikovavshego 'Tangeizer' sviashennika', 27 March 2015, http://altervision.org/putin-nagradil-ordenom-raskriti kovavshego-tangejzer-svyas hhennika-iz-novosibirska/ (accessed 10 February 2016).

'Religioznaia vera v Rossii' (2012), http://www.levada.ru/2011/09/26/religioznaya-vera -v-rossii/ (accessed 12 March 2016).

Richters, K., *The Post-Soviet Russian Orthodox Church: Politics, Culture and Greater Russia* (London: Routledge, 2012).

'Rossiiane vyskazalis' protiv prepodavaniia religii v shkole' (2013), http:// www.levada.ru/2013/03/01/rossiyane-vyskazalis-protiv-prepodav aniya-religii-v-shkole/ (accessed 12 March 2016).

'RPTs prizvala oskorblennykh v chuvstvakh veruiushikh ne bezhat' srazu v prokuraturu', 5 March 2015, http://vz.ru/news/2015/3/5/7329 84.html (accessed 5 February 2016).

Ryklin, M.N., *Svastika, krest,zvezda: Proizvedenie iskusstva v epokhu upravliaemoi demokratii* (Moscow: Logos, 2006).

Serova, O., 'Richard Wagner, Tannhäuser. Prem'era 20.12.14, ngatoib—obsuzhdaem spektakl', Discussion group on vk.com, post 23 December 2014, https://vk.com/topic-30300472_31535545 (accessed 22 January 2016).

Simons, G. and Strovsky, D., 'Censorship in contemporary Russian journalism in the age of the War Against Terrorism; historical perspective', *European Journal of Communication* 21(2) (2006): 189–211.

Simons, G. and Westerlund, D., (eds.) *Religion, Politics and Nation-building in Post- communist Countries* (Farnham: Ashgate, 2015).

'Stenogramma obshchestvennogo obsuzhdenia postanovki opery "Tangeizer' v ngatobe. 13.03.2015", http://mkrf.ru/ministerstvo/dep artament/detail.php?ID=623062&print=Y (accessed 6 February 2016).

'"Tangeizer" mstit Kekhmanu i Medinskomu', 3 April 2015, http://ria fan.ru/233415-tangeyzer-mstit-Kekhmanu-i-medinskomu (accessed 10 February 2016).

'Tangeizer. Tsenzura. Vecher s Vladimirom Solov'evym', 2 April 2015, http://www.videofan.in.ua/online/tangejzer-tsenzyra-vecher-s-vl adimirom-solovvim-02042015mp4/171131165-216644514/ (accessed 10 February 2016).

Tikhon (Shevkunov), Archimandrite, *S Bozh'ei pomoshch'iu vozmozhno vse: O vere i otechestve* (Moscow: Knizhnyi mir, 2014).

'O. Tikhon: *Tannhäuser* napravlen na razzhiganie religioznoi vrazhdy', 27 February 2015, http://sibkray.ru/news/4/873250 (accessed 22 January 2016).

Tsevan, A., 'Richard Wagner, *Tannhäuser*. Prem'era 20.12.14, ngatoib—obsuzhdaem spektakl', post 25 February 2015, discussion group on vk.com, https://vk.com/topic -30300472_31535545 (accessed 22 January 2016).

'V. Legoida: Svoboda tvorchestva ne iavliaetsia indul'gentsiei', 1 April 2015, http://ria.ru/interview/20150401/1055897768.html#ixzz3zl5l F0Qj, (accessed 7 February 2016).

'V op predlozhili sozdat' vyezdnye khudozhestvennyie sovety i eticheskii kodeks deiatelia iskusstv', 1 April 2015, http://www.vz.ru/news /2015/4/1/737635.print.html (accessed 7 February 2016).

'Velikii post i Paskha' (2015). http://www.levada.ru/2015/04/10/velikij-post-i-pasha/ (accessed 12 March 2016).

'Vtoroe kreshenie Rusi—fil'm mitropolita Volokolamskogo Illariona', (27 June 2014), http://www.pravmir.ru/vtoroe-kreshhenie-rusi-film-mi tropolita-volokolamskogo -ilariona-video/ (accessed 17 April 2016).

Wanner, C., *State Secularism and Lived Religion in Soviet Russia and Ukraine* (New York: Oxford University Press, 2012).

Willems, J. *Pussy Riots Punk-Gebet: Religion, Recht und Politik in Russland* (Berlin: Berlin University Press, 2013).

The Reception of *Leviathan* in Light of Two Soviet "Cultural Scandals": A Revival of Soviet Rhetoric and Values?

Susan Ikonen
University of Helsinki

Andrei Zviagintsev's award-winning movie "Leviathan" (2014) triggered a fierce debate among domestic audiences in Russia. It was blamed for being anti-Russian and slandering Russian life. The rhetoric of these accusations reminded many Russians of Soviet-era campaigns against writers and filmmakers. This article analyses the film's reception by different audiences, of which the most critically harsh and insistent voice was that of the Orthodox activists. The article also attempts to connect expressions of patriotism and shared identity with Soviet-era models. In this context, it discusses Stalin-era cultural control with a special focus on two Thaw-era literary scandals: the controversies about Vladimir Dudintsev's novel (1956) and Boris Pasternak's Nobel Prize (1958).

Keywords: Zviagintsev, Pasternak, Dudintsev, patriotism, cultural politics, socialist realism

Introduction

In January 2015 the Russian Internet seemed to have gone crazy. Andrei Zviagintsev's award-winning movie *Leviathan* triggered fierce discussion in which accusations were levelled at the film and its director for allegedly slandering the Russian state, the Orthodox Church, and Russian life in general.[1] The debate also rebuked those welcoming reviews, which the socially critical film won among

---

1 The film, set in a small village in the periphery of the Russian North, gives an utterly pessimistic picture of its protagonists' lives, filled with heavy drinking and constant swearing and suffering from the corrupt relations between secular and clerical authorities, at whose hands the "common man" has no justice. The Russian supporters of the film applauded this exposition as necessary, whereas its critics condemned it in harsh words.

Western commentators. In the midst of economic problems, there was a surge of antipathy towards the "West". Commentators in and outside Russia saw the film presenting social criticism in a late socialist manner, while they also saw the reactions against it repeating Soviet era patterns of cultural scandals.[2]

The journalists of the Internet newspaper *Znak* compared the 2015 "hunt for Zviagintsev" to the official outcry against Boris Pasternak in 1958, illustrating it with the ironic title "'The right thing to do is to kick him out of our country as soon as possible' — Master-Class for Medinsky and Co. from the Tormentors of Pasternak".[3] The article cited commentaries by high-level authorities, castigating Zviagintsev's "anti-Russian" film, made "on Western orders", for being "utterly opportunistic" (*zapredel'no kon"iunkturen*) and "distorting reality". These quotations were provided together with excerpts from the stenographic record of Pasternak's expulsion from the Soviet Writers Union, leaving it for the reader to draw the necessary conclusions.

This paper presents an analysis of the debate about *Leviathan* in the Russian press in 2014 and 2015.[4] While tracking the vicissi-

---

2   For an illustrative example of Western commentary, see: 'Russia's Book of Job', *The Economist* 14 February 2015, http://www.economist.com/news/books-and-arts/21643040-domestic-response-andrei-zvyagintsevs-award-winning-fi lm-leviathan-says-lot (accessed 22 April 2016).

3   P. Kharlamov, A. Zadorozhnyi and R. Ismailov. '"Samoe pravil'noe — ubrats'ia emu iz nashei strany poskoree" Master-klass dlia Medinskogo i Ko. ot muchitelei Pasternaka', *Internetgazeta Znak.com* 22 January 2015, http://www.znak.com/moscow/articles/22-01-21-38/103462.html (accessed 22 April 2016).

4   The materials used to illustrate the reception of *Leviathan* comprise of Internet newspapers and articles in the Russian central press, which have been retrieved via the Integrum database. The used newspapers are: *Komsomol'skaia pravda, Pravda kp rf, Rossiiskaia gazeta, Sovetskaia Rossiia, Novaia gazeta, Nezavisimaia gazeta* and *Metro* (Moscow). The selection was made in order to have both "official" (*Rossiiskaia gazeta*) and "critical" (*Novaia gazeta*) as well as wide-circulation views. The Communist Party newspaper (*Pravda kp rf*) was chosen to add some flavour to the discussion. Due to the electronic nature of the newspapers, no page numbers have been mentioned. It should be noted with emphasis that the fiercest debates took place in the various discussion forums of the Internet (movie forums, YouTube and Facebook sites, etc.), and that the newspapers more or less portrayed and reacted to these debates "somewhere out there", as well as gave their own, more old-fashioned journalistic reactions.

THE RECEPTION OF LEVIATHAN   127

tudes of the movie's reception among different audiences, it concentrates on the comparisons and parallels that were made between Soviet era cultural politics and current attitudes to culture and patriotism in Russia. The paper offers a historical perspective on the debate by discussing the "Pasternak case" of 1958 and tying it to an earlier, lesser-known case, caused by the publication of Vladimir Dudintsev's novel *Not by Bread Alone* in 1956.[5] These two cases present the first post-Stalinist reactions to "scandalous" works of art.[6] A closer look at the situation in the late 1950s can explain why the Pasternak case was brought up again in Russia of the mid-2010s. All three cases involved outrage and accusations of the works being anti-Soviet/anti-Russian and receiving Western praise for political reasons.[7]

---

5   For the Pasternak case, a variety of research is available, and most of the archival sources have been published. See, e.g. V.Yu. Afiani and N.G. Tomilina (Eds.), *"A za mnoiu shum pogoni..." Boris Pasternak i vlast'. 1956–1972 gg. Dokumenty* (Moscow: Rosspen, 2001); P. Mancosu, *Inside the Zhivago Storm. The Editorial Adventures of Pasternak's Masterpiece* (Milano: Fondazione Giangiacomo Feltrinelli, 2013); El. V. Pasternak et al. (eds.) *b.l. Pasternak: Pro et Contra. b.l. Pasternak v sovetskoi, emigrantskoi, rossiiskoi literaturnoi kritike. Antologiia.* Tom 2. (St. Peteisbuig. Iiistilul bogosloviia i filosofii, 2013). As to the Dudintsev case, this article utilizes archival and press materials, and also takes advantage of my previous work on the reception of his novel in the Soviet press and inside the Communist Party Central Committee. See S. Ikonen, 'Ne sotsrealizmom edinym. Obsuzhdenie romana Vladimira Dudintseva "Ne khlebom edinym" v Sovetskom Soiuze v 1956–1957 gg.', in *Politika literatury — poetika vlasti.* eds. G. Obatnin, B. Hellman and T. Huttunen (Moscow: Novoe literaturnoe obozrenie, 2014), pp. 216–233.
6   In both Soviet cases, the main "actors" behind the discussions and politics were the Soviet Writers Union and the Central Committee of the Communist Party of the Soviet Union, while Soviet press followed suit. For the Soviet press coverage of the Pasternak scandal, see: D. Kozlov, '"I Have Not Read, but I Will Say". Soviet Literary Audiences and Changing Ideas of Social Membership, 1958–66', *Kritika: Explorations in Russian and Eurasian History* 7(3) (2006). In his article Denis Kozlov introduces a comparative analysis of the reception of the "Pasternak case" and the "Sinyavski and Daniel case", relying mostly on newspaper coverage and readers' letters concerning the two cases. Kozlov attempts to analyse "language and ideas" expressed and to "note some differences" between the reactions and present "intellectual changes that those differences may suggest".
7   In short, Vladimir Dudintsev's novel *Not by Bread Alone* criticized the state of technology and the power of the (Party) nomenclature in the late 1940s Soviet Union; Boris Pasternak's *Doctor Zhivago* re-examined the Revolution and the

An inquiry into the reception of art can tell us a great deal about the debates and issues topical for a given society at a given moment. The debate about *Leviathan* and its reception in Russia brought up questions about the relations between the church and the state, the political image of Russia at home and abroad, the rise of Russian patriotism, demands on shared identity and values, and, last but not least, questions underlying the Soviet legacy and how to encounter that legacy in words and deeds, in rhetoric and practice.

Baggage from the Soviet Past? Coupling of Cultural Politics with "Patriotism"

In the Soviet Union, socialist realism became a vehicle for controlling artistic processes from an ideological point of view, which in turn defined the limits of how "realistically" one should and could portray society. When discussing societal aspects of art, the institution of (literary) criticism rose to a leading role in Soviet discourse. It served as a mediator between politics and art, and simultaneously transmitted the Party line of the time to the public.[8] Soviet rhetoric relied on certain characteristics, the most important of which was "party-mindedness" (*partiinost'*).[9] Without "party-mindedness", the speaker became an enemy — be it a potential or a real one, and thus served as a marker between cultural categories of *svoi* and *chuzhoi* ("our" and "alien").[10] Simultaneously, "party-mindedness" was a tool for explicating the ideology and for eliminating all possibilities of "other interpretations" (*inotolkovanie*) of

---

Russian Civil War; and Andrei Zviagintsev's film *Leviathan* presented the fate of a "little man" in the hands of corrupt officials in today's Russian North.

8   E. Dobrenko, 'Literary Criticism and the Institution of Literature, 1941–1953', in *A History of Russian Literary Theory and Criticism. The Soviet Age and Beyond*, eds. E. Dobrenko and G. Tikhanov (Pittsburgh, Pa.: University of Pittsburgh Press, 2011) p. 166.
9   See in further detail: A.P. Romanenko, *Sovetskaia slovesnaia kul'tura: Obraz ritora*. Izd. vtoroe, stereotipnoe. (Moscow: URSS, 2003), p. 32.
10 A.P. Romanenko, *Obraz ritora v sovetskoi slovesnoi kul'ture. Uchebnoe posobie* (Moscow: Izd-va 'Flinta' i 'Nauka', 2003), p. 74.

ideology, which in turn was represented in the viewpoint of a normative Party document.[11] Thus, for both rhetoric and pronounced values, the official line was monolithic; as to the reception of art, criticism was the vehicle through which the Party hierarchy made its views known to the public and to the artists themselves.

Most of these elements of Soviet culture and discourse became prevalent in the 1930s. Simultaneously, Soviet state patriotism was created and propagated to the mostly illiterate masses. There was a practical necessity to mobilize the people and create loyalty towards the new Soviet state, and this popular mobilization, albeit targeted at the entire Soviet people, contained the seeds for ethnically Russian nationalism. Alongside the "friendship of the peoples" rhetoric, first among the equals of the Soviet people were the Russians.[12] Despite the discussions and debates among the intellectual elites since the late 18th century, and especially the disputes between Slavophiles and Westernizes in the 19th century, modern Russian national identity was created on a nation-wide (mass) level only in the 1930s. At the same time, these were the formative years for the creation of Soviet identity (in a setting of a totalitarian society and culture in the making), a process in which Russian culture and national iconography played a crucial role and which has left an indelible mark in the various manifestations of today's Russian (patriotic) speech and demands for uniform values.

The post-war brought one more tone to this trinity of party-mindedness, socialist realism and Soviet patriotism: the utterly suspicious attitude towards the West—and the use of the "West" as a rhetorical instrument in Soviet internal discussions. The totalitarian atmosphere of the 1930s reached its zenith in cultural politics in the era of *zhdanovshchina*, named after Andrei Zhdanov, Stalin's second in charge of Soviet cultural life. Zhdanov brought Party directives and propaganda of patriotism together and inserted loyalty to not

---

11 Ibid., 78.
12 D. Brandenberger, *National Bolshevism: Stalinist Mass Culture and the Formation of Modern Russian National Identity, 1931–1956* (Cambridge: Harvard UP, 2002), pp. 43–44.

only the Soviet state but also to the Communist Party into the concept of "patriotism".[13] He initiated an attack on all Western influence, stating that the foundation of Western culture was "rotten and putrid" and that "kowtowing to bourgeois culture or playing the role of pupils" was "not becoming to representatives of forward-looking Soviet culture, of Soviet patriots".[14]

The international context of the anti-cosmopolitanism campaign of 1946 was related to animosities between former war allies, now escalating into the Cold War. As the new war unfolded, Andrei Zhdanov became its "marshal on the ideological front".[15] The infamous "Zhdanov resolutions" gave direct instructions on preferred literary and other artistic products, creating an ideal of *beskonfliktnost'* — the nonexistence of antagonisms in society. One should not expose or depict any (social) problems in artistic works, which resulted in *lakirovka* — varnishing of reality. Zhdanov died in 1948, but it was only after Stalin's death that these postulates saw their first public criticism. However, a true change would take longer to appear.

Two "Scandals" from the Early Thaw: Dudintsev and Pasternak

The questions of an appropriate artistic portrayal of Russia and the role of the "West" in Soviet internal cultural politics can best be illustrated with the first "cultural scandals" of the Thaw. They were not only characteristic of the first years' dealing with Stalin-era legacies but also set precedents for later Soviet cultural politics. Thus, in order to ponder upon the possible Soviet "baggage" in today's Russia, seemingly striving for more "centrally approved" cultural life yet wanting to dissociate itself from the full-blown Stalinist model, it is appropriate to look at the Thaw.

The 20th Party Congress in February, 1956, during which Khrushchev denounced Stalin's personality cult, was an event

---

13 R. G. Pikhoia, *Sovetskii Soiuz: Istoriia vlasti, 1945–1991* (Novosibirsk: Sibirskii khronograf, 2000), p. 48.
14 Cited in Dobrenko 2011, p. 171.
15 Pikhoia 2000, p. 48.

which changed Soviet society. The first traces of this change were seen on the literary front in the more liberal publishing policies, and it was during the summer of 1956 that Vladimir Dudintsev, an aspiring younger writer, and Boris Pasternak, an established Russian poet, submitted their novel manuscripts to *Novyi mir*. Dudintsev's was accepted, Pasternak's declined.

In a matter of months, Dudintsev's socially critical novel *Not by Bread Alone* witnessed a 180 degree turnabout from praise to condemnation. First it was acclaimed for being brave and Bolshevist-minded, and the author praised for being a true Soviet patriot.[16] Later the Soviet press gave it critical but objective accounts, and the Moscow branch of the Writers Union even considered selecting Dudintsev as their nominee for the first-ever Lenin Prize in literature.[17] Soon, however, the discussions around the novel got more controversial as some readers (including the famous writer Konstantin Paustovsky) took the novel as a call-to-arms against the whole Soviet (Party) nomenclature.[18] The Hungarian uprising, starting in late October, further scared the Soviet Party elite and escalated the Cold War. Then *Izvestiia* condemned Dudintsev's novel, criticizing the "unhealthy fuss" (*nezdorovyi azhiotazh*) around it.[19] In Party documents, expressions such as "unhealthy phenomena" or "unhealthy sentiments" were used repeatedly in the following months.[20]

A fierce press campaign against Dudintsev followed, and the mounting Western interest served as proof for the Party hierarchy

---

16 'Obsuzhdaem novye knigi', *Literaturnaia gazeta* 27 October 1956.
17 Russian State Archive of Literature and Art (rgali), F. 2464, op. 1, ed. hr. 336. Moscow branch of the Soviet Writers Union. Stenographic record of the Prose section of the Moscow branch on nominations for the Lenin Prizes. 28 November 1956.
18 The Central Archive of Social-Political History of the city of Moscow (TsAOPIM), F. 8132, op. 1, d. 9, l. 143-144. Prose section of the Moscow branch of the Soviet Writers Union. Stenographic record of the discussion event on Dudintsev's novel *Not by Bread Alone*. 22 October 1956.
19 N. Kriuchkova, 'O romane *Ne khlebom edinym*', *Izvestiia*. 2 December 1956: 2-3.
20 'Zapiska otdela kul'tury TsK kpss "O nekotorykh nezdorovykh iavleniiakh v Moskovskom otdelenii Soiuza pisatelei". Ne pozdnee 30.5.1957', in *Apparat TsK kpss i kul'tura 1953-1957. Dokumenty.* ed. V. Yu. Afiani (Moscow: Rosspen, 2001), pp. 673-682, esp. 673, 676.

of there being something inherently suspicious about the novel. The novel's societal criticism, directed at some malfunctioning aspects of Soviet life, was now seen as denigration of the whole system, as painting the whole Soviet reality in black. In contrast to the initial acclaims, the novel was now accused of being anti-Soviet, anti-patriotic and against the principles of socialist realism; Dudintsev was accused of being opposed to "us", to "our values", to "our reality". During the spring of 1957, it became clear that there would be only one way to apprehend the novel — namely, along the Party line.[21] Konstantin Simonov's change of heart (he was Dudintsev's main supporter initially), was even more illustrative: he had been in the avant-garde not only in publishing controversial pieces of literature on the pages of Novyi mir but in taking a stand to shed the Zhdanov resolutions from influencing Soviet literature.

Nikita Khrushchev's direct intervention sealed Dudintsev's fate. Khrushchev described the novel as a "slanderous essay" (klevetnicheskoe sochinenie): "We are against one-sided, dishonest and untruthful depiction of our reality, against those who collect from life only negative facts and gloat over them, who try to speak ill of and blacken (ochernit') our Soviet order".[22] As to the interest in the novel abroad, the Cultural Department of the Communist Party of the Soviet Union (CPSU) Central Committee worked out an ingenious plan. During the fiercest campaign against Dudintsev, the novel was re-published as a separate volume, which would screen from the foreign insinuations the fact that the book and its author were "forbidden".[23] This publication was used when dealing with the West, but it was not mentioned domestically: there was no mentioning of the separate volume in the Soviet press, and according to

---

21 See S. Ikonen 2014 for further details and sources in the discussions over the Dudintsev case.
22 N. Khrushchev, 'Za tesnuiu zviaz' literatury i kul'tury so zhizniu naroda', Novyi mir 9 (1957).
23 Russian State Archive of Contemporary History (rgani), F. 5, op. 36, d. 37, l. 1. Memorandum of the Cultural Department of the Soviet Communist Party Central Committee on publishing Dudintsev's novel as a separate volume. See also Russian State Archive of Literature and Arts (rgali), f. 1234, op. 18, ed. hr. 429, l. 32-33. Sovetskii pisatel' publishing house, the department of Soviet Russian prose (on publishing the novel).

Dudintsev himself, the book was kept out of reach of ordinary readers.[24]

While condemning the novel, Khrushchev did not completely exclude Dudintsev from the Soviet community — as long as the author would later work in the manner expected from a Soviet writer: "I believe that with our help and by his own will he will be able to step back onto the right path and will, together with the collective of writers, work productively for the benefit of the people, to the benefit of our Socialist Fatherland."[25] Nonetheless, Dudintsev became a persona non grata for some years, and kept more or less silent for the next thirty years. Eventually, in 1987, he published his second (and last) novel. Back in the late 1950s, however, in the tranquility of literary and Party circles, there was a scandal growing around Pasternak's manuscript.

After the manuscript of *Doctor Zhivago* was turned down by Soviet journals, Pasternak had it published abroad. The novel came out in Italian in 1957, and in 1958 it was published both in English and Russian with the help of the CIA, as we now know.[26] In October 1958, Pasternak was awarded the Nobel Prize for Literature. At this point the Soviet press condemned both the novel and its author: "We are talking about the whole spirit of the novel, its pathos and the author's view of life."[27] What was meant by the "spirit of the novel", according to the 1956 rejection letter by *Novyi mir* (now widely publicized), was the view that the novel rejected the socialist revolution and advanced the idea that the revolution had brought only suffering to the people and destroyed the Russian intelligentsia. Iuri Zhivago's "pathological individualism" filled the novel, with its hero remaining distant to the people; furthermore, the

---

24 I have discussed this aspect in more detail in: S. Ikonen, 'Kirjallisuuspolitiikan käänteitä suojasään Neuvostoliitossa — tapaus Dudintsev', *Ajan kohina: Venäläisen kirjallisuuden seuran lehti* 4 (2015).
25 Khrushchev, 'Za tesnuiu zviaz'...', p. 20.
26 P. Finn and P. Couvée, *The Zhivago affair: the Kremlin, the cia, and the battle over a forbidden book* (London: Vintage, 2015).
27 'Pis'mo chlenov redkollegii zhurnala 'Novyi mir' b.l. Pasternaku po povodu rukopisi romana 'Doktor Zhivago'. September, 1956', in *"A za mnoiu shum pogoni..." Boris Pasternak i vlast'. 1956–1972 gg. Dokumenty*, eds. V.Yu. Afiani and N.G. Tomilina (Moscow: Rosspen, 2001), p. 349.

"people" were not depicted in a way required from a Soviet novel.[28] The problem of the book, as Soviet critics saw it, did not reside in aesthetics; on the contrary, the problem was that Pasternak's novel was political to the core and served particular political goals. The book was considered deeply partial (*nespravedliv*) and historically un-objective in the depiction of the Revolution, Civil War and the post-Revolutionary years.[29]

These were fundamental problems but it was the international success that turned out to be the most serious concern for Soviet authorities. By giving his manuscript to foreign publishers, Pasternak had "disdained the elementary concept of honor and conscience of a Soviet writer and citizen". The novel depicted the October Revolution, the people who conducted it, and the entire project of building Communism in the USSR in a slanderous manner (*klevetnicheski*), which was now "hoisted as armor by the bourgeois press and taken as armament by the international reactionary forces". According to Soviet critics, awarding Pasternak the Nobel Prize had nothing to do with the objective evaluation of literary qualities of his works, which had a deeply individualist character and were far from the life of the people. "The award is tied to the anti-Soviet fuss around the novel *Doctor Zhivago* and is a completely political act, hostile to our country and directed towards fueling the Cold War."[30]

Some pieces of the novel were published in the Soviet press, and readers' commentaries were based on these excerpts, creating a Russian cliché "*ne chital, no skazhu*" — "I have not read it but I will speak out anyway".[31] In October, 1958 Pasternak was excluded from the Soviet Writers Union with nearly all members protesting against him, and the Party Central Committee let him know that were he to accept the Prize in Stockholm, he would not be granted

---

28 Ibid., 356–357, 373–374.
29 Ibid., 375–376.
30 'Predislovie redkollegii zhurnala Novyi mir k publikatsii pis'ma redkollegii zhurnala po povodu romana 'Doktor Zhivago', napravlennoe b.l. Pasternaku v sentyabre 1956 g. *Literaturnaia gazeta*, 25 October 1958', in "*A za mnoiu shum pogoni...*" *Boris Pasternak i vlast'. 1956–1972 gg. Dokumenty*, eds. V.Yu. Afiani and N.G. Tomilina (Moscow: Rosspen, 2001), pp. 376–377.
31 Kozlov, 2006.

a return back home.³² The Party authorities compared the author to a pig, with the difference that a pig would not soil its own den like the writer had done. Pasternak turned down the Nobel Prize, asking Khrushchev not to expatriate him. Paradoxically, during the same time three Soviet scientists became Nobel laureates in Physics; this achievement was trumpeted in the Soviet press. The readers were informed that the Physics award was recognition of the great achievements of Russian and Soviet scientists, whereas in the case of literature the motives were nothing but political.³³

To conclude, the limits of acceptable behavior and boundaries of expression differed in each case. Even if Dudintsev's novel did not contain enough of "party-mindedness", it did not break ties with socialist realism and Soviet values. Thus, a reasonable amount of social criticism was allowed in Dudintsev's case, albeit with caution and with (mostly rhetorical) repercussions for the author. What turned out to be "too much" was the complete disavowal of the founding event of Soviet society (as Pasternak's novel was interpreted at the time) and its values. Thus Dudintsev, although contrasted to "us", was able to remain inside the Soviet community, whereas Pasternak was expelled, as is suggested by the use of epithets such as "inner emigration" and "worse than a pig".

These two cases were Thaw-era precursors which anticipated the relations between dissenting authors and the Party and Government officials, thus marking the beginning of post-Stalinist literary and cultural politics, in which the ideological enemy—the West— had a role to play.³⁴ The praise from the West was a complicated issue: when it contradicted the Soviet self-perception, it was deemed suspicious or politically hostile, but when it lent support to positive self-understanding of the Soviet people (as in the case of the 1958 Nobel Prize for Physics), it was deemed an important form

---

32 See, e.g. A. Zadorozhnyi and R. Ismailov, '"Samoe pravil'noe—ubrat'sia emu iz nashei strany poskoree" Master-klass dlia Medinskogo i Ko—ot muchitelei Pasternaka', *Znak* 22 January 2015, newspaper for selected quotations: http://www.znak.com/moscow/articles/22-01-21-38/103462.html (accessed 22 April 2016).
33 See Finn and Couvée, 2015, p. 187.
34 In the Siniavsky-Daniel case in 1965–1966, the publication of literary works in the West served as a rallying point, resulting, this time, in actual imprisonment.

of acknowledgement. In what follows, I will explore how this dynamics works in Russian cultural production today, by analyzing the reception of Andrei Zviagintsev's *Leviathan*.

Leviathan and Its Reception in Russia

The director Andrei Zviagintsev, previously known for his films *The Return*, *The Banishment* and *Elena*, came up with the focal idea of *Leviathan* when learning about Marvin Heemeyer, who went on a rampage with a bulldozer in a small Colorado town over a zoning dispute. The rage of injustice felt by a "little man" in the face of authorities became the theme for *Leviathan*, set in Russia and written with outright associations to both religion and state (the Biblical tale of Job and the philosophical essay by Thomas Hobbes). On the shores of the Barents Sea, a mechanic refuses to sell his land to the local mayor, who then uses his connections to both secular and religious authorities to get his wish fulfilled. The film depicts a thoroughly corrupt establishment and the helplessness of the common man in the face of the authorities.[35]

Leviathan started its triumphal march at the international film festivals in April 2014, when it won the Best Film Award in Cannes. At that time the domestic controversy over the film concerned the legal ban on obscene language. Effective from 1 July 2014, new law of the Russian Federation forbade the usage of foul language in art works. The question of whether the film would become "forbidden" (i.e. not released) was concrete, yet had nothing to do with the film's subject matter. Nevertheless, the Minister of Culture of the Russian Federation, Vladimir Medinskii stated that he did not like the film and that the Russians did not drink and swear like that.[36]

---

35 Surprisingly enough, there are clear parallels between the fates of the main protagonists of Dudintsev's novel and Zviagintsev's film, as Dudintsev, too, depicted the trials and tribulations of a lone engineer struggling against the representatives of Soviet *nomenklatura* bureaucrats. Yet Dudintsev's novel was mostly within the frame of socialist realism, and was thus much more optimistic than Zviagintsev's tale.
36 E. Poliakova. '*Leviafan*: chudovishchnoe zrelishche', *Afisha* 4 June 2014, http://afisha.ngs.ru/news/more/1854001/ (accessed 22 April 2016).

In September there were speculations about whether the Russian jury would nominate *Leviathan* as the representative of Russia in the American Academy Awards. *Novaia gazeta* feared that the contemporary "patriotic hysteria" might prevent the nomination.[37] When reporting on the nomination, *Komsomol'skaia pravda* commented ironically about the movie being, perhaps, "against state cultural politics". The author of the article was happy that the Russian Oscar committee did not fear this possibility.[38] Since the film would get awards and fight its way to the Academy Awards shortlist, in the autumn the Russian press speculated about the possibility of it getting the award and listed previous Soviet and Russian films that had received either the Golden Globe or the Academy Award. In December 2014, the producer of the film, Aleksandr Rodnianskii, commented on the possible political implications of the film: "Right after its premiere in Cannes, in the very emotional atmosphere of the summer events, the film could be received as a political announcement. But we conceived the idea six years ago, and it's clear that Zviagintsev is not a political artist."[39]

At the end of the year, Vladimir Medinskii gave a speech in the Duma about the Year of Culture 2014, stating the "special successes of the Russian cinematography at festivals, including such prestigious ones like the Cannes and Venetian festivals". The *Novaia gazeta* journalist, who commented on the speech, stated that contemporary Russian "*auteur* cinematography" was actually created in many ways against the status of the Ministry of Culture and the protectors of "hoorah patriotic" ideology.[40] After all, Medinskii had stated: "We are, let me stress it one more time, from now on not going to finance projects which have an explicit defamatory (*ochernitelnyi*), anti-historical character, which spit upon our history and the deeds of our forefathers". The journalist considered problematic what it was that could be seen as "defamatory", and how

---

37 L. Maliukova, '*Leviafan* v prilive patriotizma', *Novaya gazeta* 26 September 2014.
38 D. Korsakov, 'Rossiia vydvinula na "Oskar" *Leviafana*', *Komsomol'skaia pravda* 29 September 2014.
39 V. Kichin, 'Igra na vyzhivanie'. *Rossiiskaia gazeta* 17 December 2014.
40 L. Maliukova. 'Pod kopytami dereviannoi loshadi. Kino Rossii v 2014-m: podvodim itogi', *Novaia gazeta* 24 December 2014.

this epithet could be used against all Russian cinema trying to grope for the sore spots of reality.[41]

Novaia gazeta was worried about the rise of the ideology of patriotism, its political usage and especially its connectedness to the ideology of the Russian Orthodox Church. It also contemplated that the destiny of movies and film festivals was becoming dependent not on professional evaluations but solely on the Minister of Culture, his tastes, his understanding of history and patriotism, and his whims.[42]

By mid-January 2015, the film and/or its director had already won a pile of international awards, and finally, the Golden Globe Award. On January 14, the Moscow area *Metro* newspaper titled its coverage: "Our people in Los Angeles". The governmental newspaper *Rossiiskaia gazeta* had also labelled the film "our *Leviathan*".[43] *Komsomol'skaia pravda* pondered on the question of why an internationally acclaimed movie is reprimanded back home as "anti-Russian", "gruesome", and "a mere festival hack". The opinion of a cinema specialist was that the film would not have received all these international awards had it only "denigrated" Russia, as its most ardent opponents claimed. "The international success of the film proves its absolute universality. It is ridiculous to have to be reminded, in the country of Gogol and Saltykov-Shchedrin, that patriotism of the artist is something completely different to serving the authorities or fulfilling the expectations of the people".[44] By referring to these most famous 19th century Russian social satirists, the author of the article thus contextualized the attacks by contemporaries as concentrating on populistic matters irrelevant to the art itself.

Novaia gazeta's journalist L. Maliukova pointed out that the Russian official television channels minimized the publicity around *Leviathan*'s Golden Globe Award, merely stating the fact casually,

---

41 Ibid.
42 Ibid.
43 V. Kichin, 'Evropeiskii "Oskar" ulybnulsia 'Ide'. Rossiiskaia gazeta 15 December 2014.
44 A. Pleshakova, 'Andrei Zviagintsev, - "KP" - Pobedu 'Leviafana' vosprinimaiu kak pobedu russkogo oruzhiia"', *Komsomol'skaia Pravda*, 14 January 2015.

in passing. The *Novaia gazeta* journalist speculated that had *Channel 1* or *Rossiia* had anything to do with the film, there would have been trumpeting about the movie from dusk till dawn. According to *Novaia gazeta*, some media had already called the film a "project of the West to discredit Putin's Russia", while the Minister of Culture, Medinskii, when hearing about the prize, had said in passing that winning the award indicated "the high quality of our cinematographers and their recognition on the international level".

Meanwhile, a true fight erupted on the Internet, with *Novaia gazeta* commenting: "There are only a few analytical texts, and in the flood of accusations and reprimands, the leftists and the rightists, liberals and patriots, the highest and the lowest have merged together. Some curse the film for defamation (*ochernitel'stvo*), gloominess, utter darkness. And, naturally, the author for being bribed to demonstrate the darkness of *rashki-govniashki* ("shitty Russia").[45] According to *Novaia gazeta*, the film had its supporters, but their voices were drowned out in the common chorus of resentment and bewilderment. "If there was a long search for what could unite society, here you have it: triumph of a native Russian film in the West."[46]

The head of the village of Teriberka, where the film was shot, was furious: "Teriberka is not like that! The film shows some kind of dirty and unwashed Russia. As if the film group had chosen not to pay attention to anything good: what our house of culture is like, or the library with all its multimedia systems and satellite antenna." She stated that the film was anti-Russian and precisely because of that the West liked it so much. "On the basis of *Leviathan*, contemporary Russia will come across as a dirty pit where corrupt and alcoholic people live." *Komsomol'skaia pravda* also paid attention to the

---

45 This term originates from the Minister Medinskii himself: in December 2014, while commenting on the movies, he made a statement on the state budget. This commentary prompted one member of the Cultural Committee of the State Duma to state that Medinskii was not up to his position. A. Chesova, 'Vladimir Medinskii—o fil'makh pro 'Rashkugovniashku' (obnovleno)', Village 10 December 2014, http://www.the-village.ru/village/situation/situation/1719 47-rashka_govnyashka (accessed 22 April 2016).
46 L. Maliukova. 'Takoe kino nam ne nuzhno?' *Novaya gazeta* 14 January 2015.

fact that not many people had actually seen the movie, yet were very keen to argue about it.[47]

The national fury was created by a pirate copy circulating on the internet prior to the film's Russian premiere. Some voices demanded that the film should be altogether forbidden, because it portrayed a grim and hopeless image of the country. *Nezavisimaia gazeta* wryly labelled these discussions as "truly all-Russian". The newspaper speculated about the new law on distribution certificates: "The Ministry of Culture might not allow distribution of a film that would include materials or information that discredits national culture or creates a threat to national unity and the national security of the Russian Federation, or that would undermine the basis of constitutional order." This amendment had been added to the law already in the previous summer, together with the ban on swearing, but had remained almost unnoticed. The newspaper stated that it was this second point that could present a far greater threat to the Russian cinema.[48]

The question of "depiction of life" was also present in the discussions. It reflected both a contemplative metadiscourse on socialist realism and a more straightforward attitude towards artistic expression. Andrei Maksimov, a journalist and a TV-host, noted: "Art in general is an artificial inducement: artistic truth is never on the same level as the truth of life. In no way can we unlearn the habit of evaluating art from the positions of 'socialist realism'. After all, socialism is long gone, but socialist realism has stayed. And we are very keen to evaluate cinema from the position of 'lifelike — not lifelike'."[49]

This aspect was illustrated by a *Komsomol'ka* correspondent travelling to Teriberka to watch the film together with the local people. Only a few people grumbled about the film being too gloomy,

---

47 Pleshakova 2015. ' M. Pashenkova and V. Seliverstova. 'Otvazhnii kapitan i byvshii glava poselka Valerii Iarantsev: V Teriberke kuda khuzhe, chem pokazali v 'Leviafane'!' *Komsomol'skaia pravda*, 15 January 2015; V. Seliverstova and M. Pashenkova. 'Leviafan? Net, ne videli', *Komsomol'skaia pravda*, 19 January 2015.
48 N. Grigor'eva, 'v kulture. "Oskar"' dlia Zviagintseva i 'ugrozhaiushchee' rossiiskoe kino', *Nezavisimaia gazeta*, 19 January 2015.
49 A. Maksimov, 'Strasti po Leviafanu', *Rossiiskaia gazeta*, 19 January 2015.

but when leaving the hall, people discussed how many bottles of vodka one could drink without *zakuska* (snack). The viewers had counted that the film's main hero had drank almost four during one day, and they reprimanded the film for this heavy drinking: "People do drink in Teriberka, but not that heavily!"[50] Thus, not only the critical *Novaia gazeta*, but also the governmental *Rossiiskaia gazeta* and the traditional *Komsomol'skaia pravda* included either sour, or plain ironic commentaries on the Soviet legacy still haunting Russian understanding of art as depicting life. In general, the newspapers were rather critical toward the populist outcries against the movie and sympathetic to the movie itself.

At the other extreme of the spectrum, the Communist press thought that there was nothing new or innovative in *Leviathan* and that it was stylistically identical with the "harsh realism" of *Malenkaia Vera* and *Arlekino*. These had been, according to *Pravda* KPRF, the flagship films of the era of "perestroika", which "had shattered the country with such social plagues that would have been impossible even to dream of for the generations of Soviet people, raised in the values of Socialist humanism". But now, in their mind, this kind of realism was needed to expose the oligarch leadership, hostile to the common man. The only problem was that the "commentators from the bourgeois press do not want to see this, since the main character, a worker who becomes an innocent victim of the regime, does not correspond to the liberal clichés of heroism". "Were it a martyr of Bolotnaia, the case would be different", stated *Pravda* KPRF.[51]

Questions of Ideology and Values, Then and Now

The group that was the most vehement in its condemnation of the film was a group of Orthodox activists. They criticized the film's portrayal of the Russian Orthodox Church (ROC). In Samara, 16

---

50 'Zhiteli Teriberki uvideli 'Leviafana' na bolshom ekrane i vynesli svoi verdikt: Tak pit' nel'zia!', *Komsomol'skaia pravda*, 27 January 2015.
51 *Pravda kprf*, 2.2.15. The article includes the following, characteristic line: 'Zviagintsev doesn't know where the exit lies from the dead-end where liberal reformers have led the Russian people'.

people signed a petition for the city administration to take action against the main director of the Samara theatre, actor Valeri Grishko, who had played the role of bishop in *Leviathan*. The petitioners labelled this role as a "cynical and dirty parody of the Russian Orthodox episcopacy".[52] "It hurt the feelings of all believers and, in essence, was nothing else but a buffoonery and mockery of the Russian authorities (*vlast'*) and the main confession of our country — holy Orthodoxy."[53] The actor had tried to explain, in vain, that actors sometimes had to play even Hitler.[54]

The letter-writers in Samara justified their action in terms of worldview and ideology: "The understanding of Russian reality, which dominates the film, is ideologically (*mirovozzrencheski*) improper, because from the point of view of Orthodox culture the picture of contemporary Russia looks completely different."[55] *Novaia gazeta* noted that the activists appealed to the Ministry of Culture, as if it were their ally, citing their letter: "We can't understand this kind of duplicity: how can one live at the expense of budget resources, get all advantages from the authorities and at the same time take part in cultivating an intricate vilification of Russian authorities and the Orthodox Church? One would really hope that our Ministry of Culture would resolve this strange and unhealthy (*nezdorovyi*) situation, which leads to the bewilderment of the absolute majority of our fellow citizens in Samara, who honestly love their Fatherland and honor her century-old historical traditions."[56]

---

52 A. Lvov, 'Novosti religii'. *Nezavisimaia gazeta, ng Religii*, 21 January 2015.
53 N. Fomina. 'Shershavym iazikom donosa', *Novaia gazeta*, 21 January 2015.
54 G. Portnov. "Aktera trebuiut uvolit za rol' v 'Leviafane'". *Komsomol'skaia pravda*, 20 January 2015. It is worth noting, if only for the sake of humour, that soon after, the main advocate of the letter writing, the Regional Duma deputy, Dmitri Sivirkin, also appealed to close down the Samara academic drama theatre for its forthcoming staging of the Mel Brooks' musical "The Producers". According to the activists, this musical promotes fascism and homosexuality and ridicules the War Veterans' feelings; in short, it claims the taxpayers' money should not be used for this kind of activity. The accusations led to all sorts of meetings of actors, even though the play was included in the forthcoming repertoire on paper, and not a single Rouble had been spent on it. Fomina, 2015.
55 N. Fomina, 'Nazvali familii uvazhaemykh liudei, i ia podpisal', *Novaia gazeta*, 26 January 2015.
56 '"Varvary dukha" berut v kol'tso. Svetskii kharakter gosudarstva postavlen pod somnenie', *Novaia gazeta*, 30 March 2015.

This voice from "the Samara Orthodox community" is reminiscent of Soviet rhetoric. The usage of the term "unhealthy" is one indicator of dividing people into two categorically opposite camps. The anxiety about people's "bewilderment", caused by any complex situation, recaps the Soviet experience according to which there could be only one interpretation of a given issue. This Stalin-era practice was renewed in 1957, when the CPSU consolidated its power after the chaos of 1956.

The letter from Samara also implies that the state or government (together with the ROC) is a collective entity of which every individual is a part, like it or not, and that this fact of belonging imposes certain obligations. While "party-mindedness" was the strongest Soviet rhetorical device, in the 2010s the appeal to "taxpayers' money" has taken its place. This universal and thus seemingly innocent populistic appeal has, however, a very Soviet genealogy, which, too, became apparent in the early Thaw. Amidst the complexities of de-Stalinization, in the attempt to limit its consequences, the Communist Party resorted to Lenin in 1957.[57] A certain phrase was especially cited over and over again, indicating the Party line on artistic freedom (or rather the end of it): "One cannot live in society and be free from society."[58] The budget money argument was founded on the fact that a third of *Leviathan*'s total cost was covered by financial support from the Ministry of Culture. This became a reason for the film's critics (with various backgrounds) to expand the issue from the mere reception of a movie to a wider question of cultural politics.

To further the appeal of new kinds of cultural policies, the Association of Orthodox Professionals[59] was forming an address to the Minister of Culture, asking to create an "Orthodox Hollywood", an idea incited by *Leviathan,* which the activists wanted to prevent

---

57 V.I. Lenin, 'Partiinaia organizatsiia i partiinaia literatura' (*Novaia zhizn*, n. 12, 13 November 1905), in V.I. Lenin, *Polnoe sobranie sochinenii*, tom 12 (Moscow: Gosudarstvennoe izdatelstvo politicheskoi literatury, 1960), pp. 99–105.
58 For example, Afiani, 2001, pp. 584–593. 588.
59 Assotsiatsiia pravoslavnykh ekspertov, an unofficial organization that attempts to renew the ROC but in practice seems only to discredit Patriarch Kirill.

from gaining a certificate for distribution.⁶⁰ The representative of the Union of Orthodox Citizens, Valentin Lebedev, on the other hand, stated in more diplomatic terms: "We have a free country and it's not necessary to prohibit the film's distribution. But it's important to know on what basis a significant part of the budget of an anti-Russian film was financed by the state. We will ask Medinskii about this. — The film is shot in the perestroika era genre of naturalism, in other words, dirty realism (*chernukha*). And this is exactly why it was hurriedly given various international awards due to the strained relations between the West and Russia."⁶¹

The representative of the Synodic Department of the Church and Society Relations, archpriest Vsevolod Chaplin, stated that Orthodox citizens were allowed to contact the government authorities on their own. "I have not seen the film myself, I know it only from the reviews, but it's clear that it is made for the Western audience or better still, for the Western elites, since it consciously reproduces commonplace myths about Russia and helps these myths take root."⁶²

However, there were also other opinions voiced by the official representatives of ROC. The Metropolitan of Murmansk, Simon, stated that he had liked *Leviathan* and that the movie was "honest". This was seen as a devaluation of Chaplin's words about the movie's main idea being "clearly anti-Christian".⁶³ The Metropolitan stated that the film should not be banned for its obscene language because the cursing had become "our shameful reality" and that there was no more cursing in the film than in real life. He also stated that the film invigorated the viewer as it showed the problems in the life of the country: "[The problems] are like gleaming wounds in a body from which it breaks down, suffers and dies. A complete treatment is necessary. I am heartily grateful to the director." Deacon Andrei Kuraev also accepted the film: "It's the first

---

60   O. Karmunin and M. Ivanova. 'Aktivisty prosiat sozdat' "pravoslavnyi Gollivud", *Izvestiia*. 16 January 2015.
61   Ibid.
62   Ibid.
63   'V obshchestve. rpts zovet v svetloe proshloe, gotovit narod k lisheniiam, no odobriaet 'Leviafan", *Nezavisimaia gazeta,* 26 January 2015.

movie in ages with a clearly anticlerical thematic. Not atheistic, not anti-Church, not anti-Orthodox, but exactly anticlerical".[64]

When Vladimir Medinskii spoke out in mid-January, he stated that the film, in its pursuit of international acclaim, was clearly opportunistic. But then he continued by saying how the international success of "our cinema" made him happy, and *Leviathan* was no exception. He stated that in 2014 alone, films that had received financial support from the Ministry of Culture or Cinema Foundation had received more than 30 awards at international film festivals. Medinskii did not consider *Leviathan* particularly "Russian", yet avoided answering the question about the film's "anti-Russian" character. As to the question of financing such films in the future, Medinskii stated that he personally considered that movies that not only criticised the government but openly opposed it and were filled with the "hopelessness and meaninglessness of our existence" should not be financed by the taxpayers' money. "But", he continued, "they, too, have a right to existence. The Ministry of Culture opposes categorically any forms of censorship and will never prevent their appearance on the screen."[65]

Medinskii thought it strange that there was "not a single positive hero among the main characters of the movie". He believed that the director Zviagintsev could be directed to the right path: "He is a very talented person, and I hope that in the future he will, with the support of the Ministry of Culture, make cinema in which there will be no such existential hopelessness. Cinema which makes you want to rise up, go outside and do something good, right and do it right away, here and now. Unfortunately you didn't get this feeling after *Leviathan*."[66]

To sum up, the will to outrage is probably a universal phenomenon, but in the specific context of today's Russia, it seems that Orthodox-minded activists are the fiercest moral panickers, accompanied with a growing self-assurance that their voice will be heard

---

64 '"Serdechno blagodaren rezhisseru". Mitropolit Murmanskii i Monchegorskii Simon—o fil'me Andreia Zviagintseva *Leviafan*', *Novaia gazeta*, 26 January 2015.
65 'Vladimir Medinskii: "Leviafan zapredel'no kon 'iunkturen"', *Izvestiia*, 15 January 2015.
66 Ibid.

by the highest authorities. It seems that the Kremlin is not the primary leader of Russian cultural politics and discourse, but the "active citizens" who complain about the works of art and appeal to higher authorities, and this is clearly a tendency that the authorities condone.[67]

On the other side of the debate stand the more liberal-minded people, especially journalists and professional critics, who at the same time mock the old-fashioned Soviet rhetoric and are worried about the change of cultural climate to a more black-and-white world view in general and to a socialist realist conception of art in particular.

The accusations levelled at Zviagintsev receded after a couple of months, after the Academy Award was given to the Polish film *Ida*. Zviagintsev was invited to become a member of the Academy and to be part of the forthcoming nominations[68], while the film itself boosted tourism in the village of Teriberka, with local entrepreneurs planning to organize tours to the locations of the film scenes of *Leviathan*.[69] The film got its DVD-release in Russia, only with the obscenities muted out.

Conclusions: New Values, Old Rhetoric?

The comparisons made and parallels drawn by contemporary Russians between the Pasternak case of the late 1950s and the negative reception of *Leviathan* in 2015 were related to both recent historical events and the abundance of certain 'historically grounded' rhetorical devices used by the film's opponents. On the one hand, the 2014 events that led to the overall speculations about a possible "new Cold War", triggered these parallel-seeking tendencies, both in Russia and in the West. The search by official Russia and ordinary Russians alike for a coherent cultural (and geopolitical) identity cer-

---

67 'Kto ne kormit svoiu kul'tury, budet kormit' chuzhuiu armiiu', *Izvestiia*, 17 June 2015.
68 A. Novikova, 'Andrei Zviagintsev budet prisuzhdat' "Oskara". *Komsomol'skaia pravda*, 30 June 2015.
69 M. Pashenkova, 'V tur k "Leviafanu". *Komsomol'skaia pravda*, 12 March 2015.

tainly contributed to some of the reactions to an internationally acclaimed, socially critical movie in "Cold War-ish" style. On the other hand, there were several "Soviet" elements of rhetoric present in the debate. The accusations of the "blackening" of Russian reality (*ochernitel'stvo* or *ochernit'*, *chernukha*) and depicting it only in dark colors, as well as art being slander (*kleveta*) or the depiction of reality done in a slanderous manner (*klevetnicheski*), reveal a cultural continuum of the lexicon used to describe works of art that are perceived as harmful or damaging to the image of the country, be it domestically or internationally. Thus in the case of both Pasternak and Zviagintsev, the positive foreign attention led to accusations of the works having been made "on Western orders" and having a thoroughly political purpose. The Orthodox activists' resentful appeals to the Ministry of Culture, their belief in the validity of their cause, and the Minister's own leanings to socialist realist means of representation, all contribute to the overall sentiment about the comeback of Soviet cultural politics and discourse.

Yet, more than showing a possible return to the Soviet days, the debate over *Leviathan* exemplifies the painful search for a coherent and common cultural identity, in which demands of "patriotism" play certain rhetoric roles. There are some who believe there should be an identity shared by all, and there are others who see exactly these kinds of demands of uniformity as a road towards Soviet-type monoculture. This dialogue was present in the press reception of *Leviathan*, and also illuminates one of the main differences between today's Russia and the Soviet times: journalists, commentators and critics all share a professional integrity, a will and the means to express their views openly. The traditional press has surely lost its former prestige and influence, but still it is noteworthy that even the more official newspapers could comment critically about the outrage of 2015.

At the same time, the Internet was the principal location of discourse in the "case of *Leviathan*". It was the forum where the movie was seen and discussed by ordinary Russians, and it was also the arena where Zviagintsev's own voice could be heard (in interviews) while the state television kept silent. Thus, the media environment of today is bound to restrict a possible control of reception of art (which was the condition under Soviet culture). Yet, by means of changes to state financing, the Ministry of Culture can exercise control, to a certain degree, over the production of art in the future. Soviet-era party-mindedness demanded acceptance of the postulates of the most recent Party documents as guidelines for action, and socialist realism demanded a uniform perception of reality in conformity with the overarching ideology, including the Soviet patriotic love for the Fatherland, loyalty to collectively shared values and the acceptance of their eventual superiority over the "West". *Leviathan* genuinely seems to have hurt many Russians' feelings of national pride. The populist appeal to the use of "taxpayers' money" might serve as a contemporary rhetorical device to channel the outrage of masses to a more uniform cultural output. But on whose premises will the production of culture be executed?

The reactions provoked by the film disclosed the intertwined relations between the church and the state. As the reception of *Leviathan* shows, those who are most offended will present the fiercest criticism of the work of art that offends them. In *Leviathan*, the core issue was the corrupted state-church relationship and the consequences this has on ordinary Russians. It was this thematic, which caused the patriotically-colored outcry with its challenge to the authority of the ROC as the cornerstone of Russian identity, values and national unity. Since the film addressed these issues, it was criticized for depicting these issues in the wrong way while at the same time being applauded for their truthful depiction. The ROC did not seem to have an official view about the film, which left the floor open to Orthodox "activists". The coverage of the reception of *Leviathan* thus points to a very polarized sphere of discourse, in which a certain view has a special standing: one should not be un-patriotic in the depiction of Russia. Even if casual, the statements by the Minister of Culture are being interpreted by some as the future guidelines, and by others as proof of the wrong direction of the politics of culture.

This indicates that the possible future controversies will be not so much in debates over "patriotism", but more generally about the demand for a collective understanding of shared identity and values. In this sense, ideology as a "way of seeing the world" (*mirovozzrenie*) is making a comeback. The question is, which group of people has the right to impose its value system and its *mirovozzrenie* on others. The Orthodox activists' articulations indicate that there is a fight over which authority should determine the common values of society, and that "cultural politics" becomes, once again, the vehicle with which these values are being imposed on the artists and audiences alike. An overarching ideology is still absent, but is possibly in the making. In a paradoxical manner, the authorities keep repeating that there will be no return to censorship, yet the most ardent representatives of the ROC seem to impute a certain *mirovozzrenie* even to the non-believers, while the Minister of Culture himself cultivates a Soviet-type discourse, demanding "positive heroes" in art.

Thus, the questions of church-state relations, of the political image of Russia at home and abroad, of the elements of Russian patriotism and demands on shared identity and values, as well as the task of how to encounter the Soviet legacy, were all present in the mid-2010s reception of the internationally acclaimed film *Leviathan*. It remains to be seen, whether Russian authorities and society as a whole will tolerate more nuanced and pluralistic voices and world views — or will the Leninist slogan "One cannot live in society and be free from society" and its tendentiousness towards conformity make a return in disguise?

Bibliography

Afiani, V. Yu., (ed.) Apparat TsK kpss i kul'tura 1953–1957. *Dokumenty* (Moscow: Rosspen, 2001).

Afiani, V. Yu. and Tomilina, N. G., (eds.), *'A za mnoiu shum pogoni…' Boris Pasternak i vlast. 1956–1972 gg. Dokumenty* (Moscow: Rosspen, 2001).

Pleshakova, A. 'Andrei Zviagintsev – "KP – "'Pobedu 'Leviafana' vosprinimaiu kak pobedu russkogo oruzhiia",' *Komsomol'skaia Pravda*, 14 January (2015).

Brandenberger, D. *National Bolshevism: Stalinist Mass Culture and the Formation of Modern Russian National Identity, 1931–1956* (Cambridge: Harvard University Press, 2002).

Chesova, A., 'Vladimir Medinskii—o fil'makh pro 'Rashku-Govniashku' (obnovleno)', *Village* 10 December 2014, http://www.the-village.ru/village/situation/situation/171947-rashka_govnyashka (accessed 22 April 2016).

Dobrenko, E., 'Literary Criticism and the Institution of Literature, 1941–1953'. In *A History of Russian Literary Theory and Criticism. The Soviet Age and Beyond*, ed. E. Dobrenko and G. Tikhanov. (Pittsburgh, Pa.: University of Pittsburgh Press, 2011) 163–183.

Finn P. and Couvée, P., *The Zhivago affair: the Kremlin, the cia, and the battle over a forbidden book* (London: Vintage, 2015).

Fomina, N., 'Shershavym iazykom donosa', *Novaia gazeta*, 21 January (2015).

Fomina, N., 'Nazvali familii uvazhaemykh liudei, i ia podpisal', *Novaia gazeta*, 26 January (2015).

Grigor'eva, N., 'V kul'ture. 'Oskar' dlia Zviagintseva i 'ugrozhaiushchee' rossiiskoe kino', *Nezavisimaia gazeta*, 19 January 2015.

Ikonen, S., 'Ne sotsrealizmom edinym. Obsuzhdenie romana Vladimira Dudintseva 'Ne khlebom edinym' v Sovetskom Soiuze v 1956–1957 gg.', in *Politika literatury – poetika vlasti*, eds. G. Obatnin, B. Hellman and T. Huttunen. (Moscow: Novoe literaturnoe obozrenie, 2014) 216–233.

Ikonen, S., 'Kirjallisuuspolitiikan käänteitä suojasään Neuvostoliitossa — tapaus Dudintsev', *Ajan kohina: Venäläisen kirjallisuuden seuran lehti* 4 (2015): 55–77.

Karmunin, O. and Ivanova, M., 'Aktivisty prosiat sozdat' "pravoslavnyi Gollivud"', *Izvestiia*. 16 January (2015).

Kharlamov, P., Zadorozhnyi, A. and Ismailov, R., '"Samoe pravil'noe — ubrat'sia emu iz nashei strany poskoree" Master-klass dlia Medinskogo i Ko. ot muchitelei Pasternaka', *Internet-gazeta Znak.com* 22 January 2015, http://www.znak.com/moscow/articles/22-01-21-38/103462.html (accessed 22 April 2016).

Khrushchev, N., 'Za tesnuiu zviaz' literatury i kul'tury so zhizniu naroda', *Novyi mir* 9 (1957): 3–22.

Kichin, V., 'Evropeiskii 'Oskar' ulybnulsia 'Ide''. *Rossiiskaia gazeta*, 15 December (2014).

Kichin, V., 'Igra na vyzhivanie'. *Rossiiskaia gazeta*, 17 December (2014).

Korsakov, D., 'Rossiia vydvinula na 'Oskar' Leviafana', *Komsomol'skaia pravda*, 29 September (2014).

Kozlov, D. '"I Have Not Read, but I Will Say". Soviet Literary Audiences and Changing Ideas of Social Membership, 1958–66', *Kritika: Explorations in Russian and Eurasian History* 7(3) (2006): 557–97.

Kryuchkova, N., 'O romane Ne khlebom edinym', *Izvestiia*, 2 December (1956): 2–3.

'Kto ne kormit svoiu kul'tury, budet kormit' chuzhuiu armiiu', *Izvestiia*, 17 June (2015).

Lenin, V.I., 'Partiinaia organizatsiia i partiinaia literatura', in *Polnoe sobranie sochinenii*, tom 12. (Moscow: Gosudarstvennoe izdatel'stvo politicheskoi literatury, 1960) 99–105.

Lvov, A., 'Novosti religii'. *Nezavisimaia gazeta, ng Religii*, 21 January (2015).

Maksimov, A., 'Strasti po Leviafanu' *Rossiiskaia gazeta*, 19 January (2015).

Maliukova, L., 'Leviafan v prilive patriotizma', *Novaia gazeta*, 26 September (2014).

Maliukova, L., 'Takoe kino nam ne nuzhno?' *Novaia gazeta*, 14 January (2015).

Mancosu, P. *Inside the Zhivago Storm. The Editorial Adventures of Pasternak's Masterpiece*. (Milano: Fondazione Giangiacomo Feltrinelli, 2013).

Medinskii:, Vladimir, '"Leviafan zapredelno kon"iunkturen"', *Izvestiia*, 15 January 2015.

Novikova, A., 'Andrei Zviagintsev budet prisuzhdat' "Oskar", *Komsomol'skaia Pravda*, 30 June (2015).

'Obsuzhdaem novye knigi', *Literaturnaia gazeta*, 27 October (1956): 3–4.

Pashenkova, M., 'V tur k "Leviafanu", *Komsomol'skaia pravda*, 12 March (2015).

Pashenkova, M. and Seliverstova, V.,. 'Otvazhnyi kapitan i byvshii glava poselka Valeri Iarantsev: v Teriberke kuda khuzhe, chem pokazali v 'Leviafane'!' *Komsomol'skaia pravda*, 15 January (2015).

Pasternak, El. V. et al. (eds.) *b.l. Pasternak: Pro et Contra. b.l. Pasternak v sovetskoi, emigrantskoi, rossiiskoi literaturnoi kritike. Antologiia. Tom 2* (St. Petersburg: Institut bogosloviia i filosofii, 2013).

Pikhoya, R.G., *Sovetskii Soiuz: Istoriia vlasti, 1945–1991* (Novosibirsk: Sibirskii khronograf, 2000).

Pleshakova, A. 'Andrei Zviagintsev – "KP – "'Pobedu 'Leviafana' vosprinimaiu kak pobedu russkogo oruzhiia",' *Komsomol'skaia Pravda*, 14 January (2015).

Poliakova, E., 'Leviafan: chudovishchnoe zrelishche', *Afisha*, 4 June 2014, http://afisha.ngs.ru/news/more/1854001/ (accessed 22 April 2016).

Portnov, G., "Aktera trebuiut uvolit za rol' v 'Leviafane'", *Komsomol'skaia pravda*, 20 January (2015).

Romanenko, A. P., Sovetskaia slovesnaia kul'tura: Obraz ritora (Moscow: urss, 2003).

Romanenko, A. P., Obraz ritora v sovetskoi slovesnoi kul'ture. Uchebnoe posobie (Moscow: Izd-va 'Flinta' i 'Nauka', 2003).

'Russia's Book of Job', *The Economist* 14 February 2015, http://www.econ omist.com/news/books-and-arts/21643040-domestic-response-and rei-Zviagintsevs-award-winning-film-leviathan-says-lot (accessed 22 April 2016).

Seliverstova, V. and Pashenkova, M., 'Leviafan? Net, ne videli'. *Komsomol'skaia pravda*, 19 January (2015).

"'Serdechno blagodaren rezhisseru'. Mitropolit Murmanskii i Monchegorskii Simon—o fil'me Andreia Zviagintseva Leviafan', *Novaia gazeta*, 26 January (2015).

'V obshchestve. RPTS zovet v svetloe proshloe, gotovit narod k lisheniiam, no odobriaet 'Leviafan'', *Nezavisimaia gazeta*, 26 January (2015).

"'Varvary dukha' berut v kol'tso. Svetskii kharakter gosudarstva postavlen pod somnenie', *Novaia gazeta*, 30 March (2015).

'Zhiteli Teriberki uvideli 'Leviafana' na bol'shom ekrane i vynesli svoi verdikt: Tak pit' nel'zia!', *Komsomol'skaia pravda*, 27 January (2015).

The War in Chechnya in Russian Cinematographic Representations: Biopolitical Patriotism in "Unsovereign" Times*

Andrey Makarychev
University of Tartu

The paper explores the identitarian context of Russia's cinematic narratives on the war in Chechnya. It draws on various strategies of war representation through films and uncovers their ideological and political underpinnings. The author explicates how the cinematographic imagery grounded in the Chechen war experience boosts the hegemonic discourse of the Kremlin, and then discusses whether fictional films deliver critical or counter-hegemonic arguments.

Keywords: biopolitics, biopower, patriotism

Introduction

In this paper I address the intricacies of patriotism during the two wars in Chechnya (1994–1996 and 1999–2000) as represented in Russian cinematographic narratives. These wars were the most tragic events in the first decade of post-Soviet Russia, a period known for a drastic weakening and degradation of the state. This is exactly what makes Russian patriotism of the early years of post-Soviet independence different from many other historical periods, when patriotic feelings were embodied in figures of national rulers, such as Joseph Stalin during the Great Patriotic (Second World) War, or Vladimir Putin in the course of Russia's confrontation with

---

* A preliminary version of this research was published as: A. Makarychev. 'From Chechnya to Ukraine: Biopolitical Patriotism in Times of War.' (Washington D.C.: Kennan Institute for Advanced Russian Studies, Woodrow Wilson Center, 2015) available at https://www.wilsoncenter.org/article/chechnya-to-ukraine-biopolitical-patriotism-times-war (accessed 4 June 2019).

Ukraine in 2013–2014. Against this backdrop, the 1990s look strikingly different: the decade is widely perceived as "the time of troubles", with ineffective and erratic leadership, ideological oscillations between liberalism and traditionalism, and rampant violence inside the country.

Of course, one may claim that the state, being intrinsically weak and short of positive incentives for its citizens, retained, nevertheless, the constitutive characteristic of sovereign power: the right to send people to death and take their lives. Yet the lack of strong political leadership, the disastrous state of the military and the all-encompassing feelings of insecurity all led to the widely spread perceptions of sovereignty being threatened or diminished.

My intention in this article is to reconstruct the genealogy of contemporary Russian patriotism based on a specific genre of visual representation—fiction films that are one of the most important sources of what might be called "popular geopolitics". In line with— and influenced by—the ideas of a "society of the spectacle" (Guy Debord) and the "aesthetization of politics" (Jacques Rancière), the popular geopolitical approach conceptualizes the profound changes in the structure of public policy, where rational accounts of material or physical reality are gradually superseded by narratives centered around constructed and self-imposed norms, identities, lifestyles, perceptions and other ideational phenomena.

Of course, one may claim that states instrumentally use visual and artistic imagery as an important element of their soft power toolkit.[1] However, the nature of the nexus between politics and arts goes much deeper: as Slavoj Žižek put it, the shift from the political to the aesthetic and artistic is inherent in the political itself; therefore, the arts become a terrain of ideology, mass choreography and

---

[1] B. O'Loughlin, 'Images as weapons of war: representation, mediation and interpretation', *Review of International Studies*, 37 (2011).

ideological-aesthetic experience.[2] Popular culture is thus an important domain "where power, ideology and identity are constituted, produced and materialized".[3]

One of the pivotal arguments of the popular geopolitics school is that a plethora of artistic representations opens up wider perspectives for explicating the peculiarities of regional and national identities, as compared to classical geopolitical reasoning. The most important effect of the proliferation of diverse performative forms is the extension of "the range of meanings" on which the ideas of identity appear, mature, and ultimately broaden "a space for critical thought".[4] The concept of "cultural governance" nicely reflects this trend. Even more essential is that the very "construction of the political and the type of politics it engenders"[5] becomes an inherently performative set of practices. They are based to a large extent on what might be dubbed a "pictorial turn", or "the art of viewing", which constitutes the public and the community,[6] and may extend to "visual ideologies" that control perceptions of regional and national landscapes,[7] thus contributing to the ongoing (re)construction of identity-based relations of power, as well as resistance to it.

The aesthetic shift in regional and international studies[8] can be explained by a number of reasons. One is the crisis of political language as a means of mass communication and mobilization, and the growing traction of "emotional investment" in identity-making

---

2 S. Zizek, 'The lessons of Ranciere', in *The Politics of Aesthetics*, ed. Jacques Ranciere (London and New York: Continuum, 2004), pp. 76–77.
3 K. Grayson, M. Davies and S. Philpott, 'Pop goes ir? Researching the popular culture—World Politics Continuum', *Politics* 29(3) (2009), p. 155–156.
4 D. Campbell, 'Cultural governance and pictorial resistance: reflections on the imaging of war', *Review of International Studies* 29 (2003), p. 72.
5 Grayson, Davies and Philpott, p. 156.
6 F. Moeller, 'The looking/not looking dilemma', *Review of International Studies* 35 (2009), p. 783.
7 L. Kennedy, 'Securing vision: photography and us foreign policy', *Media, Culture & Society* 30(3) (2008): 280.
8 A. Pusca, 'The aesthetics of change: exploring post-Communist spaces', *Global Society* 22(3) (2008).

strategies and their promotion.[9] Secondly, the social audience of visual representations appears larger than politically oriented groups, and includes wider public segments otherwise insensitive to rational political calculations.

> Unlike first order representations — such as a politician's speech or newspaper article — popular culture rarely makes the claim of being a true representation of the real world. [Yet] for a majority of people, it is namely these second order representations that come to play a significant role as sources of knowledge of politics and society.[10]

It is at this point that the research puzzle can be couched: what practices legitimized the patriotic discourses shaped by the war in Chechnya? In the absence of strong and commonly accepted sovereignty, what are the ideational sources of national mobilization that in the specific conditions of the Chechen war called for enormous losses of human lives?

My main operational concept is a phenomenon that I venture to call biopolitical patriotism. I claim that biopolitical mechanisms of solidarity and military brotherhood-in-arms compensated for a deficit of effectively operating state-promoted and sustained norms and/or ideologies. Following Michel Foucault, this patriotism can be dubbed biopolitical insofar as the state, being neither its engine nor key reference point, could take advantage of its potential for mobilizing the population and selectively utilizing it for political purposes. It is in this sense that the Chechen war films support and reproduce, rather than undermine and challenge, the existing relations of power and "foundational national imageries".[11]

The empirical base of this research consists of the collection of films available at the specialized Internet portal "The War in Chechnya"[12] created by a group of war veterans. To the best of my

---

9   J. Dittmer and K. Dods, 'Popular geopolitics past and future: Fandom, identities and audiences", *Geopolitics* 13 (2008), p. 440.
10 A. Kangas, 'From interfaces to interpretants: a pragmatic exploration into popular culture as international relations', *Millenium: Journal of International Studies* 38(2) (2009), p. 322.
11 G. Holden, 'Cinematic ir, the sublime, and the indistinctness of art', *Millenium: Journal of International Studies* 34(3) (2006), p. 805.
12 http://www.warchechnya.ru (accessed 5 June 2019).

knowledge, this web resource contains the fullest account of Russian movies featuring the war, and serves as a site for communication (with such interactive elements as chat, forum and quiz) between its 50,000 registered users and multiple guests. The site was created in 2009 and functions as a cultural repository of war documentaries, movies, photographs, music, books and newspaper articles, as well as an interface for public dialogue on the war in Chechnya and its effects for contemporary Russia. Out of 24 fiction films posted in this portal I have selected 17 that were made in Russia, excluding those that have already been the object of scholarly research. My analysis is focused on visual scenes, imageries and dialogues that represent or discuss the biopolitical articulations of Russian patriotic identity.

Conceptualizing Biopolitics and Bare Life

Russia's wars in Chechnya in the 1990s were not only a matter of military professionals, but required societal mobilization of ideational resources of patriotism. The complexity of this task was exacerbated by the lack of ideological justifications for a boost of patriotic pride. In times of war, the state was neither a source of attractive national values nor a possessor of strong material resources. In this sense the very concept of the state as a locus of sovereignty could have been questioned, which starting from 2000 became a pivotal point in Vladimir Putin's discourse to reconstitute a strong, powerful and independent statehood.

The idea of biopolitical patriotism, key to this article, is grounded in a conceptual distinction between sovereign power and biopower, introduced by Michel Foucault and widely used in academic discourse. The difference between the two can be grasped in at least two important respects. First, biopower takes as its object the population rather than the territory.[13] Arguably, Foucault tells

---

13 J. Joseph, 'Governmentality of what? Populations, states and international organizations', *Global Society* 23(4) (2009), p. 424.

one story of security and geopolitics paralleled by "his novel account of the other (biopolitics)".[14] In this sense, biopolitics is more about managing human beings and their bodily lives rather than possessing territories. Thus, biopolitical power is relatively insensitive to geopolitically controlling lands, which is reflected in the portrayal of Chechen landscapes in most of the movies (mountains, gorges, alpine roads that can perfectly hide snipers, etc.) as alien to Russians and even menacing. Instead, biopolitical representations are more concerned with managing lives, as well as disciplining and supervising human bodies for the sake of survival.

A further distinction stems from the works of Foucault: sovereignty presupposes "a power of death",[15] while biopolitics "promotes the life and efficiency of the body politic".[16] To put it differently, the state sends its citizens to die in the battlefields on behalf of the sovereign power, while biopolitical mechanisms help people survive. These mechanisms of biopower function at the microlevel, being entangled in a complex web of professional, corporeal and other relations. This is exactly how most of the films portray the routine of the war as grounded in "natural bases of human association" — the instinctual desire of man and woman to make love, "the social instinct of naturally gregarious human beings to live in groups among their own kind", etc. All this is largely alienated from "the political order proper [as] inscribed in the constitution, laws, institutions".[17] As a result, the hegemonic concept of identity is mostly based on corporeal practices of distinction between Self and Other, and does not necessarily imply a state-based ideology.

Giorgio Agamben's concept of "bare life" helps to better understand the milieu in which biopower functions. In the context of my study bare life designates a life without any mediating role of

---

14 M. Dillon and L. Lobo-Guerrero, 'Biopolitics of security in the 21st century: an introduction', *Review of International Studies* 34 (2008), p. 274.
15 B. Singer and L. Weir, 'Politics and sovereign power: considerations on Foucault', *European Journal of Social Theory* 9(4) (2006), p. 458.
16 N. Widder, 'Foucault and power revisited', *European Journal of Political Theory* 1(4) (2004), p. 422.
17 J.G. Finlayson, "Bare Life' and politics in Agamben's reading of Aristotle', *The Review of Politics* 72 (2010), p. 111.

public institutions or legal mechanisms.[18] It is "a form of life that is amenable to the sway of sovereign power because it is [...] caught in a sort of legal and political vacuum conducive to the permanent instantiation of exceptional practices [...] Bare life is treated as precisely an indistinct form of subjectivity that is produced immanently by sovereign power for sovereign power".[19] Russia's military offensive in Chechnya, which is referred to as "almost a war" in *Alexandra* (director Aleksandr Sokurov, 2007) and "a strange war" in *Checkpoint* (director Alexander Rogozhkin, 1998), clearly created a state of exception uncontrolled and unregulated by any law. Film heroes are usually deployed in "a limit-zone in which they no longer had anything but bare life"; they are de facto beyond political rights and political protection. Their physical lives are "reduced to the bare minimum"[20] and deprived of not only juridico-institutional, but also of economic frameworks. In *Alexandra* soldiers ask the old lady to bring them "something sweet" from the local market and then add with sorrow: "But we don't have money." In *Checkpoint* soldiers widely use bullets instead of money, and express the bare life-philosophy with an even more straightforward candor: "to devour, to take a crap, and to fuck".

The Caucasian Roulette (director Fiodor Popov, 2002) addresses another facet of "bare life", embodied by two heroines balancing between hatred and empathy. An ethnically Russian sniper who fought for the Chechens (Anna) decides to escape back to Russia, yet is chased by her possessive Chechen boyfriend who is the father of her child. In the train, she meets a Russian woman (Maria), who turns out to be the mother of a Russian soldier captured by the Chechens. The Chechen commander agrees to release her son only if the mother brings him his own child who fled together with Anna. The script of the film erases simplistic boundaries between "us"

---

18   P. Fitzpatrick, 'Bare sovereignty: Homo Sacer and the insistence of Law', in *Politics, Metaphysics, and Death: Essays on Giorgio Agamben's Homo Sacer*, A. Norris, ed., (Durham, North Carolina: Duke University Press, 2005), pp. 49–73.
19   N. Vaughan-Williams, 'The generalized bio-political border? Re-conceptualising the limits of sovereign power', *Review of International Studies* 35 (2009), p. 737.
20   J. Oksala, *Foucault, Politics, and Violence* (Evanston, Illinois: Northwestern University Press, 2012).

and "them": Maria who is driven by the utopian dream of saving her son, faces a harsh moral dilemma of being ready to take a small child away from his mother. The end of the film, with Anna's death under the train wheels and Maria's intention to take care of her hidden child, is a combination of redemption that fixes the moral superiority of the good over the evil, and the evanescence of these boundaries as a gesture of forgiveness and reconciliation.

Dysfunctional Sovereignty and Identity Split

One of the paradoxes of sovereignty lies in its deep ambiguity. What is portrayed in numerous movies as dysfunctional and corrupt statehood, unable to create positive impulses for citizens, can, however, be considered close to the Foucauldian model of sovereignty as power to take lives, which does not necessarily presuppose inclusive and sophisticated techniques of governance through enacting and empowering people.

Films give multiple examples of an obvious and deeply entrenched inability of the state to provide security and well-being for its citizens. Thus, in *Alive* (director Alexander Veledinsky, 2006), a retired Russian soldier who lost his leg on the battlefield in Chechnya, is advised to raise money for a German prosthesis, which looks symbolically ironic against the backdrop of the widely propagated triumphalist memories of the Second World War. In *The Shooting Mountains* (director Rustam Urazaev, 2011), one of protagonists complains that "we defend the border like in the stone age", i.e. with neither adequate technical equipment nor even sufficient foodstuff.

The widely spread feelings of abandonment by the state are nicely grasped in *Alexandra*: "We, the officers, wash our underwear ourselves", the main protagonist says to his grandmother and then complains about logistics: "our uniform should not be as it is. It must absorb my blood and sweat if I die". Answering his grandmother's remark "The locals don't like you here", the grandson says: "What is worse, they don't fear us. What is the need for such an army?"

As a perfect illustration of the degradation of the army, in *The Achilles Heel* (director Igor Talla, 2006) drunk and frivolous federal soldiers overtly expropriate poultry and other food from a Chechen household. Their reiteration of Putin's famous phrase *zamochim v sortire* ("We'll whack them [the terrorists] in the shithouse") sounds like a parody; it is evident that the army, in disarray, is capable only of sporadic and limited engagement in military operations.

The Crushing Force (NTV-based sketchdom, released in 2000, based on Andrey Kivinov's novel) gives perhaps the most ironic picture of the state of Russian Armed Forces in Chechnya. Three investigative police officers from St. Petersburg, who were deployed in Chechnya on a three-month mission, face the harsh reality of the dysfunctional state. Their superiors in their home city extorted foodstuff from local businessmen to provide rations for their unexpected secondment—yet instead of food, they get shampoo. Due to the erratic bureaucratic communication, nobody on the ground waits for their arrival, and they are almost de-routed back home. Ultimately they have to buy weaponry at the local market from Chechen vendors—a situation that could have been ridiculously unreal should it not have become part of reality in 2014, when Russian paratroopers sent to Ukraine were reported to be purchasing their uniforms themselves.[21] In *The Crushing Force* the protagonists kill time drafting useless reports to their superiors, routinely drinking strong alcohol and eating fish that they—evidently illegally—kill, using grenades from the ammunition. As policemen, they have to investigate cases of cattle theft, searching the locals for cow documents.

The portrayal of the state in *May* (directors Marat Rafikov and Ilya Rubinshtein, 2007) is even more grotesque. Lieutenant Pechalin, who for a few days returns to his home city from military service in Chechnya, finds his best friends working in the police, and simultaneously providing protection services for the prostitution business. "If the state is reluctant to officially recognize sex without love, it is

---

21 'Komandovanie kostromskogo polka podtverdilo poteri na Ukraine'. *Polit.ru* internet portal, 27 August 2014, http://polit.ru/news/2014/08/27/victims/ (accessed 20 April 2016).

unfortunate, but I will help with this", one of his fellow policemen says, thus creating another zone of biopolitical indistinction between law enforcement and criminality, the legal and the illegal.

Yet the state is not only blatantly immoral and corrupt — it is a vague institution with uncertain boundaries of powers and competences. In *The Sniper* (director Arman Gevorgian, 2012), the protagonist who has been wounded in Chechnya, after recovery returns there not by the order of his military command, but in his vacation, to finalize an unfulfilled assignment of liquidating a Chechen commander. The Russian sniper's return to the battlefield is not motivated by his loyalty to the state, but by the ethos of *esprit de corps* that generates a patriotic momentum. The state — as exemplified by the Russian military command — is not the key driver for the hero and does not directly spearhead his behavior, but watches him at a distance and obviously capitalizes on the results of his personal courage and the sense of camaraderie. "They are acting at their own risk and discretion", a high-ranking military officer reports to his superior about the sniper's self-planned mission in Chechnya. This remark betrays a deeply troublesome logic behind the policies of the state, which can utilize the allegiances and commitments of its citizens without bearing formal responsibility for their actions or duly protecting them. The events in eastern Ukraine in 2014, with numerous Russian volunteers fighting "at their own discretion and risk" on behalf of Russia without even being properly named and buried after their deaths, is a good example of the broad possibilities of the state to stay aside and even deny sending their armed people on a military mission.

Checkpoint further problematizes the complex relations between the biopolitical bonds cementing the combating army and the state. Its plot exhibits the grass-roots biopolitical order being interrupted by the legal order that belongs to the domain of sovereign power. One of the Russian soldiers, nicknamed Krysa, is accused of shooting a Chechen woman in a sporadic firefight, and then detained upon the requests of Chechen residents and the order of the federal military authorities, in spite of vehement resistance of Krysa's immediate superior, who takes the detention as a personal insult. This unfortunate sovereign interference, legal yet illegitimate, turns into a tragedy: in the final scene the local Chechens drop Krysa's mutilated body near the checkpoint where he served. This denouement only confirms the ambiguous nature of sovereignty: what on the surface appears to be a humiliating exposure of its purely symbolic nature, under deeper scrutiny reveals the constitutive right of the sovereign power to take people's lives. Regardless of what happened to Krysa after his detention (he could be kidnapped by the Chechens, or intentionally given to them as a symbolic compensation for the death of the Chechen woman), the narrative unveils the sovereign intervention, with law as its key instrument, as deeply inimical to the norms of biopolitical solidarity constitutive of the military corps.

Such a state incarnates the Foucauldian model of sovereign power as based on the thanatopolitical/necropolitical[22] function of executing human beings trapped in the zone of indistinction generative of bare life. A perfect example of danger, emanating from a malfunctioning and inhumane state, occurs in *The War is Over, Forget It* (director Valery Kharchenko, 1997). The film epitomises a decomposing sovereignty, personified by a general with patriotic views, who forces soldiers to decorate his apartments with carpets; contract soldiers, who rape a soldier's mother; a minister whose mistress misuses huge funds meant for reconstruction works in Chechnya, etc. The heroine, in a desperate attempt to save her son from the dangers of serving in Chechnya, sells her apartment to pay a bribe to a corrupt military officer, yet the deal ultimately fails. The final scene of the film impresses by its cruelty: the son, who unexpectedly comes back as a deserter, is killed by the military police in front of his mother's eyes. This scene reveals the malignant nature of sovereignty at its purest: the state physically and literally exerts its "right to kill" instead of protecting the lives of its citizens. To put it in Foucauldian terms, the bloodletting on behalf of the state is a

---

22 C. Aradau, 'What is left of biopolitics?' *Radical Philosophy: Philosophical Journal of the Independent Left*, May–June (2012), http://www.radicalphilosophy.com/reviews/individualreviews/whats-left-of-biopolitics (accessed 20 April 2016).

ritual of power in which "punishment had to be performed in excess, and such an excess had to be turned into a form of spectacle, to generate awe in those witnessing the performance of power".[23] A hollow sovereignty, void of positive content, thus degenerates into a killing inhumane machine.

The State/Motherland Distinction and Biopolitical Patriotism

It is the radically negative imagery of the state that constitutes a key problem for patriotic narratives, however rudimentary and underconceptualized they might be. The distancing from the state makes officers in *The Honor is Mine* (director Viktor Buturlin, 2004) engage in attempts to differentiate the state from an imagined motherland. In a desperate attempt to justify his mission in the military, a Russian officer maintains that he serves "the motherland, not the assholes", thus drawing an ethical line between the deplorable reality on the ground and its normatively appealing mythical opposite. Along similar lines, *The Sniper* shows a conflict between the Moscow-based headquarter officers on the one hand, and those who fight on the ground and thus have stronger claims to represent the motherland on the other, a rather common topic in war movies that portray high-up staff as disconnected from the realities on the ground.

Yet the idea of "mother Russia" as an ethical antidote to the dangerously dysfunctional state remains largely abstract and fuzzy. In *The Honor is Mine*, the protagonist is seconded from his military unit in Chechnya to St. Petersburg with the stressful mission of delivering the body of a killed soldier to his mother, which turns in an exploration of "what the motherland looks like". The "normal life" of a peaceful St. Petersburg that the officer encounters is a good illustration of what Putin's hegemonic narrative would later dub as "the malignant 1990s" — the world of greed and money, in which the Chechen clans are important players. The officer ends

---

23 Jabri 2006, p. 830.

up rejecting the "wild capitalism" of the 1990s, and ultimately repudiating both lucrative prospects for a job and romantic engagement with a young business woman. This highly negative portrayal of post-Soviet civilian life as morally unacceptable, if not vicious and sinful, becomes the key argument for representing the army not only as an alternative to the steady degradation of society, but as a wishful embodiment of a better — and overtly remasculinized — Russia.[24]

The same contrast between the military and civilian life is discernible in *The Shooting Mountains*. For its hero, a young border guard lieutenant, life outside the military is a source of threats: having returned to see his pregnant wife, he is detained by the police on account of a fray with a Caucasian thief who intended to steal his wallet. The police officer demands that he revoke his formal claims against the offender, who immediately finds protection from a powerful personality in the local Georgian community. It is only the sudden intervention of federal security officers, the lieutenant's superiors, who restore justice and release him from unfair detention and possible accusations of "fuelling inter-ethnic hatred". This narrative culminates in a scene announcing President Putin's decree that relegates the border guard troops to the administrative supervision of the Federal Security Service (FSB) — a move that stretches far beyond bureaucratic policies and that was met with enthusiastic applause by an assembly of border guard officers.

A similar story is narrated in *The Thunder Gates* (director Andrey Maliukov, 2006), where for most characters the army is an escape from personal problems and tragedies in their private lives — the wife's betrayal, relatives' deaths, children's sickness, etc. Against this backdrop, the army is portrayed as an institution that plays an important social role and even rectifies social injustice. In *The Yomp* (director Andrey Maliukov, 2002), too, the hero comes from an orphanage with a criminal record, yet in the army he finds his true identity and unravels his best qualities.

---

24 O. Riabov and T. Riabova, 'The remasculinization of Russia? Gender, nationalism, and the legitimation of power under Vladimir Putin', *Problems of Post-Communism* 61(2) (2014), pp. 23–35.

A similarly mundane story is shown in *The Dead Field* (director Alexander Aravin, 2006): one of its heroes is an orphan, who finds the real sense of his mission only in the army. What is more, he refuses to meet his stepfather who comes to see him in Chechnya: in a desperate hate gesture, the soldier takes a grenade and threatens "to kill everyone" should the stepfather approach him. Again, the army features in this context as a shelter protecting servicemen against the complexities and vicissitudes of their civilian lives, usually replete with injustice and bad memories.

Against this background, during the Chechen wars of the 1990s, Russian patriotism took a biopolitical form in the sense that the state, without being a promoter of national identity, nevertheless appropriated patriotic sentiments and capitalized on them. This demonstrates that "biopolitics and sovereign power should not be posed antithetically — they rather complement each other by causing disciplinary effects".[25]

This complementarity is discernible in *Alexandra*, too. "I am poor. I live in tents. We are all divorced", laments the film's hero, thus attesting that even the family as a social institution is sidelined in the everyday structures of unmediated, bare life. This is what questions the very existence of nation as a political community that, in Alexandra's logic, ought to be based on generation-to-generation liaisons beyond existing ethnic or religious divides ("I will help you when you come to St. Petersburg", she promises a Chechen boy before leaving). In a short verbal bickering, her grandson accuses her of being too possessive, ignoring the difference between generations and disregarding his individuality, to which Alexandra polemically replies: "Can you imagine a young Caucasian telling his grandmother that he is an autonomous individual?" This dialogue betrays Sokurov's allusion to the biopolitical background of the idea of the nation as an equivalent to family as community, regulated by its intrinsic norms rather than by state interventions.

Many other films construct and display a boundary between the "bare life" in the military and a "normal life" that, in the meantime, is externalized either as replete with injustice (for instance, *The*

---

25 Singer and Weir, pp. 445–446.

Honor is Mine), or as "incomprehensible" (in *The Check Point*, one of the Russian soldiers confesses that in Chechnya "all people look alike"). It is this boundary, distinctly exhibited in *The Dead Field*, *The Honor is Mine*, and *Alexandra*, that is conducive to the transformation of exceptional measures initially meant to be provisional, into a lasting characteristic that can not be confined to the military and is extrapolated to the whole society.[26] A peculiar Russian patriotism, born on the battlefields of Chechnya, expanded from the military "state of exception" to the vernacular discourses by filling them with a biopolitical content: "When back home, I'll batter those who didn't serve in the Army, instead courting our girls", pledges a young Russian soldier only minutes before being killed in battle. This spontaneous declaration of self-assertion is meant to legitimize his possessive desire to protect those who did not ask for his protection — a line of conduct that the Russian state itself often deems quite legitimate.

The De-politicizing Effects of Biopolitical Patriotism

As in other wars, soldiers and officers fighting in Chechnya, products of bare life, are incapable — and reluctant — to think in political or legal categories. All political terms in their words are vulgarized: "If something happens, consider me a national patriot", one of the soldiers says before going to "the shithouse" (*The Check Point*). In a more general sense, soldiers are incapable of a fully fledged civil and political life outside the military and even may feel an aversion to it. In *Alexandra*, the eponymous heroine deplores that her grandson, who is serving in Chechnya, "is unable to do anything but shoot". "What do you read?", she asks him, and receives the answer: "Nothing". "What films do you watch?", she keeps interrogating him, only to hear: "You'd better not know".

This self-detachment from politically divisive categories translates into a deep miscomprehension of the underlying political reasons for the Chechen war. There are numerous scenes in which the

---

26   J. Oksala, 'Violence and the biopolitics of modernity', *Foucault Studies* 10 (2010), pp. 29–30.

protagonists discuss the causes of the conflicts, yet all of them betray a deep sense of confusion and the lack of a narrative that could justify or explicate the war. The most typical and common arguments for a sovereign power—territorial (Chechnya is part of the Russian Federation) and legal (the Russian Army restores the constitutional order)—are completely missing in these narratives.

A scene from *The Dead Field* illuminates the embarrassment that communications with the Chechens cause for Russians. A local resident, evidently intended to bewilder a Russian soldier, challenges him by asking: "Who are you?", and receives a simple answer: "A Russian soldier". "If you are a Russian soldier, what then are you doing here?", the Chechen guy continues his unfriendly inquiry. This question is so confounding that it provokes an aggressive reaction from the Russian side: "Do you want me to give you a swat?". This verbal exchange reveals a surprising dyslexia—all rational political arguments endlessly articulated in the official discourse (the war on terror, protection of Russia's territorial integrity against armed separatists, the restoration of the constitutional order, etc.) are strikingly absent from the lexicon of those who are supposed to practically implement them.

In *Alexandra*, a singular infusion of political meanings in the film narrative is equally perplexing. "I know that I shouldn't say this to you, but please, let us go, we are tired and can't put up with all this"—a Chechen adolescent pathetically says to Aleksandra who can't find the proper words to respond. "It is not that easy", she replies, which attests to the crisis of communication between the two. The film ends with a scene of emotional unity between Alexandra and the local Chechen women, whom she befriends, yet there are still "many questions to ask"—for example, "how can they [the Chechens] capture people and keep them under the earth".

All this leads to an inability to articulate the *finalité politique* of the Russian mission. In *The Thunder Gates*, a Russian soldier desperately asks: "What do they [the Chechens] need?". Giving no answer to this simple question, the filmmakers engage with historical parallels, presuming that the revolt in Chechnya was a revenge for the Soviet Union's war in Afghanistan. This interpretation, close to conspiracy theories, can be found in *The Purgatory* (director Alexandr

Nevzorov, 1997). The film also contains an illuminating scene in which a Chechen commander talks to a Russian officer blocked in his tank, trying to convince him to surrender and then work for the Chechens. The Russian trooper leaves the long tirade of his Chechen counterparts without a single word, and prefers an agonizing death to treason. What is noteworthy is not his choice as such, but the fact that this gesture of patriotic self-sacrifice is mute and not sustained by any explanatory argument. This impossibility of communication attests to the futility and irrelevance of rational arguments in a situation of radical alterity.

In *The Yomp*, a Russian officer serving in Chechnya claims: "We are here to prevent the country from being turned into a scrapyard". This abstract mission statement attempts to place the military operation in a domestic context, yet leaves obscure who exactly intends to "turn the country into a scrapyard", and how the war can prevent this from happening. Another explanation of this film's hero is no less vague: "I serve in Chechnya to make all of you safe from coffins coming to your city". This reasoning portrays the war as something almost metaphysical and transcendental, which necessarily requires heroic self-victimization of self-sacrifice. This logic unveils a vicious circle: to protect people from dying you need to risk your own life, and this is exactly what cements biopolitical patriotism.

The biopolitical kernel of Russian post-Soviet patriotism, devoid of references to rational categories and deeply traumatic, is perfectly explained by Zakhar Prilepin in his novel *Sankya*. Its hero, a young Russian nationalist, avers: "I am ready to live under any type of authority should it protect and maintain our territory and regenerate the population. Today this is not the case", and then adds an even stronger biopolitical statement:

> There is no ideology nowadays; it is instincts that are ideological…The soil, the honor, the victory, the justice—neither of those fundamentals needs an ideology. Love necessitates no ideology… There is only a sense of kinship, that's it. The comprehension of what is going on in Russia is based on neither a certain body of knowledge nor on intellectual casuistry that can be used to deconstruct everything, but on the feeling of cognation. It grows in human beings from childhood, and it cannot be got rid of. If you feel that Russia is tantamount to your wife, as in Alexander Blok's poetry, then you treat it as

your wife. In a biblical sense — as someone with whom you are deeply engaged and pledged to live until death… And in this case you have no choice… All what is genuine denies the very idea of choice.[27]

It is exactly this version of biopolitical (without room for making individual decisions based on conventional wisdom or rationale) patriotism that surged in Russia as a reaction to the Euro-Maidan in Ukraine, followed by mass-scale public support for the annexation of the Crimea and the instigation of pro-Russian separatism in Novorossiya (Eastern Ukraine). The patriotic wave, commenced in 2014, was a direct — and much more solidified — extension of the biopolitical patriotism that emerged during the Chechen war. This type of patriotic narrative does not need the idea of a modern, effective, rational and socially caring state as a condition for its functioning. The idea of a well-governed state is supplanted by a biopolitical reasoning in which the nationalist discourse is self-constitutive and self-reproducing on the basis of belonging to a mentally constructed, valorized and symbolized community of like-minded compatriots.

The Imperial and the Post-colonial

Paradoxically, the war unveiled that both parties in the deadly conflict, Russians and Chechens, shared a post-colonial desire to "raise up from the knees", yet the drastically dissimilar ways they did so only alienated them from each other. Both Russian imperial policies and the Chechen contestation of them are narrated in a language full of biopolitical allusions. In *The Check Point*, a local Chechen girl, who brokered sexual services for Russian soldiers, turns out to be a sniper and ends up killing one of them. A reverse — yet in a way symmetrical — situation is represented in *The Captive* (director Alexei Uchitel, 2008), a story of implicitly homoerotic feelings of a Russian soldier for his young Chechen hostage. The plot, saturated with multiple corporeal and intimate allusions, ends with the Russian soldier killing his Chechen captive for trying to ask the passing Chechen fighters for help.

---

27   http://sankya.ru/ (accessed 4 June 2019).

In most films, Russian identity is portrayed as morally superior to that of her enemies, which in the view of some analysts borders on racism.[28] *The Yomp* not only displays many scenes against the backdrop of Orthodox churches as material reminders of Russian historical grandeur, but also deconstructs Chechen identity as fake or mythical by explicating the Chechen motivation for the war with greed for money. In many other movies, the Chechens are portrayed as money-hungry bandits, who seize hostages and demand ransoms for them. In *The Achilles Heel*, this narrative reaches its nadir. The Chechen commander whose people capture Russian hostages, explains his rationale in a business-like manner, trying to involve the captives in his business. This is how he demands ransom from the violently captured and incarcerated female Moscow journalist: "This is a profitable business. You can ask your employer to make your face widely known and to open a charity bank account to raise money for your release".

Love and romantic engagement can be another reference point to foment an imperial "We"-narrative. In *The Achilles Heel* the hero, the Moscow businessmen Maxim, who is captured by Chechen guerillas along with the pretty Russian female journalist Liza, falls in love with her and does his best to escape from captivity with her. Obviously, this puts him in direct confrontation with the head of the Chechen gang, who intentionally avoids clear identifications with palpable meanings. "The war has generated thousands of nobodies, including me and you", the Chechen commander says, thus offering a mode of communication bereft of any possible relations of representation. Interestingly enough, in The *Shooting Mountains* a local Chechen leader is characterized as "someone with neither kin nor tribe behind", whose father renounced him—a perfect model of non-identity short of discernible social characteristics.

Yet in *The Achilles Heel*, the real identity-making figure is the son of the Chechen commander Ruslan, who oscillates between his possessive father and the Russian couple whom he ultimately helps to flee. The scene with his father on his knees, asking Ruslan to

---

28   D. Gillespie, 'Defense of the realm: the 'new' Russian patriotism on screen', *The Journal of Power Institutions in Post-Soviet Societies* 3 (2005).

come back, symbolizes the destruction of his parental role and the vindication of the moral superiority of the Russian couple.

The Chechen collective Self can also be deconstructed through the exposure of splits between "good Chechens" and "bad Chechens". In *The Yomp*, the armed Chechen bandits shoot dead envoys from the local village, who are unhappy with the war and demand a stop to the hostilities. In *A Matter of Honor* (director Andrey Chernykh, 2007), the hero is an ethnic Chechen fighting against the local mafia and its high-level protectors in Moscow. These examples are meant to decompose ethnicity and the concomitant ethnic solidarity as key drivers for the Chechen political community.

Another way to break up the Chechen identity is through closely associating local rebels with foreign mercenaries, who visually incarnate inimical otherness (Arabs, black people etc.). Their appearance legitimates the war as external aggression, with explicit references to "female snipers from Ukraine" (*The Sniper*) and Lithuania (*The Purgatory*) — countries that in the hegemonic discourse of the Kremlin are portrayed as "Russia-unfriendly" and under the sway of "malignant Western influence".

In *The Russian Victim* (directors Elena Lyapicheva, Irina Maletina and Mikhail Dobrynin, 2006), the historical parallels between the war in Chechnya and imperial traditions are much more accentuated. The script makes direct references to the legacy of the tsarist regime and Orthodoxy as the incarnations of the "real" Russia. The historical narrative leads to a direct challenge of the post-Soviet Russian state as being gripped by greedy oligarchs, who are portrayed as national traitors. One of them, visually resembling the Russian tycoon Boris Berezovsky, who played a key political role during the Yeltsin regime, in a telephone conversation with his high-ranking interlocutor exposes the narrative of national betrayal: "The first Chechen war was quite good for everybody. We were destroying cities and then were rebuilding them. Yet the trouble is that nowadays the *siloviki* [i.e. military and security services] are rising in power. We need to teach them a lesson and make clear who is in charge in Russia". Direct parallels with the conspiracy against the tsar about a century ago articulate the key message of the movie quite distinctly: Russia falls victim to domestic disloyalties and can survive only as a centralized—perhaps, authoritarian and monarchic—state with Orthodoxy as its ideological core.

Another reference point of the imperial articulation of Russian identity is the Soviet era. The films discussed here contain explicit or implicit comparisons between the Russian state in the 1990s and the Soviet Union. In *The Yomp*, one of protagonists claims that Russian and Chechen officers, who nowadays fight each other, have been serving together in Afghanistan "for a strong, united power". The enemies of today were brothers-in-arms a couple of decades ago: in Afghanistan in the 1980s, the Chechen commander Sayd saved the life of the Russian Major Makarov.[29] In *The Shooting Mountains*, one of the protagonists pledges to throw away his Soviet-era uniform but not until the army regains its former strength, respect and reputation—a remark that nicely fits in with the Russia-dominated discourse of glorifying Soviet values.

Conclusions

This study revealed an important paradox in the biopolitical core of the Russian collective identity that emanates, following the vocabulary of Giorgio Agamben, from the domain of bare life. On the one hand, biopolitical patriotism, grounded in the spirit of combat friendship and a sense of military duty, does not necessarily imply unconditional loyalty to the state. In many respects it constitutes an alternative to the corrupt, inefficient and malfunctioning state that—perhaps, not always intentionally—relegates its citizens to the conditions of bare life, leaving them without due protection and placing them beyond institutional and even legal contexts.

Yet on the other hand, the state aptly capitalizes on the proliferation of biopolitical patriotism and even manages to manipulate its zealots. The Kremlin, with all its attempts to contrive a national

---

29 A similar scene is displayed in "The House of Fools" (director Andrei Konchalovsky): a Russian officer who came to sell the dead body of a Chechen fighter to rebels' commander, found out that the latter saved his life in Afghanistan. Ultimately he refused to take money and left with the words: "I owe you a debt".

idea(l), remains short of ideological authenticity,[30] reducing ideological articulations to moral rhetoric and a metaphysical fight between the forces of good and evil.[31] Against this backdrop, it is biopolitical solidarity emanating beyond—but appropriated by—the state that constitutes a core element of quasi-ideological constructs of patriotism and nationalism, transformable to the vague and loosely articulated ideas of the "Russian world" as a family-like organic community, or Russia's civilizational self-sufficiency.

It is in this sense that one may see the gradual transformation of politics into biopolitics, envisioned by Agamben as producing "a state of bareness, meaning lawlessness that is systematic and lethal".[32] In a situation of bare life, people can be easily manipulated by state propaganda and turn a blind eye to rational arguments that are often substituted by memories of bygone times of glory. Yet these memories, as the case of the Chechen war makes clear, could be stressful and ambiguous, only adding confusion to the imperial narratives about the past.

The controversial exchanges of mutually deconstructing narratives in the Chechen war films make any role identity either incomplete or intentionally blurred. It also turns biopolitical patriotism into a mostly intuitive "readiness to die and to kill for an abstraction capable of so much harm".[33] In Prilepin's explanation, it is the idea of love—in a wider sense—that justifies and substantiates the unconditionally primordial patriotism based on human allegiances rather than on a state-steered ideology. The ideological emptiness of the sovereign power makes this type of patriotism an imitation of love because it "is love of a false object, an object that

---

30 L. Storch, 'Bezydeinost' kak sovremennaia 'Russkaia Ideia'. "*Ekho Moskvy*" web portal, 28 August 28 2013, http://leonidstorch.livejournal.com/18760.html (accessed 20 April 2016).
31 A. Morozov, 'Sem' novostei rossiiskoi vnutrennei politiki: kak umiraet politicheskoe', *Slon*, 10 October 2013, http://vpratus.livejournal.com/8026.html (accessed 20 April 2016).
32 E. Vogt, 'S/Citing the Camp', in *Politics. Metaphysics, and Death. Essays on Giorgio Agamben's Homo Sacer*,. Andrew Norris, ed., (Durham: Duke University Press, 2005), pp. 74–106.
33 G. Kateb, George, *Patriotism and Other Mistakes* (New Haven and London: Yale University Press, 2006), p. 8.

is not an object, but one of those dream substances, mock realities".[34] As the developments in Russia after the war in Chechnya demonstrated, the huge disappointments about the ability of the central power to spearhead the nation might trigger a deep sense of desperation, deprivation and abandonment, which can be overcome by a new mobilization of resources of patriotism and nationalism, however illusory their substance might be.

Bibliography

Aradau, C., 'What is left of biopolitics?', *Radical Philosophy. Philosophical Journal of the Independent Left*, May–June (2012). http://www.radicalphilosophy.com/reviews/individual-reviews/whats-left-of-biopolitics (accessed 4 June 2019).

Campbell, D, 'Cultural governance and pictorial resistance: reflections on the imaging of war', *Review of International Studies* 29 (2003): 57–73.

Dillon, M. and Lobo-Guerrero, L., "Biopolitics of security in the 21st century: an introduction", *Review of International Studies* 34 (2008): 265–292.

Dittmer, J. and Dods, K., 'Popular geopolitics past and future: Fandom, identities and audiences", *Geopolitics* 13 (2008): 437–457.

Finlayson, J., "Bare Life' and Politics in Agamben's Reading of Aristotle', *The Review of Politics* 72 (2010): 97–126.

Fitzpatrick, P., 'Bare sovereignty: Homo Sacer and the insistence of Law', in *Politics, Metaphysics, and Death: Essays on Giorgio Agamben's Homo Sacer*, ed. A. Norris (Durham, North Carolina: Duke University Press, 2005) 49–73.

Gillespie, D., 'Defense of the realm: The 'new' Russian patriotism on screen', *The Journal of Power Institutions in Post-Soviet Societies* 3 (2005).

Grayson, K., Davies, M., and Philpott, S., 'Pop goes ir? Researching the popular culture–world politics continuum', *Politics* 29(3) (2009): 155–156.

Holden, G., 'Cinematic ir, the sublime, and the indistinctness of art', *Millenium: Journal of International Studies* 34(3) (2006): 793–818.

Jabri, V., 'Shock and awe: Power and the resistance of art', *Millenium: Journal of International Studies* 34 (3) (2006): 819–839.

Joseph, J., "Governmentality of what? Populations, states and international organizations', *Global Society* 23(4) (2009): 424.

O'Loughlin, B., 'Images as weapons of war: representation, mediation and interpretation'. *Review of International Studies*, 37 (2011): 71–91.

---

34 Ibid, p. 17.

Kangas, A., 'From interfaces to interpretants: A pragmatic exploration into popular culture as international relations", *Millenium: Journal of International Studies* 38 (2) (2009): 317-343.

Kateb, G., *Patriotism and Other Mistakes* (New Haven and London: Yale University Press, 2006).

Kennedy, L., 'Securing vision: photography and us foreign policy', *Media, Culture & Society* 30(3) (2008): 279-294.

"Komandovanie kostromskogo polka podtverdilo poteri na Ukraine", Polit.ru internet portal, 27 August 2014, http://polit.ru/news/2014/08/27/victims/ (accessed 20 April 2016).

Moeller, F., "The looking/not looking dilemma". *Review of International Studies* 35 (2009): 781-794.

Monastireva-Ansdell, E., 'Trapped in the prisoner scenario: the first Chechen war and Sergei Bodrov's 'Prisoner of the Mountains", *Studies in Russian and Soviet Cinema* 8(2) (2014): 98-119.

Morozov, A., 'Sem' novostei rossiiskoi vnutrennei politiki: kak umiraet politicheskoe', *Slon*, 10 October 2013, http://vpratus.livejournal.com/8026.html (accessed 20 April 2016).

Oksala, J., 'Violence and the biopolitics of modernity', *Foucault Studies* 10, November (2010): 23-43.

Oksala, J., *Foucault, Politics, and Violence* (Evanstone, Illinois: Northwestern University Press, 2012).

Pusca, A., 'The aesthetics of change: Exploring post-Communist spaces", *Global Society* 22(3) (2008): 369-386.

Riabov, O. and Riabova, T., 'The remasculinization of Russia? Gender, nationalism, and the legitimation of power under Vladimir Putin', *Problems of Post-Communism* 61(2) (2014): 23-35.

Singer, B. and L. Weir, 'Politics and sovereign power: Considerations on Foucault". *European Journal of Social Theory* 9(4) (2006): 443-465.

Storch, L., 'Bezydeinost' kak sovremennaia 'Russkaia Ideia'. *Ekho Moskvy web portal*, 28 August 2013, available at http://leonidstorch.livejournal.com/18760.html (accessed 20 April 2016).

Vaughan-Williams, N., 'The generalized bio-political border? Re-conceptualising the limits of sovereign power'. *Review of International Studies* 35 (2009): 729-749.

Vogt, E., 'S/Citing the Camp'. In *Politics. Metaphysics, and Death. Essays on Giorgio Agamben's Homo Sacer*, ed. A. Norris (Durham: Duke University Press, 2005).

Widder, N., 'Foucault and power revisited', *European Journal of Political Theory* 1(4) (2004): 411-432.

Žižek, S., 'The Lessons of Ranciere'. In *The Politics of Aesthetics*, ed. Jacques Ranciere. (London and New York: Continuum, 2004).

Zakhar Prilepin, the National Bolshevik Movement and Catachrestic Politics

Tomi Huttunen and Jussi Lassila
University of Helsinki

This article examines the Russian writer and publicist Zakhar Prilepin, a visible representative of Russia's patriotic currents since 2014, and a well-known activist of the radical oppositional National Bolshevik Party (NBP) since 2006. We argue that Prilepin's public views point at particular catachrestic political activism. Catachresis is understood here as a socio-semantic misuse of conventional concepts as well as a practice in which political identifications blur the distinctions defining established political activity. The background for the catachrestic politics, as used in this article, was formed by the 1990s post-Soviet turmoil and by Russia's weak socio-political institutions, which facilitate and sustain the space for the self-purposeful radicalism and non-conformism — the trademarks of NBP. Prilepin's and NBP'S narrated experience of fatherlessness related to the 1990s was compensated by personal networks and cultural idols, which often present mutually conflicting positions. In Pierre Bourdieu's terminology, Prilepin and the Nationalist Bolshevik's case illustrate the strength of the literary field over the civic-political one. Catachrestic politics helps to conceptualize not only Prilepin's activities but also contributes to the study of the political style of the National Bolshevik Party, Prilepin's main political base. As a whole, the paper provides insights into the study of Russia's public intellectuals who have played an important role in Russia's political discussion in the place of well-established political movements.

Keywords: Prilepin, catachresis, National-Bolshevik Party, post-Soviet Russia, literature and politics, conservatism, radicalism

Introduction

When the Belarusian-Ukrainian writer Svetlana Aleksievich won the Nobel Prize for literature in October 2015, the writer and publicist Zakhar Prilepin criticized the decision of the committee in the newspaper *Izvestiia* for not awarding it to a "real Russian" writer instead.[1] According to Prilepin, the real Russian writers he mentions—namely Yevgeny Yevtushenko, Viktor Pelevin, Vladimir Sorokin, Vladimir Makanin, Fasil' Iskander and Andrei Bitov—are all worthy of the award. Each of them can surprise the Nobel Committee, which does not want to repeat the previous mistakes made in awarding the prize to Russian writers.[2] By "mistakes" Prilepin referred to those Russian Nobel laureates in literature—Ivan Bunin, Alexander Solzhenitsyn and Joseph Brodsky—whose views, according to him, dramatically challenged the Committee's anti-Russian stance since awarding the prize: the émigré writer Bunin appeared to be a Russophile, Solzhenitsyn was a Russian nationalist and Brodsky appeared to be a "xenophobic imperialist."[3] Prilepin asserted that Aleksievich was awarded the prize because she cannot surprise the committee: "A good female journalist who thinks that Russia has always killed, kills, and will kill everyone and Russians will never cease to be slaves," simply demonstrates that "The Nobel Committee recognizes the Russian literature only when the Russian submarines move around Europe."[4]

At first sight, in terms of Russia's political trend and chilled relations with the West since the Ukrainian crisis, the aforementioned views are anything but exceptional. However, there are aspects which are worth mentioning regarding the very commentator and his role in Russia's overall conservative and anti-Western socio-cultural mainstream. First, Prilepin is not just a writer who occasionally succeeded in commenting on the issue in the relatively eminent Russian newspaper *Izvestiia*, known for its politically conformist views since the early 2000s. By 2015, he had become one of the most popular writers in Russia, particularly after the publication of his novel *Obitel'*, although he was already a success in 2006, when he received positive reviews for his autofictional novel *Sank'ia*. The government's official newspaper, *Rossiiskaia Gazeta*,

---

1 Z. Prilepin, 'Svetlana Rossii!', Izvestiia, 9 October 2015, available at http://izves tia.ru/news/592832 (accessed 15 January 2016).
2 Ibid.
3 Ibid.
4 Ibid.

greeted the author of *San'kia* as the new Maksim Gorky.[5] Prilepin's nationwide popularity certainly resonates with the Russian mainstream public and its desire to see the "new Gorky" as an intellectual authority for the nation's social and national conscience. This, indeed, resonates with Russia's arguable legacy of a literature-centered and writer-centered culture. In late 2014 and early 2015, Prilepin conducted occasional trips to the Donbass Region to demonstrate support for the pro-Russian rebels and civilian population.[6] His trips received wide resonance and positive feedback in the Russian media, which fits well with the state-controlled patriotic publicity, to which the majority of Russians largely conform. Besides his obvious literary success and outspoken pro-Russian views, positive perception of Prilepin has been boosted by his image: brawny masculine looks, born in 1975, with a record as a war-veteran of the Chechen wars. Against this background, it is not surprising that Prilepin has become a member of the eminent nationalist conservative think tank *Izborsk Club*, led by Alexander Prokhanov, Russia's leading nationalist-Stalinist publicist and writer.[7] The personal link behind this membership can be found in the mutual admiration between Prilepin and Prokhanov, expressed not least in the latter's laudatory views of *San'kia*.[8] It is thus no wonder

---

5   P. Basinskii, 'Novyi Gorky iavilsia'. Rossiiskaia gazeta 15 May 2006, available at: http://www .rg.ru/2006/05/15/sanjka.html (accessed 15 January 2016).
6   K. Fatkullin, 'Zakhar Prilepin rasskazal o svoikh poezdkakh v Donbass', Russkaia Sluzhba Novostei 25 April 2015, available at http://rusnovosti.ru/posts/371516 (accessed 15 January 2016).
7   Alexander Prokhanov (b. 1938) has been one of the most durable and visible nationalist publicists and writers in Russia who gained visibility in the Soviet semi-dissident nationalist literary movement since the late 1960s. During perestroika, he actively worked against Gorbachev and the liberalization of the system, and since the collapse of the Soviet Union has been the editor-in-chief of the ultra-conservative and nationalist newspaper Zavtra, which has been the central platform for anti-western and pro-Stalinist segments of Russia's political discussion. In 2012, Prokhanov became the chair of the Izborsk club (for more, see http://www.izborsk-club.ru/).
8   A. Prokhanov, 'Prilepin stal dlia menia otkrytiem'. San'kia.ru, available at http://sankya.ru/otzivi/aleksandr-prohanov-prilepin-stal-dlja-menja-otkritie m.html (accessed 8 February 2016). This is also seen in the television program Chai s Zakharom, hosted by Prilepin since January 2016 and run by the conservative channel Spas, to which Prilepin invited Prokhanov as his first guest.

that Prilepin has ended up on the documentary film *Prezident* of the famous pro-Kremlin television host Vladimir Solov'ev, screened in the state television channel *Rossiia 1*, which draws an unswerving picture about Putin's greatness and the need for Putin as the country's president.⁹

However, Prilepin's image as a semi-official public literary patriot is controversial because of his well-known oppositional stance and activism as a visible representative of the National Bolshevik party, or rather, the Natsbol-movement (NBP). For NBP and Eduard Limonov, a radical writer and the party's ultimate personification, bourgeois-type stability and order, public and political conformism as well as Russia's gradual adaptation to global repercussions of capitalism — that is, the overall development of post-Soviet Russia including the Putin-era — has been the enemy number one. In particular, this controversy is manifested in Prilepin's inclination to position himself as a kind of disciple of Limonov. Unsurprisingly, just one day before Prilepin's reaction on Aleksievich's Nobel Prize in *Izvestiia*, Limonov expressed sexist views in the same forum by attacking Aleksievich, who, according to Limonov, "reminds one more of those pitiful moms who must sit in a committee of soldiers' mothers than a writer who would dare to challenge the (Belorussian) regime".¹⁰ A further aspect of this controversy lies in Prilepin's list of ideal candidates for the Nobel Prize. Indeed, many of them represent those "anti-Russian" views for which Aleksievich became Prilepin's target. It is possible to evaluate writers and their literary products regardless of the political views these products imply (that is, literature is literature and politics is politics), but it is Prilepin's public role and his political engagement that makes this list controversial and illuminating. On the one hand, he canonizes

---

Available at https://www.youtube.com/watch?v=E4U-Fe7DVkM (accessed 8 February 2016).
9   Prezident, Documentary film by Vladimir Solov'ev 2015, available at http://russia.tv/video/show/brand_id/59329/episode_id/1193264/video_id/1165983/ (accessed 15 January 2016).
10 E. Serzhan, 'Eduard Limonov: Nobelevskuiu premiiu segodnia vruchaiut vsem podriad'. *Izvestia* 8 October 2015, available at http://izvestia.ru/news/592786 (accessed 15 January 2016).

certain authors in the history of literature, regardless of their political views, and, on the other, he uses this same canon for emphasizing his own public and political role as a writer.

The above-mentioned controversy that dominates Prilepin's public activity is in our focus. From the viewpoint of the Kremlin's tactics of divide and rule, Prilepin can be seen as an ideal figure on account of his youthful, intellectual and rebel-like patriotic conformism. In this vein, the oppositional appeal and danger can be harnessed for the support of the regime's conservative, pro-Russian, and at least, non-Western stance in order to prevent the formation of potential anti-regime coalitions. In Prilepin's particular case, this makes sense since he played a visible role in the anti-regime protests in 2011–12, and his links to influential oppositional actors and figures are well known.[11] Prilepin represents an insightful case in Russia's patriotic cultural production in dissemination of anti-Western and pro-Russian views via numerous interviews, talk shows, radio programs and newspaper columns. In this article, we analyze Prilepin's literary and political activities in order to clarify his position as a literary-oriented public intellectual in Russian society. We argue that incessant controversies of Prilepin's views can be interpreted as catachrestic politics. Catachresis is understood here as a socio-semantic misuse of conventional concepts as well as a practice in which political identifications blur the distinctions defining established political activity. The background for catachrestic politics, as understood in this article, was formed by the 1990s post-Soviet turmoil and by Russia's weak socio-political institutions, which facilitate and sustain the space for the self-purposeful radicalism and non-conformism—the trademarks of the NB movement. Prilepin's and NBP's narrated experience of fatherlessness re-

---

11 This concerns his extensive networks and links with liberally oriented cultural actors but also to visible anti-Kremlin political instances, like the television channel Dozhd', and figures, Aleksei Naval'nyi in particular. Well before the escalation of protests in 2011–12, Prilepin and Naval'nyi were establishing a nationalist-democratic oppositional movement Narod in 2007, whose manifesto is available at http://www.apn.ru/publications/article17321.htm (accessed 8 February 2016).

lated to the 1990s was compensated by personal networks and cultural idols, which often present mutually conflicting positions. In Pierre Bourdieu's terminology, Prilepin's and NBP's case illustrates the strength of the literary field over the civic-political one. Catachrestic politics as a conceptualization helps not only make sense of Prilepin, but also contributes to the study of the political style of the National Bolshevik Party, Prilepin's main political base. As a whole, the paper aims to provide insights into the study of Russia's public (literary-oriented) intellectuals, who have played an important role in Russia's personalistic political discussion. This discussion appears significant at the expense of surrounding, weakly established, political parties.

The first section of the article introduces Eduard Limonov, Prilepin's main idol and the leader of NBP, followed by a discussion on NBP's political style, and on how this style has been understood in terms of conversion between literary and political capitals. We locate NBP in-between the fields of the literary-artistic and political production, since NBP is the essential background in exploring controversies, endemic for Prilepin's public position. In the second part, we analyze catachrestic politics in light of our interviews with Prilepin and Nizhny Novgorodian activists of the Natsbol movement. We argue that because of the particular nature of this politics, its symbolic resources for a serious political alternative are ultimately limited. Prilepin's primary step towards his literary and public success, the autofictional novel *San'kia*, occupies a central role in this political articulation. It illustrates the importance of literary and artistic idols alongside with the commonly and collectively felt rootlessness and fatherlessness. At the same time, the major controversies of Prilepin's public views are largely crystallized in his attempts to animate conservatism and to emphasize the stagnant nature of liberalism. The data of the article comprises interviews of Prilepin and of Natsbol-activists in Helsinki and Nizhny Novgorod in 2013 and 2014 as well as interviews and articles of Prilepin in the Russian media.

NBP, Limonov and Conversion between Literary and Political Capitals

Previous studies on NBP have mainly approached the movement's role either in terms of the post-Soviet nationalism and fascism,[12] or discussed its leader Eduard Limonov.[13] These frameworks are more or less justified considering Limonovs's public views. For instance, in April 2015 Limonov declared that besides the annexation of Russian-speaking territories, Russia needs a people's revolution, a full-scale nationalization of private property, the deportation of the "super-rich" (*sverkh-bogatykh*), and the establishment of the progressive socialist model à la Venezuela.[14] However, his revolutionary dreams and flirtation with totalitarian solutions have unavoidably inflated in the course of time in terms of providing shocking effects and novelty that a potential revolutionary movement requires. Indeed, over the course of NBP's 23-year existence,[15] Limonov's comments like these have brought nothing exceptional into the ideological hotchpotch of the movement. They have remained as utopian as they were in the first issues of NBP's catechism, the newspaper *Limonka*, whose print version ran between 1994 and 2002. In this respect, the durability of the movement as well as the enduring charisma of Limonov as Prilepin's main idol and of numerous artistically oriented Russian youngsters in post-

---

12 M. Mathyl, 'The National Bolshevik Party and Arctogaia: two neo-fascist groupuscules in the post-Soviet political space', *Patterns of Prejudice* 36(3) (2002), pp. 62–76.; M. Laruelle, 'Aleksandr Dugin: A Russian Version of the European Radical Right?' (2001), available at https://www.wilsoncenter.org/sites/def ault/files/OP294.pdf (accessed 15 January 2016).
13 V. Sapon, 'Apostles of the "Other Russia": Mikhail Bakunin and Eduard Limonov on Paths of Radical Social Transformation', *Russian Politics & Law*, 43(6) (2005); A. Rogatchevski, *Eduard Limonov: A Critical Study*, Ph. D Thesis, Department of Slavonic Languages and Literatures, University of Glasgow (Glasgow, 1998); A. Rogatchevski, 'The National Bolshevik Party (1993–2001): A Brief Timeline'. *New Zealand Slavonic Journal*, 41 (2007), pp. 90–112.
14 E. Limonov, 'Za rabotu, tovarishchi !', *Drugaia Rossiia* 13 April 2015, available at http:// drugros.ru/news/4247.html (accessed 15 January 2016).
15 In 2007 NBP was declared an extremist organization and disbanded. Since then it has continued its political existence as a non-registered party Drugaia Rossiia (Another Russia), though members are still constantly referred to as "natsbols."

Soviet Russia, prompt a closer examination of the NBP and its central figure, Limonov.

Mikhail Sokolov's analysis of reasons behind NBP's popularity among the post-Soviet nationalist movements[16] sheds light on the questions relevant to the discussion of Prilepin's idols, literary as well as political ones. In comparison with another major post-Soviet nationalist movement of the 1990's, *Russian National Unity* (RNE), whose core supporters were less educated and had a background in security and army instances, NBP appealed to young cultural intellectuals and university people, who found in Limonov a revolutionary, as well as a cultural and literary hero.[17] In approaching multiple symbolic peculiarities of the movement, Viktoriia Sukovataia points out that "Limonov introduced to Russian literature a new type of 'ideal hero', simultaneously cosmopolitan and patriotic, a cynical and romantic intellectual who had absorbed a significant layer of world cultural values as well as purely Russian ones."[18] Adopting Pierre Bourdieu's concept of "capitals" to the aftermath of the Soviet Union's collapse, one can argue that the supporters and members of NBP lacked social and "institutional capital" typical of the Soviet-era cultural intelligentsia.[19] Limonov's hatred of the Soviet cultural elite has been a repetitive feature in his novels and writings,[20] and it is not far-fetched to link this distaste to his social background and reputation as a hooligan and semi-criminal. In terms of Limonov's gradual success as a self-educated writer, it was this "outsidedness" with regard to societal and cultural institutions, which framed his biographically oriented literary style. Sokolov points out that besides Limonov, the other key founders of NBP — Alexander Dugin and Yegor Letov — were self-

---

16 M. Sokolov, 'Natsional-Bol'shevistskaia partiia: ideologicheskaia evoliutsiia i politicheskii stil', in *Russkii Natsionalizm. Ideologiia i nastroenie*, ed. A. Verhovskii (Moskva: SOVA, 2006).
17 Sokolov 2006.
18 V. Sukovataia, 'Eduard Limonov in Search of a "New Masculinity"', *Russian Politics & Law*, 46(1) (2008), pp. 20–30.
19 Sokolov 2006, 155–159.
20 Ibid., 155.

educated intellectuals as well.[21] In this vein, NBP's radical, anti-institutional, anti-bourgeois and non-conformist political style was central for its success, while it was successful for Limonov as well.

Following Bourdieu, Sokolov discusses NBP's chaotic style as a profitable conversion between the cultural and political "capitals". Limonov's literary works create a habitus of a social and political radical, whose biographical dimension is redeemed by the activism and existence of a radical political movement, and conversely, the reputation of this movement can be converted into a symbolic (and economic) capital of Limonov's books.[22] Sokolov's approach has an explanatory force particularly in Russia, in which political movements have been overly personalistic and leader-dependent. Nevertheless, when the crucially important aspect of style in Natsbols' and Limonov's own activism is reduced to histrionics, controversies of this style remain unexplained regarding the ideas that they possess. This particularly applies to Prilepin as an influential actor in Russia's conservative patriotic mainstream. In other words, how can we explain the controversy between Prilepin's political identification with Natsbols and his current patriotic — and conformist — conduct?

Catachrestic Politics

Let us continue with Bourdieu's views on the political field with regard to its respective rules and the navigation of social agents in and between various fields. Seeing the political field as historically institutionalized and hierarchized towards exclusive professionalism, we may agree with Sokolov's previous assertion regarding the conversion of cultural capital into a political one among figures like Limonov, in other words, among those who felt left out from the political (and economic) arrangements, which, in the case of the Soviet Union and Russia, appeared to be earthmoving. While the political field affects everyone and might receive attention from many citizens, it is eventually accessible only to the few. As Bourdieu writes:

---

21 Sokolov 2006, pp. 155–159.
22 Ibid., pp. 155–159.

> (A)politicism, which sometimes takes the form of anti-parliamentarism and which can be channelled into various forms of Bonapartism, Boulangism and Gaullism, is fundamentally a protest against the monopoly of the politicians, and represents the political equivalent of what was in previous periods the religious revolt against the monopoly of the clerics.[23]

This certainly applies to Russia and the overall apoliticalness of Russians.[24] However, Bourdieu's reference to particular political regimes in the history of France are revealing since they all resulted as a larger access to power in the political field. NBP's national bolshevism has never succeeded in this regard, and there are good grounds to argue that it has never seriously calibrated its political message for any realistic chances of getting into power. Why is this the case? In Bourdieu's terms, in Russia the literary artistic field has had an institutional autonomy and power to view political and social issues from the standpoints of the rules of its own field (i.e. the historical and political impact of literature in Russia). Conversely, the narrowness and closeness of Russia's political field has allowed a relatively sustainable political movement on its margins. Without a realistic chance and incentive to calibrate its message towards the rules of the political field (that is, towards a realistic competition between ideas in solving problems), NBP's marginal position sustains symbolic struggles according to the rules of the literary artistic field.

To rephrase this in terms of Yuri Lotman's cultural semiotics,[25] NBP strives to maintain its dynamic peripheral (cultural, political and geographical) position in relation to the centre. Thus, the movement is maintaining its weak level of structuration, since this means, according to Lotman, the constant emergence of new cultural meanings and texts but not any established languages.[26] In other words, the access to the centre would establish a more stable

---

23   P. Bourdieu, *Language and Symbolic Power* (Cambridge, ma: Harvard University Press, 1991), pp. 175 et seq.
24   According to the Levada Center poll in late 2013, 67 % of Russians were not, or not at all, interested in politics, while only 1 % professed to be 'very interested in politics' (28 % professed to be 'rather interested', and 4 % could not answer). *Levada-Tsentr*, 'Interes k politike', 16 December 2013, available at http://www.levada.ru/old/16-12-2013/interes-k-politike (accessed 15 January 2016).
25   Y. Lotman, *Universe of the Mind. A Semiotic Theory of Culture* (London and New York: I.B. Tauris, 1990), pp. 127 et seq.
26   Ibid.

political message. In its peripheral position, this *trope* appears catachrestically in relation to the centre, that is, the field, or system, of politics. Jacques Derrida defines catachresis as "a distortion in a language use" as follows:

> (T)he violent and forced abusive inscription of a sign, the imposition of a sign upon a meaning which did not yet have its own proper sign in language. So much so that there is no substitution here, no transport of proper signs, but rather the irruptive extension of a sign proper to an idea, a meaning, deprived of their signifier.[27]

In other words, catachresis is something in which linguistic (or symbolic) resources of a speaker do not meet with objects that the speaker wants to describe. From the speaker's viewpoint, the given catachresis is close to aphasia which can be understood either as a speaker's neuro-linguistic disorder related to his/her mother tongue,[28] or as a socio-cultural phenomenon. The latter can be termed as a symbolic aphasia, discussed particularly with regard to post-Soviet Russia in which larger groups and cohorts of a society show notable restrictions, or not-yet-established creativity, in naming social and cultural phenomena.[29] The other side of catachresis concerns its general semantic dimension embedded in all symbolic systems, particularly in natural languages. The classical example in many languages, including English, is the expression *legs of a chair* which points at the use of an old word in describing something new that does not have a name yet (a meaning which did not yet have its own proper sign): the things which carry the chair, are named according to legs of a living being. In this respect, catachresis can be seen the semantic poverty of any language.

In terms of this poverty, the political dimension and potential of catachresis is best described by Ernesto Laclau, who approaches

---

27 J. Derrida, *Margins of Philosophy* (Brighton: Harvester Press 1982), p. 255.
28 H. Lehečková, 'Assessment and Treatment of Aphasia in Czech'. *Folia Phoniatr Logop* 64 (2012), available at http://www.karger.com/Article/Pdf/340013 (accessed 15 January 2016).
29 S. Oushakine, 'The Quantity of Style—Imaginary Consumption in the New Russia'. *Theory, Culture & Society* 17(5) (2000); S. Oushakine, 'In the State of Post-Soviet Aphasia: Symbolic Development in Contemporary Russia'. *Europe-Asia Studies*, 52(6) (2000); S. Oushakine, '"We're nostalgic but we're not crazy": Retrofitting the Past in Russia.' *The Russian Review* 66(7) (2007).

politics as a natural and never-ending attempt towards hegemony. This never-ending attempt is crystallized in his conceptual broadening of catachresis. According to Laclau, catachresis (*legs of a chair*),

> can be generalized if we face the fact that any distortion of meaning has, at its root, the need to express something that the literal term would simply not transmit. In that sense, catachresis is more than a particular figure: it is the common denominator of rhetoricity as such...if the empty signifier arises from the need to name an object which is both impossible and necessary, from that zero-point of signification which is nevertheless the precondition for any signifying process, the hegemonic operation will be catachrestical through and through.[30]

Despite Laclau's theoretical understanding of catachresis is central for our conceptualization, we emphasize the concept's empirical value for Prilepin's as well as NBP's cultural production. Laclau's assertion is applicable to any new, or "real," political initiative, when politics is seen as a discursively conducted never-ending attempt towards hegemonic closures. In addition to this, NBP provides a tangible context and case for the necessary experience and need to address political issues, which, however, from NBP's standpoints, appear to be impossible. In other words, whereas for Laclau politics as such is a catachrestical cycle—momentarily erupted initiatives for new meanings whose eventual catachresis is challenged by new initiatives—Prilepin and NBP adds a concrete empirical facet to Laclau's theoretical standpoint, representing politics that remains and aims to remain catachrestical.

San'kia and the Deprived Generation

The 1990s in Russia can be seen as Laclau's zero-point of signification (the need to name an object which is at the same time necessary and impossible). Besides the 1990s as the zero-point of signification, the decade appears to be the experience of non-belonging to the family unit, the experience of rootlessness or orphanage. Indeed, according to Igor Smirnov's study on the catachrestic worldview in the historical avant-garde, these elements are essential for the social

---

30 E. Laclau, *On Populist Reason* (London & New York: Verso, 2005), pp. 71-72.

catachresis—the trope of non-belonging.[31] For the young Natsbols, the experience of orphanage in the society and the non-belonging to the 1990s' ideological atmosphere were cured and solved by the new type of party, which appeared as the warmly welcoming family. This is tangibly expressed by a key representative of Nizhny Novgorodian Natsbols in our interview in 2014. He described his leaving from Sakhalin to the European part of Russia in the 1990s. His father was "more leftist" than the party's mainstream at the end of the USSR, and after the collapse, the father became involved in radical movements. Via his father he found the newspaper *Limonka* in the mid-1990s. This experience was his major motive to leave Sakhalin and in 1998 he ended up in Nizhny Novgorod. Soon, together with friends, he organized the first group of NBP in the city. They conducted an attack on McDonald's restaurant with a slogan "Hamburgers for America—Dostoevsky for Russia" (*Amerike gamburger—Rossii Dostoevskii*). He became a party member officially in 1999, and as a 17-year-old teenager came to Moscow for networking in newspapers and met with Trotskyists, who took care of him, gave him fried potatoes, the "smell of which was far more important than any of the newspaper stuff." In the "bunker" (headquarters of NBP), he met "young men in black and tattoos all over while mothers were walking around quietly."

The description above is very close to the way the main protagonist in Prilepin's *San'kia* experiences his becoming a member of the party of *Soiuzniki*. The obvious prototype of Soiuzniki is NBP, while its leader Kostenko's explicit prototype is Limonov, originally Savenko. San'kia had recently buried his father—described in the funeral episode related to absurdities of the Russian winter—and had "left" his mother, the family unit, in order to find his real family among the party in Moscow:

> ... there is only this kinship and nothing else. Understanding what is happening in Russia does not depend on how much you know or intellectual casuistry which you can use to wash up any definitions, any questions, it depends on the feeling of kinship that grows in you already when you are a child, and then you have to live with it, because you cannot escape it. If you

---

31   I. Smirnov, 'Katahreza'. *Russian Literature* xix(1) (1986), pp. 57–64.

feel that Russia is for you, like for (Alexander) Blok in his poems, a wife, then you experience her as a wife. A wife in the Biblical sense, with her you are going to live your life to the end. Blok understood it perfectly.[32]

The notions of kinship, blood relation (*rodstvo*) and fatherlessness (*bezottsovshchina*) appear decisive for San'kia in his inner dialogues, trying to understand the meaning of Russia, on the one hand, and the party and its members in his own life, on the other:

> But you do not have a father either (...) Not a bloody thing... Fatherlessness in search of what we need as the sons... We are the fatherlessness in search of what we need as the sons...
> You're lying. There are also *soiuzniki* with fathers. But they don't need fathers... Because what kind of fathers are those? They are not fathers. That's why I'm not lying.
> But how about mothers, then? What about mothers? They know only that they need their sons at home...[33]

In the late 1990s — early 2000s, the Natsbol-protagonist becomes commonplace in contemporary Russian prose: in our interview Prilepin named Viktor Pelevin, Nataliia Kliuchareva, Dmitri Bykov, Sergey Shargunov and himself as authors treating the subject. The Natsbol-protagonist is an obvious representative of the so-called "Generation bmp" (*Bez Menia Podelili*, "it was dealt out without me"), a notion first used by the political commentator Stanislav Belkovsky and emphasized by Prilepin himself.[34] Initially it refers to the immediate post-Soviet generation that was born in the 1980s, and became involved in the NBP movement. They experienced the fall of the Soviet Union as a tragedy. The years that followed were frustrating, filled with the sense of non-belonging to the surrounding society as if all the positions were decided and distributed without listening to them. This was the new post-Soviet generation, which did not treasure Yeltsin's romantic revolution at all; they were far too young in the early 1990s, while in the late 1990s they were looking for "fried potatoes" in Limonov's bunker.

---

32 S. Prilepin, 2015 (2006), pp. 185–186:
33 Ibid, pp. 138-9:
34 Z. Prilepin, 'Pokolenie bmp — 'Bez Menia Podelili'', *Novaia Gazeta*, 26 September 2011, available at http://www.novayagazeta.ru/arts/48672.html. (accessed 15 January 2016).

Prilepin himself was 17 when his father died in 1992. In our interview, conducted in December 2013, Prilepin described his early 1990s as a mixture of non-belonging, fatherlessness and poverty, projected into negative experiences of that time. He constantly stressed his experiences of the kinship with the "NBP orphans," the fatherless youth. In line with Limonov's self-educated anti-bourgeois intellectual role, Prilepin also highlighted his self-educated background as an occasional journalist in a tabloid instead of emphasizing his university degree (in philology) from the Nizhny Novgorod State University. His "universities", in keeping with Maxim Gorky, were the war in Chechnya and working in OMON groups, after which he met Limonov for the first time: "I asked him, when the revolution is going to happen in Russia. He answered: 'In 1999, Zakhar'. 'OK', I said, 'call us then, we are ready to fight'." After the economic default in 1998, Prilepin lost his job: "For months we did not have any money, for a year or so we lived in a barrack eating some cabbage, it was a terrible time. I was looking for work as a *merchandiser* in Nizhny Novgorod, and eventually I found a job as a journalist for cheap tabloids." This became the starting point of his literary career. A notable tension arises from Prilepin's overall conservative stance with regard to his willingness to emphasize the importance of radical hooligan avant-garde poets as his literary idols. Here we can see an obvious link to NBP's literary artistic capital and its enduring legacy. Indeed, on several occasions, the NBP representatives have defined themselves as radical avant-garde artists, that is, "more avant-gardist than others."[35]

Prilepin's Liberal Stagnation and Conservative Vitality

For Laclau, catachresis is a conceptual metaphor for politics in the sense that any concept is and remains open to re-definition. Prilepin, however, does not solely aim at providing new meanings for partic-

---

35 A. Raikov, 'Kul'turnaia sostavliaiushchaia natsional-bol'shevisma', available at http://theory.nazbol.info/index.php?option=com_content&view=article&id=196:2010-01-09-11-15-33&catid=30:the-community&Itemid=49 (accessed 15 January 2016).

ular political positions, but he incessantly and deliberately appropriates "old" meanings as well. In this respect, Prilepin's position is in line with the current (2014–2015) Russian conservative and patriotic mainstream, while he can also be identified as a conservative radical oppositional leftist. He identifies himself as a patriotic conservative, but the basis of this identification is principally constructed vis-à-vis his radical and oppositional position, outlined in his *Sank'ia* and repeated in our interviews as well as public appearances. Consequently, he aims to create his radical and oppositional reputation as a person, who is not liberal and whose views do not contradict conservatism and traditionalism. A further challenge emerges from his current role as a famous writer in relation to his vague vision of leftism. In this case, literary and economic success must be distanced from its capitalist underpinnings, and in particular, his leftism consists of the need to be distanced from traditional communists and the Soviet-like nomenklatura, as has been commonplace for Limonov as well. These controversial identifications can be illustrated as in Table 1 (arrows refer to distancing forces).

Table 1   Prilepin's controversial identifications

Conservative	⬅➡	Radical
Right wing	⬅➡	Left wing
Patriot	⬅➡	Opposition
Literary tradition	⬅➡	Avant-garde
Family unity	⬅➡	Fatherlessness
Conventional	⬅➡	Experimental

In this vein, Prilepin aims to represent Russian cultural and literary traditions and its overall conservative conduct with an unconventional and oppositional pathos, which supposedly challenges the experienced Western-liberal hegemony. This conservative demand, however, does not propose the symmetrical change into a conservative hegemony but is a demand for "vitality" (*zhivoy*). This notion can be found in his criticism of the Nobel laureate Aleksievich as a writer who cannot cause any surprise. This vitality is not exclusively linked to a united success of the state, that is, patriotism as a sort of unconditional receipt for the state's collective success. Rather, Prilepin's frames patriotism as oppositional, non-(or anti) liberal in terms of challenging any conformist peace.

Prilepin's seemingly durable experience of the 1990s appears to be a key facet to his distaste of liberalism and claims of liberals' lasting dominance. It seems that Russia's current patriotic mainstream and the marginal position of liberals has not diminished this experience. Consequently, his emphases on vitality resonate with the mode of identification typical for Natsbols of the 1990s, in counterposing political power from a position which lacks institutional and political capital for making real decisions. Thus, the list of writers, who Prilepin sees optimal for the Nobel Prize in his criticism against Aleksievich, and who largely contradict Prilepin's own political views, exemplifies his willingness to resort to this vitality (unpredictability) as a political value. In other words, Prilepin's vitality is close to subversion and conflictuality, both overly controversial in respect to the official patriotic policies based on ideals of stability and order, but highly common to Natsbols in sustaining a political reputation via a literary-artistic reputation. For instance, in an interview in the independent television channel *Dozhd'* — for which Prilepin hosted the program under his name in 2013 — Prilepin welcomed the debate on the return of the name of Stalingrad for the city of Volgograd, because "the only peaceful place is the cemetery" (*spokoyno tol'ko v kladbishche*).[36] For Prilepin, it seems that this peace — here the unanimous condemnation of Stalinism — is something which is ultimately linked to the experienced conformist liberal hegemony, applicable also to Putin's regime at least before 2014. While leftism could figure as a logical component in challenging the Western liberal hegemony and the experienced capitalism — as a political synonym for Prilepin's vitality — it is conservatism (e.g. motherland, Russian language, family) that stands as the major alternative to the Western liberalism for Prilepin (as

---

36 'Zakhar Prilepin: Stalin — eto naivysshaia tochka razvitia tsivilizatsii', *Dozhd'* 19 February 2013, available at https://tvrain.ru/teleshow/harddaysnight/zahar_prilepin_stalin_eto_naivysshaja_tochka_razvitija_tsivilizatsii-337066/ (accessed 15 January 2016).

well as for the political mainstream).[37] However, since he systematically aims to maintain his oppositional and radical Natsbol stance, the experienced Western liberal surroundings is seen as bourgeois. In other words, a key element in Prilepin's catachresis of politics and of its definitions is the equation of liberalism with bourgeois. This can be seen as an explicit fidelity to Limonov's anti-bourgeois revolutionary stance but also a highly "glocalized" understanding of liberalism. For Prilepin, this means overall negativity emerging from the 1990s economic policies, in which the historical conservatism and anti-revolutionary reputation of the bourgeois are stretched to the notion of liberal and liberalism.

The crisis and war in Ukraine has provided a welcome setting for Natsbols and Prilepin in this respect — along with other Russian nationalists who have been involved in fights in the Donbass[38] — since the military volunteerism is the concrete proof of patriotic vitality and engagement against the "bourgeois" liberal mainstream.[39] This includes the official, "specious" support for Donbass as well as those with an anti-war or, pro-Kiev position. Nonetheless, Prilepin is overtly reluctant to identify his political opponents among the liberal opposition, particularly when it comes to representatives of literature. In line with his admiration of "vitality" — a kind of meta-ideological framework for his eclectic political and literary sources — he praises the historical link between literature and political power in Russia. In an interview in *Svobodnaia Pressa* in September 2015, a web-publication whose editor-in-chief he is himself, he puts himself onto the real progressive patriotic side of the *limonovtsy*, at the same time praising his literary colleagues at the liberal side as well while they demonstrate the overall vitality of literature in Russian politics:

---

37 'Zakhar Prilepin duel' protiv liberalov'. TV ROSSIIA, programma PravDa 11 November 2013, available at https://www.youtube.com/watch?v=_vb6m6ZQDow (accessed 15 January 2016).
38 M. Laruelle, 'The three colors of Novorossiya, or the Russian nationalist myth-making of the Ukrainian crisis', *Post-Soviet Affairs* 32(1)(2015).
39 Z. Prilepin, 'Sorvite s nikh pogony', Svobodnaia Pressa 4 May 2015, available at http://svpressa.ru/society/article/120737/ (accessed 15 January 2016); Z. Prilepin, 'Deshevle vyrastit' odnogo patriota, chem dat' skidku na million', Svobodnaia Pressa 30 May 2015, available at http://svpressa.ru/blogs/article/123627/ (accessed 15 January 2016).

> *Svobodnaia Pressa*: Do literature and the writer have a chance to reclaim the lost dominance over minds? Or do we need to change the format?
> Prilepin: Literature has a brilliant dominance over minds. One part of society is fed by the truth of (Boris) Akunin, (Liudmila) Ulitskaia, Vladimir Sorokin, Andrei Makarevich and (Viktor) Shenderovich. The influence of these writers on intellectuals in Russia is simply tremendous. If these personalities try, they will gather a huge, 50,000-participant march in the capital without a problem. Another part of society carefully listens to Alexander Prokhanov, Iunna Morits, Olesiya Nikolaeva, Dmitry Ol'shanskiy and Sergey Shargunov. Pupils of Eduard Limonov were the first who went to Crimea and Donbass when everything was only at the beginning. Today hundreds of limonovtsy fight in Luhansk as well as in Donetsk. There are whole units in which they form the major part of fighters. What do you think, are there any other examples in the world where a writer—no matter whether he is a political actor as well—can mobilize his readers and supporters to the battle for freedom? Russia is still a literature-centred country. Literature does not speak to tens of millions, but instead, to hundreds of thousands of the most active. And that's enough.[40]

A further catachrestic dimension of Prilepin's activism is related to his willingness to identify himself as a representative of *narod*, people, boosted by his semi-peripheral locus in Nizhny Novgorod with regard to Moscow. However, this popular frame, seemingly suitable for strengthening his anti-liberal stance, is concurrent with his vision of being a Limonov-type new radical, representative of the anti-bourgeois cultural aristocracy of passion and of the new power elite. In 2010, he concluded this vision of "vitality" as follows by playing with the letters of NBP:[41]

> It's time to recognize: a living and real aristocracy with its codex of honour, mythology, heroes and legends, is already here.
> It's name is—(The) New Bolshoi (great) Project. More precisely, a pseudonym. You know the name with these three letters. The only thing that remains is to seize power..

In depicting this "new aristocracy" more closely, Natsbols have regularly emphasized their cultural and literary basis (in Russian, *kul'turnaia sostavliaiuschaia*) by canonizing certain representatives of

---

40 G. Bobrov, 'Povorot mirovoi istorii', *Svobodnaia Pressa* 28 September 2015, available at http://svpressa.ru/society/article/132759/ (accessed 15 January 2016).
41 Z. Prilepin, 'Novaia aristokratiia uzhe zdes', *Limonka* (2010), available at http://limonka.nbp-info.com/345_article_1226841295.html (accessed 12 October 2015).

literary history along with the NBP leaders. Limonov even applies the notion of *pantheon* in this context, naming somewhat surprisingly the Japanese writer of estrangement, Yukio Mishima, French author Louis-Ferdinand Céline and the English dandy and immoralist Oscar Wilde as his predecessors. The party pantheon consists of well-known artists and public intellectuals, such as Limonov, punk musician Yegor Letov, esoteric philosopher and fascist-nationalist publicist Aleksandr Dugin (these three were the founders of NBP), jazz pianist and avant-garde composer Sergey Kuriokhin and rock poet Dmitry Reviakin, not to forget Prilepin himself. Prilepin's own canon includes certain representatives of cultural history often (catachrestically) of anti-canonized authors. Socialist realist Leonid Leonov, Boris Kornilov, Vladimir Lugavskoy, Anatoly Mariengof, and Sergey Esenin (who is, however, canonized in 20th century Russian literature). It seems obvious that Kornilov, Esenin and Mariengof appear in Prilepin's *pantheon* for local patriotic reasons. Esenin was born in Ryazan, as was Prilepin, while Kornilov and Mariengof were from Nizhny Novgorod, Prilepin's home city.

On the other hand, Esenin and Mariengof, central representatives of the poetic group of the Imagists, turned into passionate chauvinist nationalists and Slavophiles in the early 1920s. The Russian National Bolshevik ideologist, Nikolay Ustrialov, and his so-called *smenovekhovtsy* movement, was supposedly an inspiration for the Imagists' chauvinism in the 1920s.[42] It is worth mentioning that three years after Esenin's death, Ustrialov wrote an essay about him. It dealt with a poet who loved his fatherland more than anything. According to Ustrialov, Esenin was a confident patriot writing love poetry for Russia, his beloved. Eventually, as to the poet's reaction to the October revolution, Ustrialov declared that Esenin lived the revolution organically, also quoting his poem: "My mother is this country, / I am a Bolshevik!" This poem became a

---

42   T. Huttunen, '"Not Back To Pushkin, But Forwards Away From Him": On the Russianness of Russian Imaginism.' *ACTA SLAVICA ESTONICA vi. Studia Russica Helsingiensia et Tartuensia xiv. Russian National Myth in Transition* (2014), available at http://www.ruthenia.ru/National_myth/Huttunen_Tomi.pdf (accessed 15 January 2016).

perfect declaration of a former village poet Esenin, who became a nationalist Bolshevik in the city of Moscow after finding his new family unit in the hooligan group of the Imagists.

In discussing NBP's historical roots and Prilepin's pantheon of Russian Imagists, it is important to note that immediately after the October revolution, the Imagists were collaborating eagerly with the Bolsheviks, receiving privileges and financial aid. They were also in close contact with the "Chekists" — officers of the notorious Soviet security organization before and during Stalin's regime — a phenomenon that is present in both Limonov's and Prilepin's biography. Limonov had a worshiping relationship with his father, who was an officer of Stalin's NKVD,[43] while, Prilepin (as mentioned above) was a soldier of OMON, Russia's special troops, in the Chechen wars in 1996 and 1999. In the spirit of these historical parallels, the participation of Iakov Bliumkin — Socialist-revolutionary Bolshevik and agent of the Cheka, who gained a reputation by murdering the German diplomat Wilhelm von Mirbach in 1918 — in the Imagists circle and "literary life theatre" was also an essential feature of this phenomenon.[44]

Conclusion

This article has examined Zakhar Prilepin, one of the most popular writers and controversial public intellectuals, who has actively advanced patriotic and conservative views for Russia's domestic audiences since 2014. Since then, Prilepin has also become the most "official" incarnation of the Natsbol movement. Traditionally, the most influential and valued realm of cultural production in Russia has been literature, and, thus, it is not surprising that literature has

---

43 E. Carrere, *Limonov*. (Helsinki: Like, 2013).
44 In particular, Imaginists' famous hooligan public collective performances are worth mentioning in this context as predecessors of various performances of natsbols: The literary trial of the Imaginists (November 1920), the literary trial on contemporary poetry by the Imaginists (November 1920), Imaginist writings at the Strastnoy Monastery wall, Renaming the streets of Moscow according to the Imaginist poets, or their attempt to organize a "General Mobilisation." For instance, in terms of the latter, the official publication of natsbols after Limonka was titled as Total Mobilisation.

been of utmost importance for the movement. Moreover, the movement's birth within the chaos of the Soviet Union's disintegration and the general sense of dissatisfaction in the "new Russia", is intrinsically linked to particular literary and cultural idols, which compensate for the experience of the social and political orphanage. Prilepin is, and identifies himself as, a representative of the post-Soviet generation, which experienced severely the loss of the system but was allowed to read, see and hear novelties, which were completely absent and alien to Soviet society. Limonov's aesthetic and nostalgic thirst for totalitarianism and anti-Westernism, along with his extremist openness and radicalism certainly spoke to young Prilepin along with thousands of others who felt bereft in the 1990s.

Russia's writer-centered perception of literature — canonized writers or the panthéons of writers — fits well with Russia's person-centered politics. It is not too far-fetched to say that political movements and parties in Russia are not run by ideologies but by persons.[45] In this respect, NBP is not a radical exception in Russia's post-Soviet political landscape, but rather a radical exemplification of it and its endemic features: personalistic movements and eclectic political ideas.

In depicting Prilepin's cultural production in line with the Natsbol movement, we have argued that it can be fruitfully termed as catachrestic politics. NBP's birth and story is part of this overall conceptualization. While rootlessness and fatherlessness are inseparable elements of the movement's catachresis, followed by a strong fidelity to revolutionary-type idols, catachresis is a kind of symbolic necessity for the movement whose principal identity is to be peripheral and revolutionary in relation to any established center. While a real challenge to any political regime requires a populist rupture — a combination between new and old societal demands in an accessible format for the masses[46] — Natsbols are an anti-populist movement, even in the field of Russian nationalism. The Natsbols'

---

45 A comprehensive viewpoint to aspects and dimensions of Russia's patronal governance, see H. Hale, *Patronal Politics: Eurasian Regime Dynamics in Comparative Perspective* (Cambridge: Cambridge University Press, 2015).
46 E. Laclau, *On Populist Reason* (London and NY: Verso, 2005).

revolutionary and literary oriented message is ultimately unresponsive to any institutional compromise between elitist, covert and personalistic literary sources and to more appropriate and realistic practices in the field of politics. Russia's restricted and authoritarian political system, apolitical sentiments and the valued legacy of "writers who are more than simply writers" sustains Prilepin-like figures whose political weight is fed by literary achievements and distinctions.

Bibliography

Basinskii, P., 'Novyi Gorky iavilsia', *Rossiiskaia gazeta*, 15 May 2006, http://www.rg.ru/2006/05/15/sanjka.html (accessed 15 January 2016).

Bobrov, G., 'Povorot mirovoi istorii', *Svobodnaia Pressa* 28 September 2015, http://svpressa.ru/society/article/132759/ (accessed 15 January 2016).

Bourdieu, P., *Language and Symbolic Power* (Cambridge, Massachusetts: Harvard University Press, 1991).

Derrida, J., *Margins of Philosophy* (Brighton: Harvester Press, 1982).

Fatkullin, K., 'Zakhar Prilepin rasskazal o svoikh poezdkakh v Donbass', *Russkaia Sluzhba Novostei* 25 April 2015, http://rusnovosti.ru/posts/371516 (accessed 15 January 2016).

Hale, H.E., *Patronal Politics: Eurasian Regime Dynamics in Comparative Perspective* (Cambridge: Cambridge University Press, 2015).

Huttunen, T., '"Not back to Pushkin, but forwards away from him": on the Russianness of Russian imaginism'. *ACTA SLAVICA ESTONICA vi. Studia Russica Helsingiensia et Tartuensia xiv. Russian National Myth in Transition* (2014), http://www.ruthenia.ru/National_myth/Huttunen_Tomi.pdf (accessed 15 January 2016).

Laclau, E., *On Populist Reason* (London and New York: Verso, 2005).

Laruelle, M., 'Aleksandr Dugin: A Russian Version of the European Radical Right?' (2001), https://www.wilsoncenter.org/sites/default/files/OP294.pdf (accessed 15 January 2016).

Laruelle, M., 'The three colors of Novorossiya, or the Russian nationalist mythmaking of the Ukrainian crisis', *Post-Soviet Affairs* 32(1) (2015): 55–74.

Lehečková, H., 'Assessment and treatment of aphasia in Czech'. *Folia Phoniatr Logop* 64 (2012): 165–168.

Limonov, E., 'Za rabotu, tovarishchi !', *Drugaia Rossiia* 13 April 2015, http://drugros.ru/news/4247.html (accessed 15 January 2016).

Lotman, Y., *Universe of the Mind. A Semiotic Theory of Culture* (London and New York: I.B. Tauris, 1990).

Mathyl, M., 'The National Bolshevik Party and Arctogaia: two neo-fascist groupuscules in the post-Soviet political space', *Patterns of Prejudice* 36(3) (2002): 62–76.

Oushakine, S., 'The quantity of style — imaginary consumption in the New Russia', *Theory, Culture & Society* 17(5) (2000): 97–120.

Oushakine, S., 'In the state of post-Soviet aphasia: symbolic development in contemporary Russia', *Europe-Asia Studies* 52(6) (2000): 991–1016.

Oushakine, S., '"We're nostalgic but we're not crazy": Retrofitting the past in Russia', *The Russian Review* 66(3) (2007): 451–482.

Prezident, Documentary film by Vladimir Solov'ev (2015), http://russia.tv /video/show/brand_id/59329/episode_id/1193264/video_id/116 5983/ (accessed 15 January 2016).

Prilepin, Z., *San'kia* (Moscow: Ad Marginem Press, 2015 [2006]).

Prilepin, Z., 'Novaia aristokratiia uzhe zdes', *Limonka* (2010), http://lim onka.nbp-info.com/345_article_1226841295.html (accessed 12 October 2015).

Prilepin, Z., 'Pokolenie bmp — 'Bez Menia Podelili'', *Novaia Gazeta* 26 September 2011, http://www.novayagazeta.ru/arts/48672.html (accessed 15 January 2016).

Prilepin, Z., 'Stalin — eto naivsysshaia tochka razvitia tsivilizatsii', *Dozhd'* 19 February 2013, https://tvrain.ru/teleshow/harddaysnight/zah ar_prilepin_stalin_eto_naivysshaja_tochka_razvitija_tsivilizatsii-337 066/ (accessed 15 January 2016).

Prilepin, Z., 'Svetlana Rossii!', *Izvestiia*, 9 October 2015, http://izvestia.ru/ news/592832 (accessed 15 January 2016).

Prilepin, Z., 'Sorvite s nikh pogony', *Svobodnaia Pressa* 4 May 2015, http:// svpressa.ru/society/article/120737/ (accessed 15 January 2016).

Prilepin, Z., 'Deshevle vyrastit' odnogo patriota, chem dat' skidku na million', *Svobodnaia Pressa* 30 May 2015, http://svpressa.ru/blogs/arti cle/123627/ (accessed 15 January 2016).

Prokhanov, A., 'Prilepin stal dlia menia otkrytiem'. *San'kia.ru*, http://san kya.ru/otzivi/aleksandr-prohanov-prilepin-stal-dlja-menja-otkritie m.html (accessed 8 February 2016).

Raikov, A., 'Kul'turnaia sostavliaiushchaia natsional-bol'shevisma', http: //theory.nazbol.info/index.php?option=com_content&view=articl e&id=196:2010-01-09-11-15-33&catid=30:the-community&Itemid=49 (accessed 15 January 2016).

Rogatchevski, A., 'Eduard Limonov: A Critical Study.' PhD Thesis, Department of Slavonic Languages and Literatures, University of Glasgow (Glasgow, 1998).

Rogatchevski, A., 'The National Bolshevik Party (1993–2001): A Brief Timeline'. *New Zealand Slavonic Journal* 41 (2007): 90–112.

Serzhan, E., 'Eduard Limonov: Nobelevskuiu premiiu segodnia vruchaiut vsem podriad', *Izvestia* 8 October 2015, http://izvestia.ru/news/59 2786 (accessed 15 January 2016).

Sapon, V., 'Apostles of the "Other Russia": Mikhail Bakunin and Eduard Limonov on Paths of Radical Social Transformation', *Russian Politics & Law* 43(6) (2005): 43–61.

Smirnov, I., 'Katahreza'. *Russian Literature* xix(1) (1986): 57–64.

Sokolov, M., 'Natsional-Bol'shevistskaia partiia: ideologicheskaia evoliutsiia i politicheskii stil''. In *Russkii Natsionalizm. Ideologiia i nastroenie*, ed. A. Verhovskii (Moscow: SOVA, 2006).

Sukovataia, V., 'Eduard Limonov in search of a "new masculinity"', *Russian Politics & Law* 46(1) (2008): 20–30.

'Zakhar Prilepin duel' protiv liberalov'. *tv Rossiia, programma PravDa* 11 November 2013, https://www.youtube.com/watch?v=_vb6m6ZQ Dow (accessed 15 January 2016).

The Religious Identity of Modern Orthodox and Hasidic Jewry in St. Petersburg

Elena Ostrovskaya
Saint Petersburg State University

This article describes the results of field research into religious Jewry of St. Petersburg. I analyze biographies of Modern Orthodox and Hasids of Lubavitcher traditions (or the Chabads as they call themselves), who in the aftermath of the Soviet Union's disintegration in the 1990s chose observance as their self-identity and lifestyle. The paper is aimed at answering the following questions: how do modern Jewish identities differ from one another among the St. Petersburg observant Jewry raised in non-religious families and Soviet schools? How do they coordinate their collective identity with other Jewish communities around the world? To conceptualize my research, I have used Giddens and Beck's theories of modernity, while my methodology draws on the use of biography and biographical narrative in ethnographic studies. I argue that individual reflexivity gained new importance for both Modern Orthodox Jews and the Chabads in the post-Soviet religious liberation and the arrival of new religious influences. However, whereas Modern Orthodox Jews emphasize the autonomy of their subject position and stress the meaning of individual dogma, the Chabads foreground the primacy of tradition when reflecting on their identity as religious Jews.

Keywords: biographical narrative, reflective subjectivity, religious Jewry, observant Jews of St. Petersburg

The term "observant or religious Jewry" (*religioznoe evreistvo*), frequently used in my research, is a term employed by the Chabad, Modern Orthodox, and Litvak respondents, to distinguish between Jewish ethnicity and Judaism. The identity of St. Petersburg observant Jewry originated between 1990 and 2015 in two contrasting sources: Soviet Jewish traditions and new influences brought to Russia by religious missionaries. There is hardly any sociological or anthropological research on religious Jews in Russia in general and none in St. Petersburg in particular. One of the reasons for this is their isolation.

In the course of this study, which I conducted in 2015, I made forty interviews in four key communities in St. Petersburg: the Modern Orthodox Jews, the Litvak, the Reformists, and the Chabad,[1] and visited a number of community centers. For the Modern Orthodox, most of the interviews were conducted via Skype or during the respondents' visits to St. Petersburg. The respondents were 32–67-year-olds, who had been active members of the given religious groups for at least 10 years. These people grew up in the Soviet atheistic tradition and then adjusted to a more pluralist post-Soviet society. At the beginning of the 1990s, my informants quickly seized the new liberty to make choices concerning their religious identity and it was during this time that their spiritual search began. In this article, I focus on the Modern Orthodox and the Chabad, because these groups feature two different ways of combining traditions and individual reflexivity.

The Modern Orthodox community of the observant Jews of St. Petersburg is both a unique and novel example of an invisible and transnational community. The shared experience of the Jewish University and work life has defined their biographies, their identity, as well as their social and political positions. Most of them, guided by Religious Zionism, ended up moving to Israel. However, having settled there, they were never integrated into the social and cultural life of Israel, but rather maintained a translocal identity. The latter is characterized by a Soviet heritage as well as by Jewish Orthodox values.

The second group discussed, the Chabads, has combined the Soviet heritage, embraced by Lubavitcher Hasids, with the Western vision of the Chabad movement, promoted by missionaries from the US and Israel. The Chabad respondents aspire to building a solid religious community — an ethnic and religious transnational network of the Chabad organizations — the purpose of which is to enforce Hasidic dogmas and traditions. The characteristic features of

---

[1] As for the Modern Orthodox, most of the interviews were conducted via Skype or during the respondents' visits to St. Petersburg.

the Chabad of St. Petersburg are their local diversity, their ambition to become a leading Jewish group in the world, and their reserved attitude towards the non-Jewish outsiders. I argue that the practice of excluding outsiders is a defense mechanism, resulting from years of persecution and brutal repression the Soviet government launched against them to curb their pursuit of freedom of conscience and religion.

Jewish Modernity: Theory and Methodology

The theoretical frame of this article engages the concept of reflective subjectivity, central to Anthony Giddens and Ulrich Beck's theory of modernity, as well as the method of biographical narrative. The approach to the biographical method has gone through a major change in social science. The so-called "biographical turn" in the early 21st century was a result of the 20th-century rise of the sociological theory of modernity. In fact, when discussing reasons for this turn, most European scholars refer to the new understanding of subjectivity in modern and late modern societies.[2] Theorists of modernity claim that the key characteristic of today's societies, apart from the risks and the insecurity, is the emergence of a reflective individual confronted by a post-traditional environment, manifesting and advocating ideological pluralism.[3] According to Giddens, in post-traditional societies an individual discovers his/her identity through a biographical narrative: "In the post-traditional order of Modernity, and against the backdrop of new forms of mediated experience, self-identity becomes a reflectively organized endeavor. The reflective project of the self, which consists in the sustaining of coherent, yet continuously revised, biographical narratives, takes place in the context of multiple choice as filtered

---

2 P. Chamberlayne, J. Bornat and T. Wengraf, *The Turn to Biographical Methods in Social Science: Comparative issues and examples* (London, New York: Routledge, 2000).

3 U. Beck, *Risk Society* (London: Sage, 1992); U. Beck and U.E. Ziegler, *Eigenes Leben. Ausflüge in die unbekannte Gesellschaft, in der wir leben* (München: Verlag C.H. Beck, 1997); P. Berger, B. Berger, and H. Kellner, *The Homeless Mind: Modernization and Consciousness* (Harmondsworth: Penguin Books, 1973).

through abstract systems."[4] The biographical method allows a researcher to reconstruct the choices available for a reflective identity construction in a unique account of events, facts, and experiences.

In my research this method has enabled me to reconstruct the narratives of individual religious identities of the respondents and the ways in which they see themselves as part of the religious group.[5] The respondents shared with me their life stories, recounted with a specific narrative emphasis; they recount their life story relating it to a historical background. The narrations feature the transitional period from 1990 to 2015, when observant Jews were abandoning Soviet practices of secret observance in favor of an open lifestyle, which implies a unique time, space, and worldview.

Biographical narrative is extremely useful for a hard-to-reach population group study.[6] These are groups which are usually unapproachable due to their occupation, health condition, lifestyle, or social isolation. The Jewish religious groups reviewed in this research are highly secretive—for two reasons. Firstly, in accordance with the *Halakha*,[7] they exclude non-Jews. Secondly, their isolation results from years of persecution in the Soviet Union. Many respondents aged 47 or older said that history might repeat itself because the outside world is hostile, especially in Russia, with its grim

---

4   A. Giddens, *Modernity and Self Identity: Self and Society in the Late Modern Age* (Cambridge: Polity Press, 1991), p. 5.
5   In the analysis of these narratives, I used methodologies developed by Thomas Wengraf and Fritz Schütze. T. Wengraf, *Qualitative Research Interviewing Biographic Narrative and Semi-Structured Methods* (London: Sage Publications, 2001); F. Schütze, 'Biography Analysis on the Empirical Base of Autobiographical Narratives: How to Analyse Autobiographical Narrative Interviews, Part II', *Biographical Counselling in Rehabilitative Vocational Training. Further Educational Curriculum*. (EU Leonardo da Vinci Programme, 2008), http: www.biographicalcounselling.com/ (accessed 27 August 2015).
6   The EU commissioned biographical research into hard-to-reach population groups, which resulted in some outstanding projects. For example, sostris (Social Strategies in Risk Societies) has developed not only interesting topics in keeping with the democratic doctrine of the EU, but also a methodology. The leading scholars in the project, Thomas Wengraf and Prue Chamberlayne, also created a new biographic-narrative interpretative method (bnim).
7   *Halakha*—the laws and statutes of Judaism, regulating religious, family and social life of Religious Jews.

past and somber present with respect to anti-Semitism. For these reasons, surveying the observant Jews was a challenging experience, which required a creative approach and inventive techniques.

Snowball or respondent-driven sampling are often used in the study of hard-to-reach communities. However, these methods suggest having an access to such groups, which was not the case in this research. After a number of vain attempts to approach observant Jewry and interview them, I decided to use the small-world method, which is based on the idea that through their connections, people are linked to a much greater number of people unfamiliar to them.[8] Therefore, I constructed a graphics within my social circles. Since I was targeting particular respondents, I referred to those in my circles who were likely to have a Jewish background or connections. Indeed, I found my prospective informants at a distance of three to six "handshakes". Unfortunately, this did not facilitate the sampling.

In telephone and electronic communication with addressees suggested by informants, I made some disastrous mistakes in using incorrect words and idioms defining sacred topics used or avoided by particular observant communities. A revealing example is my telephone conversation with a prominent leader of a St. Petersburg yeshiva (a religious school or a place to study) and an acclaimed expert in the religious written heritage. At first, he was willing to help with the sampling. When I introduced myself and explained the purpose and reason for my research, he enquired whether I was a Jew and which religion I practiced. On hearing my replies, he said that he would not be able to help since he did not understand who I was looking for. "It's impossible to convert to Judaism! We do *Teshuvah* and *Giyur*. I have no clue who you need. If you could revise it and text me later." That was the first and the last time we talked. Such incidents made me think of an interpreter who would explain to me the framework and vocabulary of Petersburg Jewry, someone who would find and negotiate with prospective respondents.

---

8 D.J. Watts, *Small Worlds: The Dynamics of Networks between Order and Randomness.* (Princeton, New York: Princeton University Press, 1999).

Many scholars, who have used the snowball method, say that first respondents tend to distort and shift sampling,[9] which was the case in this research too. Initially, my plan was to interview observant Jews between 32 and 50 years of age. Having faced negative feedback on my replies to questions about my nationality and religion, I realized that I could go through it over and over again with no positive outcome. Therefore, having collected a dozen interviews through the snowball method and having acquired access to the community, I turned to respondent-driven sampling. On completing the interview, I would ask each interviewee to enroll another candidate. Many of those surveyed not only gave names and contact information of prospect interviewees, but also encouraged them to participate. In consequence, the age category of the respondents widened.

Respondents were selected in accordance with their membership in one of the Petersburg religious communities, which helped to avoid common lapses concerning snowball and respondent-driven methods. The aim was to include respondents who would represent the same community, but whose answers would be different from those of other community members. For example, parents of targeted respondents would say that there were very few contacts they could give since everybody had left. Later, I learnt that "everybody" implied their children and their friends who had moved to Israel. I interviewed those by Skype and asked them for contacts of people they knew through other acquaintances to avoid any distortions.

Another typical feature in the respondent-driven sampling is that those surveyed are likely to choose candidates who could create a certain image of the community. This proved problematic when negotiating with community leaders. The solution was to

---

9   D.D. Heckathorn, 'Respondent-Driven Sampling: A New Approach to the Study of Hidden Populations', *Social Problems* 44(2) (1997), pp. 174–199; D.D. Heckathorn., S. Semaan, R.S. Broadhead, J.J. Hughes, 'Extensions of Respondent-Driven Sampling: A New Approach to the Study of Injection Drug Users Aged 18–25.' *AIDS and Behavior* 6(1) (2002): 55–67; D. D: Heckathorn, 'Snowball versus Respondent-driven sampling', *Sociological Methodology*. 41(1) (2011), pp. 355–366.

ease restrictions and include younger respondents into sampling. These tend to be more sociable and most of them have many connections. As far as extremely guarded religious Jewry was concerned, full access was out of question. Nevertheless, with more information and contacts, I was able to recognize the saturation point after which the narratives appeared to repeat similar elements.[10]

Observant Jewry of St. Petersburg

Over the last 25 years, St. Petersburg observant Jewish communities have undergone a significant transformation. Of the people I interviewed, the respondents in their forties or older had no religious background and associated Jewish identity as people belonging to the same ethnicity rather than the same confession. This generation has given rise to two underground groups: the Lubavitcher Hasids or Chabad and the so-called "Litvaks". Each group has its origins in the traditions of Russian Judaism. Hasidic (which means "piety" in Hebrew) Judaism is a branch of Orthodox Judaism that promotes Jewish mysticism. It originated in the 18th century under the first Lubavitcher rabbi Shneur Zalman of Liady (1747–1812) and quickly caught on in Ukraine, Lithuania, Belarus, Romania and Hungary. In Russia, this teaching was named Chabad, which is a Hebrew acronym for "Chochmah" (Wisdom), "Binah" (Understanding), "Da'at" (Knowledge). In 1951, Rabbi Menachem Mendel Schneerson became the seventh Rebbe of Chabad-Lubavitch and was at the head of the movement until his death in 1994. Thereafter the community underwent a crisis and schism, which affected Chabad across the world.

---

10 I need to say a few words about the ethical side of the research: I provided each respondent with full information about myself including Internet resources. When communicating with a prospective respondent through correspondence or face-to-face, I stated that I was doing independent research into St. Petersburg religious Jewry with no sponsorship and tight deadlines; therefore, I would not press them for answers. Respondents would ask me where the biographies would be published and I explained to them that I would incorporate only fragments of the full text in my articles with names substituted by for letters. Furthermore, I suggested that they should check the transcript and read the article beforehand. The respondents, whose interviews were used in the article, read it.

The Litvaks borrow from the Lithuanian movement, founded in the xviii century by Rabbi Elijah Ben Shlomo Zalman as a reaction against Hasidism. His followers were called *Misnagdim*, which means an opponent. Later with the spread of this movement and with the creation of educational centers specializing in the study of the Jewish written heritage in Russia, USA, Britain, and Germany, the name Litvak would start to refer to any Hasidism opponent regardless of their residence or community. While conducting this research, I met very few actual Soviet Litvak adherents, for most of them emigrated to the USA or Israel in the 1980s. Some would come back as missionaries to revive the observant lifestyle in St. Petersburg. The majority of the biographical narratives accounted in my study represent the age group from 32 to 52, who were born and raised in St. Petersburg and joined the community in the 1990s.

Both Modern Orthodox and Chabad can be ranked as religiously moderate, which means they do not totally shut themselves away from the outsider world like the Litvaks. In fact, unlike the Litvaks, they do not expect adherents to follow all prescriptions to the letter. I also studied the St. Petersburg Reformist community, founded by American Reformist missionaries. They are open to debate with outsiders over political and dogmatic issues. What is more, Reformists are lenient to such unorthodox practices as a female Rabbi. However, a characteristic feature for other observant Jewry is their separation from the world of outsiders, known as the *goyim*. Religious Jewry in St. Petersburg is a closed community. In fact, seclusion is part of their identity. During the interviews, the respondents frequently said: "I have no wish to explain it to non-Jews." This differentiation between "us" and "others", "Jews" and "*goyim*", is the only feature common to all observant communities. The interviews suggest that observant Jews are convinced that a non-Jew will never understand them and their position in today's world.

In terms of the calendar and chronology, St. Petersburg observant Jewry is somewhat unique. When asked about their date of birth, the adult respondents were able to use both the Russian/Christian as well as the Jewish chronology, while the younger interviewees did not know how they correspond. Their letters and the most noticeable events in the lives of their outstanding leaders are dated according to the Jewish chronology. Every year the Grand Choral Synagogue of St. Petersburg issues a calendar for St. Petersburg Jews. They consult it when making an appointment or organizing the week. From the majority of the surveyed observant Jews from St. Petersburg, I have learnt that the Synagogue calendar is a unique attribute and a significant part of the observant identity of the city. This concept was thoroughly explained by the chief information officer of The Grand Choral Synagogue:

> Our calendar is a communication tool. Before starting our information office, we decided to go and see how they manage things in Moscow. Their trademark was a newspaper. They didn't bother about keeping up with the new high-tech stuff. All they needed then was a weekly paper with 40,000 subscribers, which we couldn't afford. To them it was a distinctive sign: you are one of us if you get the newspaper. I thought of a calendar as an alternative. So, we could send it out, and it would be both a tool of communication and a distinctive marker. The question "why don't you subscribe to the calendar?" would be a good excuse for starting a dialogue. If a person has any interest in Jewish culture, he'd certainly be interested in our religious festivals. The logic was simple. We immediately knew we wouldn't reduce it to beautiful pictures. Surprisingly, not many understood it. But we persevered. We want the calendar to tell our story so that anyone who gets it says: "This is how we do it in St. Pete". And anyone who sees it would know it was made in Petersburg. That is not as easy as it seems, as every calendar has its own topic. Every year a topic of the year is chosen. Last year it was Jewish homes and buildings, which have to do with the Jewish history of Petersburg. Commemoration is an important part of our work, we cannot afford any mistake in any name or any date.

The interactive religious calendar, available on the St. Petersburg Grand Choral Synagogue website, creates guidelines for everyday life for the Chabad intellectuals of Petersburg. It not only introduces Jewish chronology to observant Jews brought up in the Soviet period who are unfamiliar with it, but also gives information about special annual events and festivals and their celebration in different Chabad communities around the city. Besides, the calendar is a distinctive marker, which helps to differentiate between the insiders and the outsiders. The only way to get hold of this calendar is to subscribe to it in a Synagogue. It builds a Synagogue-individual-Synagogue reciprocal link.

In addition to the understanding of time, the topography of the observant community is also unique. The Jewish microcosm provides for everything and eliminates the necessity of any interaction with the outside world, except for the use of public transport, healthcare, monetary transactions, or marketplace. Although they walk the same streets as other people, the religious Jews of St. Petersburg restrict themselves to a limited set of destinations.

These are the Jewish religious centers, synagogues (minyanim), Jewish kindergartens, schools, educational centers, kosher stores and the homes of other observant Jews.

Religious Jewish life is committed to a religious day and week schedule with a crowning Shabbat feast and to a restricted diet and behavior, which ban non-kosher cafés, restaurants and venues meant for the "others". The practice of secluding from the outside society and excluding the outsiders from the community are defense mechanisms, evolved through years of persecution and brutal repression the Soviet government launched against Jews to curb their pursuit of freedom of self-identification and religion. The tragic incidents of violent attacks on those with "the fifth paragraph"[11] and religious convictions have been rendered by *refuseniks*[12] and passed down from generation to generation in Jewish families. During my field work, at the end of the interview, most respondents over 50 would lend or give me the books about those times. This period includes the Great Patriotic War, which hit Jews hard, and the Soviet dictatorship up to the 1980s, when observant Jews were persecuted, imprisoned or put to death.

Tradition and Religious Authority in Modern Orthodoxy and Chabad

The Modern Orthodox community is organized as translocal, with members scattered around the world. I call this community "Petersburg Jewish University and the New Jewish School" (PJU-NJS).

---

11 The fifth paragraph was a euphemism of the Soviet era, used to refer to Jewish passports. In Soviet times, ethnicity was recorded in the passport, and therefore a mandatory item of any questionnaire on biographical data was the fifth in order of filling – the paragraph which contained a question on ethnicity.

12 *Refusenik* is a Soviet term, defining a person who applied for immigration to Israel and turned into an outcast when their application was rejected.

Twelve out of twenty interviewees identified themselves as Modern Orthodox or *kippot serugot* (knitted kippot). Most of them left Russia for Israel, some settled in the us. Those few who stayed in St. Petersburg chose not to join any religious community. The former proved either to have graduated from the Petersburg Jewish University,[13] or to have worked at the New Jewish School.[14] All of these people mentioned the PJU as a place, which was crucial for the formation of their Jewish religious identity. Later these people left for Israel, where they started to put Judaica studies into practice in many different institutions and places. They have been working for *Knizhniki* Publishing House, teaching Hebrew and Jewish traditions inside and outside schools. Nothing has been written about this invisible community. I came across it only accidentally when analyzing the biographical narratives collected during my field work.

The outlines of the Chabad tradition belong to the seventh Lubavitcher Rabbi—Rabbi Menachem Mendel Schneerson (1902–1994), who called on the young Chabad emissaries to launch a global mission of propagating the ideals and values of religious Jewry worldwide. The ambitious plan was to facilitate Jewish consolidation by teaching not only the outer forms of observance, but also its deeper meanings.[15] The commitment to religious prescriptions is the most evident feature of the Chabad tradition. This compliance with religious prescriptions makes the St. Petersburg Chabad adherents both conspicuous and unapproachable. The Chabad men wear black wide-brimmed hats, black and white attire, and a beard. They pray three times a day in a synagogue. Trying to fulfill the commandments to the letter, most of them choose to work in community centers, Grand Choral and Small synagogues, yeshivas and schools.

---

13 The Jewish University was founded in 1989 and functioned in its original educational project science 1997. Then it was reorganised and renamed to St. Petersburg Institute of Jewish Studies.
14 The Educational Association New Jewish School was founded in 1998 to assist teachers across CIF countries in writing educational programs and teaching in Jewish schools.
15 S. Heilman and M. Friedman, The Rebe. The Life Afterlife of Menachem Mendel Schneerson (Princeton, Oxford: Princeton University Press, 2010), 161–162.

The Chabad women are responsible for running the house, cooking kosher food, and fulfilling routines in the prescribed way. They are true to the kosher style: a long skirt, a neck and arm covering top, a wig, with or without makeup depending on the calendar. You can hardly run into a Chabad woman on the street. She is usually a mother of at least 5-6 children, involved in the cultural life of the community. Allegedly, they are bound to communicate only with the women belonging to the same community center, which has a Rabbi and a Synagogue (minyan) of its own. Female respondents stress their reluctance to socialize outside the community. There are differences in the lifestyle of women from the Rabbis' surrounding group, described above, and that of the common Chabad women from the district community. The former do not work, they have their multiple children to look after, and they are active members of the club. Some might work at Chabad girls' schools. In contrast, the latter usually have a secular occupation, work in different parts of the city, have no more than three children and rarely attend women's clubs.

The two discussed movements of observant Jewry differ from each other in their approach to the tradition and the individual freedom to construct their religious identity. The PJU-NJS interviewees often claim that a Rabbi and even a Synagogue are of secondary importance compared to their personal faith. The respondents rely on their own knowledge of Judaism when interpreting their life and the world. In their biographical narratives, the informants stressed that they had never wished to belong to or to join any collective, that they were interested in unusual people, books, subjects, and cultures. For the PJU-NJS people, an observant Jew is autonomous and independent. In their narratives they often mention that they do not turn to a Rabbi, synagogue or community for guidance or help. The PJU-NJS respondents need these only for the sake of expensive *mikvah*[16] or some specific prayers. Nevertheless, having settled

---

16 Mikvah—a pool for ritual bathing, immersion in which is prescribed on certain days during the holidays for intimate relationship or to prepare for the wedding. Mikvah are divided into male and female, they are thoroughly cleaned after each use. Mikvah is built in a synagogue. It is difficult and expensive to maintain.

in Israel, they keep in touch, consolidate to maintain traditions of the Soviet intelligentsia, exchange books, fly all the way to see the performance of a Soviet singer or actor and cooperate in academic research into Judaism.

In contrast, the Chabad respondents arrange their narratives so that they are perceived as part of a solid ethnic and religious community. In their narratives, subjective reflection seems to begin after joining the Chabad. It is defined by the acquired framework of Chabad's *Weltanschauung*. The Lubavitcher Hasidism puts a big emphasis on self-reflection, mysticism, signs and sustainable communication with the Divine. The above listed characteristics were brought by the Chabad missionaries, who came to stay in the 1990s. From the Soviet Hasids, the contemporary Chabads have adopted the conviction that charismatic religious continuity is maintained through consanguinity. Their commitment to this idea becomes evident through the analysis of different biographical narratives, where they give careful accounts of their observant ancestry. Some claimed to be the descendants of the priests (Cohens). Besides, they were likely to embark on stories of persecution during the Soviet times.

The Experiences of "Coming Back" in the Biographies of Modern Orthodox Jews

The differences in the way in which the Chabad and Modern Orthodox groups conceptualize their religious identities is especially evident in their accounts of their experiences of "coming back" and initiation. For Modern Orthodox Jews, the *Teshuvah* ("comingback" or rejoining the Jewish religious tradition) or the *Giyur* (conversion to Judaism) happened either after the introduction into the PJU elite or upon entering the PJU, (a narrative most common for the 36–45-year-old respondents), or following years of continuous reflection on the world, life and its meaning (most common for the 51–62-year-old respondents).

The 36–45-year-old respondents would cite their non-religious but ethnically Jewish parents as the main influence which eventually encouraged them to join Religious Jewry. Respondents' accounts as well as their parents' narratives have revealed a similar motive: in the turbulent 1990s, placing the children in a Jewish school was a way to secure their future. Besides, a degree from a Jewish university was seen as a much sought-after ticket to Israel. Few parents would have expected their children to become observant in the end, which they did after graduating, visiting Israel and embarking on academic research into Judaism. Most of the respondents said they had been attracted by the intellectual atmosphere, approachable peers, enchanting texts, and the unique opportunity to reflect, share ideas and teach others. Below I cite two illustrative narratives.

> In my school years everybody knew that student dormitory on Kievskaia str next to the Frunzenskaia subway station. The university itself was housed in some sort of a culture house far off, near the Kirovsky plant. We came there to celebrated Jewish festivals. Study, party, hang out or spend the Shabbat. This was a great party of all ages, students, pupils and tutors all together. I was the youngest, but I never felt it. Everybody was young, happy and having fun. We studied the Mishnah, started on the Talmud, even though we knew very little Hebrew. Those who were two month senior would teach others. It was really free then, before it became an institution. Different autonomous individuals came together to study and communicate.

Another illustration of a path to the PJU-NJS community is the narrative of a 41-year-old female respondent D. from a non-religious family, who left her home town Sevastopol for St. Petersburg at 17 to enter the university and then stayed for good. Unlike the other respondents, she does not have Jewish relatives. She became interested in Judaism, joined the community PJU-NJS, entered PJU, and did *Giyur* when studying in Israel. The respondent became a religious Jew after joining the PJU-NJS:

> It was hobby, which brought me to the university. I failed the entrance exams, took a preparatory course and went to live in the Peterhoff student dormitory. There I met the local Jews who told me about the Jewish University. I knew a little about Jews and Judaism. My new friends were really special. They studied at the biology department and also attended the Judaism Institute, then the Jewish University. They said that they had discovered their true Jewish identity there. Me and the other students inspired by their stories decided to enter it. I succeeded. A year later I was doing Oriental Studies ... I did *Giyur* in Israel. Before that I had been practicing Judaism. It all started in the Jewish University. I did have interest in some far-eastern

philosophies, but it was more of a read to me, not something real. What carried me away was the lifestyle in general rather than a one-off life example. In fact, I knew some really pious Muslims, who were my closest friends, but I never wanted to become one. It was a different case with Judaism. A combination of life and studies, the idea of studying as a lifestyle attracted me most. That was what I had been longing for.

The examples discussed above address a key moment in the biographical narratives of respondents, affiliated with PJU-NJS. They strive to join a group of Petersburg intellectuals, freed from conformity and compliance. The respondents wanted to consolidate with those who had a voice of their own. The identity portrayed in the narratives of PJU-NJS adherents is characterized by reflective individualism, which started in the family and formed during the university years. The parents of the 36–45-year-old respondents were engaged by the ideals of non-conformism, open mindedness, and creative expression in the Khrushchev era. Their parents encouraged them to read contemporary literature, to embrace their individuality, and to be in control of their lives. As a result, the respondents from this age group have grown as latent dissidents, who value individualism and intelligence. Judaism and observance taught at Jewish University brought them together.

Another group within the PJU-NJS community involves the 51–62-year-old respondents, who have either never immigrated or have returned shortly thereafter. Most of them graduated from technical institutions, so they have no background in the Arts. Some used to be dissidents, associated with the so-called "St. Petersburg spiritual underground", where they read banned literature, met to debate and to learn religious traditions. The majority were Jews by mother and father, but did not observe. They generally turned to religion in the 1990s when they met the charismatic D. A 59-year-old male respondent from a non-religious family of Petersburg Jews with a degree in engineering gives the following account:

> I can't say I was ever into Jewish studies, although I would try learning something occasionally. I did read books like most engineers. There was even some academic stuff by Gasparov, Averintsev, who were tagged the intellectual engineers. I had no academic ambition, it was just pastime. We would discuss books over a cigarette. We wanted to reflect on things. For us the Soviet Union was finished; we had no interest in it. Then philosophical

questions arose. I got to think about the concept of a scientific worldview. I read further. I started to teach others the supremacy of Greek civilization. When I was giving one of my speeches, my counterpart concluded that I sounded like a Jew. At first, I thought she was being mean. A "Jew" was a taboo word in Soviet times. Then, I learnt she meant no offence. In fact, she was involved in the Jewish Renaissance project. Her friends had left the country and she was looking for like-minded people. I learnt about D. and became interested. At the time he was hiring people to do editing work for him. The only requirement was good Russian. Someone introduced me to D. who turned out to be an eloquent speaker. I didn't understand a word of his speech, though. I remember asking him about the Jewish heritage: "Do you mean there's something more to the Bible and Sholem Aleichem?" I was shocked to learn that there were another 60 thousand books. My imagination could hardly accommodate that many. It was a staggering figure. This exact number opened a whole new world for me. The world I knew nothing about. So, a gradual revelation started. Meanwhile, D. ventured at creating a university. If you had only seen it in 1989! It was a mess. Doors with all those plates saying "Armenian studies", "Azerbaijan studies". They only managed to launch Korean and Jewish courses; the other doors were sealed. Nevertheless, the Jewish department was thriving.

This narrative is a good example of the emphasis placed on self-reflective intelligence so common within the PLU-NJS respondents. The respondent was attracted to Judaism due to its rational approach and non-European character. His account shows how chaotic and free the first years of PJU were, with no hierarchy whatsoever. Studies are generally described as an introduction to a fascinating world of texts.

D. taught An Introductory course in Jewish civilization which consisted of 6 brilliant lectures. Everyone was carried away, and so was I. Rabbis that lectured us were a different case. They freaked me out. I didn't know how a Soviet person could approach them without causing offence. Religion was a delicate issue; you needed to do your homework before asking questions. How wrong I was. Our Rabbis were friendly Misha Korets, Weingart. They were willing to answer any questions we had. After meeting them, I began to read every single Jewish book translated into Russian. Meanwhile, D. embarked on some new projects. We did the Beit Midrash. He explained to us that we would study sacred texts in Hebrew. It was beyond me, yet D. talked me into it. At first, I was playing the card of an atheist with an academic interest. I thought they would shoo me away, but they didn't, as if it didn't matter at all. Then it started to kick in. The texts I was reading were appealing to me. It was a mystical experience. I felt as if I was about to unravel the mystery. Finding answers to life mysteries was not the main goal. What mattered most was the beauty of the texts. They were absolutely unique, different from any western writing. At some point I realized that I needed to somehow connect to this heritage. Most of the texts write: "we read...", but there's no "we", only them. The things said in those books have got to be a part of your everyday life, but they were not part of mine. The only way to find the clues to the texts was to become observant. When you observe the prescriptions, you tune in, prepare yourself for finding the right answers.

This respondent portrays the mystical experience of reading sacred texts, which facilitated his way to observance. Again the appeal of the tradition lies not in the certainty of the religion, but its openness to individual reflection. For this respondent, the main value of the sacred books is not that they would contain "answers", but the experience of studying them.

"Coming Back" and Initiation in the Chabad Community

There are eight Chabad rabbis-emissaries, who were raised in Israeli or American religious families with traditional Jewish values. They came to St. Petersburg from Israel and the US with a mission to revive Judaism in Russia. They learned to speak Russian when living in St. Petersburg; they have adapted to the city, or rather created in it a space fitted to the Lubavitch standards. All of the key figures of the regional Chabad communities are following the ideological guidelines of these Rabbis. A distinct group of the 61-and-over Chabads became aware of their Jewish ancestry and decided to support the revival of Hasidism. Some of them were *refuseniks* (denied permission to emigrate). Eventually, they did leave for Israel in the 1980s or 1990s, only to return with a Chabad mission and to start building a community, regardless of the environment or funds.

Initially, the 32–54-year-old Chabad respondents turned to religion in the turbulent 1990s for mundane reasons. Most of them had a Jewish mother or a Jewish father and therefore went to a Jewish school, but only later rediscovered their national identity in the hard times of the collapse of the Soviet Union. In their narratives, a more thorough reflection of their religious and social identity begins in the years after entering the Chabad community of St. Petersburg. A 35-year-old female respondent, born in Moscow to a Jewish mother, married to a missionary, is now living in St. Petersburg and working in a Jewish school. She entered religious Jewry in the senior grades of a Jewish school, where she was sent by her mother. This had no religious implications. The mother thought an ordinary school would not help her daughter withstand the turbulent teenage years. The year spent in a Litvaks school did not make a difference for the respondent. Then she went to a Litvaks school for girls in Israel. There were not many options left for her at the time of perestroika.

> Most of my schoolmates applied for this program. So did I. We went to Sohnut, an organization which processed the applications. In the end, I got into the Naale Academy. The name of the program was *We Start at 16*, which implied that we would finish school at 16 and stay on in Israel. My mom was tough. I had never left home even for a summer camp. Now I was to go to a foreign country. I was looking forward to it. After all I could come back any time. I ended up in a similar religious community that I had resented in the Moscow Litvak school. I wanted to go out with boys, do the stuff other teenagers did. All that Torah, scriptures were of some interest, but I never took them close to heart.

After her return from Israel, the respondent briefly worked as a journalist. The family did not have funds to send her to university. Eventually, the respondent's mother helped her to enroll in Jewish studies at the Peoples' Friendship University of Russia (PFUR). There she met fellow Chabad students, who were close to her in terms of age and outlook. Below I give her account of her path to joining the observant community and entering its cultural continuum.

> Chabad was fun. They didn't moan about the past or tell sad *refusenik* stories. They were energetic and young, only two years older or the same age as me. Our tutors were also young. They taught us that Judaism could be fun and trendy. Everything started to fall into place. I was still living on the outskirts, while those placed in the Moscow dormitory would go to the synagogue, attend religious festivals, which I hardly did. One Saturday I went to a disco. I knew it was wrong, but that was in theory. I remember thinking what am I doing here. What was next? Another disco, another boyfriend. The same routine. Yawn. I had enough of this life and I made up my mind to become observant. Later on, I learnt about the pullfrom-above concept, which means

that God calls on you and then waits for your response. That was how I felt. I didn't go through a miraculous recovery after a serious illness. Nothing of that sort. I simply couldn't go on like that.

Even though the Chabad community sets strict rules for its members, this respondent describe the Chabad community as "fun" and "trendy" in contrast to the restrictive life of the Litvak communities. Though she followed the rules of the Litvak school, religion did not come "close" to her "heart". Her coming to observance was her choice in the more permissive environment. However, she explains this both as an individual decision or "response", and a call made by God.

The following is an account of a 41-year-old female respondent, a patrilineal Jew from St. Petersburg, where she received her degree. Her parents left for Israel in the 1990s, while she stayed, joined the Jewish world, socialized with Jewish families and contributed to the organization of the St. Petersburg Choral Synagogue. After careful speculation and a number of incidents, she and her husband decided to take *Giyur*. Below she describes factors, which a religious court considers when reaching a verdict on whether to grant the permission:

> I began to take charge of things. I went to the Rabbi. We came with my husband. They knew him in the Synagogue. He was some sort of technical support responsible for creating the website and setting up the technical base. He was familiar with the Rabbi, whose computer he repaired more than once. We had been no strangers to them and very much a part of the community by then. So, we both voiced our wish to take *Giyur* so that our inner and outer lives would be balanced. We had always thought of ourselves as Jews in the first place and had always tried to be so. We wanted our children to be raised and taught as Jews. We wanted to make things in a proper way, to keep up. On the whole, that was it; and we were pretty welcomed. I've heard a lot of less fortunate stories. I'm in charge of a group about *Giyur* in the social network Vkontakte. Many people have been writing to me about their futile attempts, years of pleading, rejection and despair. I don't know why it happens. It took us only a year, which is way too fast.
> What is needed then? I can't say there is a set list of requirements or books to learn. The main thing is involvement in the community. You've got to communicate with the majority of members, participate in the majority of projects, attend classes, observe and have some knowledge of prescriptions. Meanwhile, you need to collect recommendations proving that you attended, heard and they remembered you. In the end you bring a pile of recommendation letters to Moscow for an interview with the Rabbi in charge.

> The court is based in Moscow, they don't have Petersburg headquarters. After the interview it might take a long time before you are eventually invited to court. There you will be tried.
> They would ask questions to make sure you observe prescriptions in your everyday life. They might ask you about peeling an apple on Shabbat, ways and timing for making a salad. You may have to cite the words of blessings for every meal or extra lines in prayers on holidays. Correct answers would prove that the person has observed for at least one year. You can only learn these things through asking and copying. These are a part of a Chabad family's routine. Then, in a year you will be given a certificate. It's hard to describe this feeling when you get it. It's like falling in love for the first time. Totally overwhelming.

This extensive transcript is given in full as a brilliant example of a considered reflection on selective criteria for prospective Chabad members taking *Giyur*. The respondent acknowledges a certain arbitrariness in the admission. She also talks about the strict demands for the *Giyur*. The candidate should be involved in the Chabad community and religious activities. They should have a decent position and status with observant Jewry, show good knowledge of Kashrut, namely: food restrictions, ritual purity requirements. However, she complies with the religious authority of the people, deciding together with her husband to take the *Giyur*. For her, the initiation is a powerful spiritual experience and she describes the *Giyur* as an exhausting, time-consuming procedure, aimed at letting in the best of the best.

Conclusion

St. Petersburg religious Jewry is a difficult community to reach. They aim to limit their contacts with the outside world and are haunted by the memories of persecution during the Soviet times. Observant Jews of St. Petersburg oppose the lifestyle and values of ethnical Jewry as well as that of outsiders. They have their own sacred calendar and a sacred urban topography. Nevertheless, the observant Jewish communities in St. Petersburg are also involved in various translocal and transnational networks.

The Modern Orthodox respondents belong to a special community type, which I call the invisible community of the Petersburg Jewish University-New Jewish School (PJU-NJS). Despite being scattered across the world, the members of this community share a collective, translocal religious identity, manifested in continuous communication. Religious Zionism plays an important role in the political views of this community and all Modern Orthodox adherents are striving to move to Israel. Nevertheless, due to their stress on individualism, they are reluctant to join any Israeli religious communities, even those located in their place of residence. The Modern Orthodox Jews I interviewed often questioned all religious authority and instead, presented the Jewish tradition as something that invites one to individual reflection rather than provides certain answers. The people from the PJU-NJS are engaged in Judaic studies, or scientific study of the written heritage of Judaism. In their biographical narratives, they portray themselves as autonomous intellectuals.

Unlike the Modern Orthodox community, both the Chabad youth and the descendants of the Lubavitcher Hasids are indifferent to Religious Zionism. The decedents of the Soviet Hasidism are prone to seclusion, segregation, and dissidence. They seem to reproduce the Soviet-time local traditions of collectivism, meritocracy and paternalism. Another distinguishing feature is gender disposition and a varied repertoire of roles and statuses. St. Petersburg has a complex Chabad infrastructure of local synagogues, kindergartens, schools, workshops for men and women, societies, etc. However, the novel features in this community are a neutral attitude to home affairs and bigger interest in transnational policies of the Chabad network. Even though the Chabads discovered or chose their religiousness in the same environment of new opportunities and the social upheaval as Modern Orthodox Jews, in their biographical narratives they are less prone to describe the conversion or the "coming home" as a personal, deliberated choice, but rather as something that takes place "naturally" or is caused by the "call of God". Unlike the Modern Orthodox individualists, the Chabad respondents conceptualize their religious identity within the framework of tradition.

References

Beck, U. *Risk Society* (London: Sage, 1992).

Beck, Ulrich and Ziegler, Ulf Eerdmann *Eigenes Leben. Ausflüge in die unbekannte Gesellschaft, in der wir leben*. (München: Verlag C.H. Beck, 1997).

Berger, P., Berger, B. and Kellner, H. *The Homeless Mind. Modernization and Consciousness* (Harmondsworth: Penguin Books, 1973).

Bertaux, D. a Kohli, M. 'The Life Story Approach: A Continental View'. In *Life Story Research*, vol. I, ed. B. Harrison (Los Angeles, London, New Delhi, Singapore: Sage, 2008) 42–65.

Chamberlayne, P. and Rustin, M. 'From Biography to Social Policy.' Final Report of the sostris Project. University of East London, Centre for Biography in Social Policy (1999). http://cordis.europa.eu/documents/documentlibrary/76095551EN6.pdf (accessed 21 April 2016).

Chamberlayne, Prue, Joanna Bornat, and Tom Wengraf. *The Turn to Biographical Methods in Social Science Comparative issues and examples*. (London, New York: Routledge, 2000).

Denzin, N.K. 'The reflexive interview and a performative social science.' *Qualitative Research* I (2001): 23–46.

Duncan J.W. *Small Worlds: The Dynamics of Networks between Order and Randomness* (Princeton, New York: Princeton University Press, 1999).

Giddens, A. *Modernity and Self Identity: Self and Society in the Late Modern Age* (Cambridge: Polity Press, 1991).

Hackstaff, K.B., Kupferberg, F. and Négroni, C. eds. *Biography and Turning Points in Europe and America* (Bristol: Policy Press, 2012).

Heckathorn, D.D. 'Respondent-Driven Sampling: A New Approach to the Study of Hidden Populations', *Social Problems* 44(2) (1997): 174–199.

Heckathorn, D.D., Semaan, S. Broadhead, R.S. and Hughes, J.J. 'Extensions of Respondent-Driven Sampling: A New Approach to the Study of Injection Drug Users Aged 18–25', *AIDS and Behavior* 6(1) (2002): 55–67.

Heckathorn D.D. 'Snowball versus Respondent-driven sampling', *Sociological Methodology* 41(1) (2011): 355–366.

Heilman, S. and Friedman, M. *The Rebe. The Life Afterlife of Menachem Mendel Schneerson* (Princeton and Oxford: Princeton University Press, 2010).

Roberts, B.H. *Biographical Research* (Buckinghamand Philadelphia: Open University Press, 2002).

Schütze, F. 'Biography Analysis on the Empirical Base of Autobiographical Narratives: How to Analyse Autobiographical Narrative Interviews, Part II'. *Biographical Counselling in Rehabilitative Vocational Training. Further Educational Curriculum*. (EU Leonardoda Vinci Programme, 2008) http: www.biographicalcounselling.com/ (accessed 27 August 2015).

Wengraf, T. *Qualitative Research Interviewing Biographic Narrative and Semi-Structured Methods* (London: Sage Publications, 2001).

About the Contributors

Sanna Turoma is an Academy of Finland Fellow at the Aleksanteri Institute at the University of Helsinki, where she also directs the cultural studies cluster at the Finnish Center of Excellence in Russian Studies. She is the author of *Brodsky Abroad: Empire, Tourism, Nostalgia* (University of Wisconsin Press, 2010) and co-author of *Empire De/Centered: New Spatial Histories of Russia and The Soviet Union* (Ashgate, 2013) with Maxim Waldstein, a Finnish-language textbook of Russian literary history (2011, 2015), and a forthcoming volume *Cultural Forms of Political Protest* (Routledge, 2017) with Birgit Beumers, Alexander Etkind, and Olga Gurova. She has edited several special issues in Russian Studies for international journals.

Kaarina Aitamurto holds the position of post-doctoral researcher at the Aleksanteri Institute at the University of Helsinki. Her doctoral dissertation analysed Russian contemporary Paganism and nationalism. In her recent research, she focuses on Muslim minorities in ethnically Russian areas and the rise of Islamophobia. She is the author of *Paganism, Traditionalism, Nationalism: Narratives of Russian Rodnoverie* (Routledge, 2016) and co-editor of *Modern Pagan and Native Faiths in Central and Eastern Europe* (Acumen 2013) and *Migrant Workers in Russia: Global Challenges of the Shadow Economy in Societal Transformation* (Routledge, 2016).

Tomi Huttunen is professor of Russian literature and culture at the University of Helsinki. He specializes in and has published widely on historical avant-garde literature, montage principle, semiotics of culture, Russian rock poetry and contemporary literature.

Susan Ikonen has an ma in History and Russian Language and Literature from Helsinki University. She is preparing her PhD thesis on Soviet Thaw-era and late socialist cultural politics and literary discussions, concentrating on the case of Vladimir Dudintsev. She has published scholarly articles on her topic in Russian and in English.

Boris Knorre is associate professor at the Faculty of Humanities of the National Research University – Higher School of Economics. His interests include sociology and philosophy of religion, social anthropology, politization of religions and church-state cooperation. He has authored the monograph *In Search of Immortality: Fyodorov's Religious-Philosophical Movement* (Moscow, 2008) and more than 100 articles on contemporary religious communities, including Orthodoxy, paganism in Russia, New-Age and neo-orientalistic cults.

Irina Kotkina is an independent scholar. She has published widely on Russia's cultural policy, opera, and theatre. Her most recent publications include "Utopian Literature and Utopian Political Thinking in Present-Day Russia", *Russian Review 7* (October 2016), "Eurasianism and Contemporary Russian Cultural Politics – Case of the Ministry of Culture", *Art, Society and Politics in (Post)Socialism* (ed. Anreea Lazea), Editura Universitatii de Vest Timisoara, 2015, pp. 15–34, and (co-authored with Mark Bassin) "The Etnogenez Project: Ideology and Science Fiction in Putin's Russia," *Utopian Studies* 27:1 (2016).

Jussi Lassila works as a postdoctoral researcher at the Aleksanteri Institute of the University of Helsinki. His core areas of interest are political discourse analysis and post-Soviet identity politics. The second edition of his monograph *The Quest for an Ideal Youth in Putin's Russia ii: The Search for Distinctive Conformism in the Political Communication of Nashi, 2005–2009* was published by Ibidem in 2014 (first in 2012). His has also published articles in *Europe-Asia Studies*, *Canadian Slavonic Papers*, and *Demokratizatsiia*.

Andrei Makarychev is Guest Professor at Johan Skytte Institute of Political Science, University of Tartu, Estonia. His areas of expertise are Russia-eu relations, post-Soviet countries, mega-events in Eastern Europe and Eurasia, and biopolitics. He is a co-editor of *Changing Political and Economic Regimes in Russia* (Routledge, 2013). He has published articles in leading journals such as *Global Governance*, *International Spectator*, *European Regional and Urban Studies*, *Problems of*

Post-Communism, Demokratizatsiia, Journal of International Relations and Development, Europe-Asia Studies, Journal of Eurasian Studies, and *Welttrends,* as well as book chapters in edited volumes.

Elena Ostrovskaya works as a professor at the Saint-Petersburg State University. Her doctoral thesis analyzed contemporary Russian Buddhist convert communities, and her Habilitation thesis expounded her theory of institutionalization of traditional religious ideologies. Her current study focuses on the observant Jewry within the post-Soviet cultural space. She is the author of seven books, among which the most popular in Russia are *The Tibetan Buddhism, The Religious Model of Society,* and *The Buddhist Communities of Saint-Petersburg*. Ostrovskaya has published numerous articles on the theory and methodology of sociological studies and field research.

Mikhail Suslov, PhD in history, is a Marie Curie researcher at the Uppsala Center for Russian and Eurasian Studies, Uppsala University. His academic interests include Russian intellectual history, cultural history of the Orthodox Church, and geopolitical ideologies. His most recent publication is Suslov (ed.), *Digital Orthodoxy in the Post-Soviet World* (Stuttgart: ibidem-Verlag, 2016).

SOVIET AND POST-SOVIET POLITICS AND SOCIETY
Edited by Dr. Andreas Umland | ISSN 1614-3515

1   Андреас Умланд (ред.) | Воплощение Европейской конвенции по правам человека в России. Философские, юридические и эмпирические исследования | ISBN 3-89821-387-0
2   *Christian Wipperfürth* | Russland – ein vertrauenswürdiger Partner? Grundlagen, Hintergründe und Praxis gegenwärtiger russischer Außenpolitik | Mit einem Vorwort von Heinz Timmermann | ISBN 3-89821-401-X
3   *Manja Hussner* | Die Übernahme internationalen Rechts in die russische und deutsche Rechtsordnung. Eine vergleichende Analyse zur Völkerrechtsfreundlichkeit der Verfassungen der Russländischen Föderation und der Bundesrepublik Deutschland | Mit einem Vorwort von Rainer Arnold | ISBN 3-89821-438-9
4   *Matthew Tejada* | Bulgaria's Democratic Consolidation and the Kozloduy Nuclear Power Plant (KNPP). The Unattainability of Closure | With a foreword by Richard J. Crampton | ISBN 3-89821-439-7
5   *Марк Григорьевич Меерович* | Квадратные метры, определяющие сознание. Государственная жилищная политика в СССР. 1921 – 1941 гг | ISBN 3-89821-474-5
6   *Andrei P. Tsygankov, Pavel A.Tsygankov (Eds.)* | New Directions in Russian International Studies | ISBN 3-89821-422-2
7   *Марк Григорьевич Меерович* | Как власть народ к труду приучала. Жилище в СССР – средство управления людьми. 1917 – 1941 гг. | С предисловием Елены Осокиной | ISBN 3-89821-495-8
8   *David J. Galbreath* | Nation-Building and Minority Politics in Post-Socialist States. Interests, Influence and Identities in Estonia and Latvia | With a foreword by David J. Smith | ISBN 3-89821-467-2
9   *Алексей Юрьевич Безугольный* | Народы Кавказа в Вооруженных силах СССР в годы Великой Отечественной войны 1941-1945 гг. | С предисловием Николая Бугая | ISBN 3-89821-475-3
10 *Вячеслав Лихачев и Владимир Прибыловский (ред.)* | Русское Национальное Единство, 1990-2000. В 2-х томах | ISBN 3-89821-523-7
11 *Николай Бугай (ред.)* | Народы стран Балтии в условиях сталинизма (1940-е – 1950-е годы). Документированная история | ISBN 3-89821-525-3
12 *Ingmar Bredies (Hrsg.)* | Zur Anatomie der Orange Revolution in der Ukraine. Wechsel des Eliteregimes oder Triumph des Parlamentarismus?| ISBN 3-89821-524-5
13 *Anastasia V. Mitrofanova* | The Politicization of Russian Orthodoxy. Actors and Ideas | With a foreword by William C. Gay | ISBN 3-89821-481-8
14 *Nathan D. Larson* | Alexander Solzhenitsyn and the Russo-Jewish Question | ISBN 3-89821-483-4
15 *Guido Houben* | Kulturpolitik und Ethnizität. Staatliche Kunstförderung im Russland der neunziger Jahre | Mit einem Vorwort von Gert Weisskirchen | ISBN 3-89821-542-3
16 *Leonid Luks* | Der russische „Sonderweg"? Aufsätze zur neuesten Geschichte Russlands im europäischen Kontext | ISBN 3-89821-496-6
17 *Евгений Мороз* | История «Мёртвой воды» – от страшной сказки к большой политике. Политическое неоязычество в постсоветской России | ISBN 3-89821-551-2
18 *Александр Верховский и Галина Кожевникова (ред.)* | Этническая и религиозная интолерантность в российских СМИ. Результаты мониторинга 2001-2004 гг. | ISBN 3-89821-569-5
19 *Christian Ganzer* | Sowjetisches Erbe und ukrainische Nation. Das Museum der Geschichte des Zaporoger Kosakentums auf der Insel Chortycja | Mit einem Vorwort von Frank Golczewski | ISBN 3-89821-504-0
20 *Эльза-Баир Гучинова* | Помнить нельзя забыть. Антропология депортационной травмы калмыков | С предисловием Кэролайн Хамфри | ISBN 3-89821-506-7
21 *Юлия Лидерман* | Мотивы «проверки» и «испытания» в постсоветской культуре. Советское прошлое в российском кинематографе 1990-х годов | С предисловием Евгения Марголита | ISBN 3-89821-511-3
22 *Tanya Lokshina, Ray Thomas, Mary Mayer (Eds.)* | The Imposition of a Fake Political Settlement in the Northern Caucasus. The 2003 Chechen Presidential Election | ISBN 3-89821-436-2
23 *Timothy McCajor Hall, Rosie Read (Eds.)* | Changes in the Heart of Europe. Recent Ethnographies of Czechs, Slovaks, Roma, and Sorbs | With an afterword by Zdeněk Salzmann | ISBN 3-89821-606-3

24 *Christian Autengruber* | Die politischen Parteien in Bulgarien und Rumänien. Eine vergleichende Analyse seit Beginn der 90er Jahre | Mit einem Vorwort von Dorothée de Nève | ISBN 3-89821-476-1

25 *Annette Freyberg-Inan with Radu Cristescu* | The Ghosts in Our Classrooms, or: John Dewey Meets Ceauşescu. The Promise and the Failures of Civic Education in Romania | ISBN 3-89821-416-8

26 *John B. Dunlop* | The 2002 Dubrovka and 2004 Beslan Hostage Crises. A Critique of Russian Counter-Terrorism | With a foreword by Donald N. Jensen | ISBN 3-89821-608-X

27 *Peter Koller* | Das touristische Potenzial von Kam''janec–Podil's'kyj. Eine fremdenverkehrsgeographische Untersuchung der Zukunftsperspektiven und Maßnahmenplanung zur Destinationsentwicklung des „ukrainischen Rothenburg" | Mit einem Vorwort von Kristiane Klemm | ISBN 3-89821-640-3

28 *Françoise Daucé, Elisabeth Sieca-Kozlowski (Eds.)* | Dedovshchina in the Post-Soviet Military. Hazing of Russian Army Conscripts in a Comparative Perspective | With a foreword by Dale Herspring | ISBN 3-89821-616-0

29 *Florian Strasser* | Zivilgesellschaftliche Einflüsse auf die Orange Revolution. Die gewaltlose Massenbewegung und die ukrainische Wahlkrise 2004 | Mit einem Vorwort von Egbert Jahn | ISBN 3-89821-648-9

30 *Rebecca S. Katz* | The Georgian Regime Crisis of 2003-2004. A Case Study in Post-Soviet Media Representation of Politics, Crime and Corruption | ISBN 3-89821-413-3

31 *Vladimir Kantor* | Willkür oder Freiheit. Beiträge zur russischen Geschichtsphilosophie | Ediert von Dagmar Herrmann sowie mit einem Vorwort versehen von Leonid Luks | ISBN 3-89821-589-X

32 *Laura A. Victoir* | The Russian Land Estate Today. A Case Study of Cultural Politics in Post-Soviet Russia | With a foreword by Priscilla Roosevelt | ISBN 3-89821-426-5

33 *Ivan Katchanovski* | Cleft Countries. Regional Political Divisions and Cultures in Post-Soviet Ukraine and Moldova| With a foreword by Francis Fukuyama | ISBN 3-89821-558-X

34 *Florian Mühlfried* | Postsowjetische Feiern. Das Georgische Bankett im Wandel | Mit einem Vorwort von Kevin Tuite | ISBN 3-89821-601-2

35 *Roger Griffin, Werner Loh, Andreas Umland (Eds.)* | Fascism Past and Present, West and East. An International Debate on Concepts and Cases in the Comparative Study of the Extreme Right | With an afterword by Walter Laqueur | ISBN 3-89821-674-8

36 *Sebastian Schlegel* | Der „Weiße Archipel". Sowjetische Atomstädte 1945-1991 | Mit einem Geleitwort von Thomas Bohn | ISBN 3-89821-679-9

37 *Vyacheslav Likhachev* | Political Anti-Semitism in Post-Soviet Russia. Actors and Ideas in 1991-2003 | Edited and translated from Russian by Eugene Veklerov | ISBN 3-89821-529-6

38 *Josette Baer (Ed.)* | Preparing Liberty in Central Europe. Political Texts from the Spring of Nations 1848 to the Spring of Prague 1968 | With a foreword by Zdeněk V. David | ISBN 3-89821-546-6

39 *Михаил Лукьянов* | Российский консерватизм и реформа, 1907-1914 | С предисловием Марка Д. Стейнберга | ISBN 3-89821-503-2

40 *Nicola Melloni* | Market Without Economy. The 1998 Russian Financial Crisis | With a foreword by Eiji Furukawa | ISBN 3-89821-407-9

41 *Dmitrij Chmelnizki* | Die Architektur Stalins | Bd. 1: Studien zu Ideologie und Stil | Bd. 2: Bilddokumentation | Mit einem Vorwort von Bruno Flierl | ISBN 3-89821-515-6

42 *Katja Yafimava* | Post-Soviet Russian-Belarussian Relationships. The Role of Gas Transit Pipelines | With a foreword by Jonathan P. Stern | ISBN 3-89821-655-1

43 *Boris Chavkin* | Verflechtungen der deutschen und russischen Zeitgeschichte. Aufsätze und Archivfunde zu den Beziehungen Deutschlands und der Sowjetunion von 1917 bis 1991 | Ediert von Markus Edlinger sowie mit einem Vorwort versehen von Leonid Luks | ISBN 3-89821-756-6

44 *Anastasija Grynenko in Zusammenarbeit mit Claudia Dathe* | Die Terminologie des Gerichtswesens der Ukraine und Deutschlands im Vergleich. Eine übersetzungswissenschaftliche Analyse juristischer Fachbegriffe im Deutschen, Ukrainischen und Russischen | Mit einem Vorwort von Ulrich Hartmann | ISBN 3-89821-691-8

45 *Anton Burkov* | The Impact of the European Convention on Human Rights on Russian Law. Legislation and Application in 1996-2006 | With a foreword by Françoise Hampson | ISBN 978-3-89821-639-5

46 *Stina Torjesen, Indra Overland (Eds.)* | International Election Observers in Post-Soviet Azerbaijan. Geopolitical Pawns or Agents of Change? | ISBN 978-3-89821-743-9

47 *Taras Kuzio* | Ukraine – Crimea – Russia. Triangle of Conflict | ISBN 978-3-89821-761-3

48 *Claudia Šabić* | "Ich erinnere mich nicht, aber L'viv!". Zur Funktion kultureller Faktoren für die Institutionalisierung und Entwicklung einer ukrainischen Region | Mit einem Vorwort von Melanie Tatur | ISBN 978-3-89821-752-1

49 *Marlies Bilz* | Tatarstan in der Transformation. Nationaler Diskurs und Politische Praxis 1988-1994 | Mit einem Vorwort von Frank Golczewski | ISBN 978-3-89821-722-4

50 *Марлен Ларюэль (ред.)* | Современные интерпретации русского национализма | ISBN 978-3-89821-795-8

51 *Sonja Schüler* | Die ethnische Dimension der Armut. Roma im postsozialistischen Rumänien | Mit einem Vorwort von Anton Sterbling | ISBN 978-3-89821-776-7

52 *Галина Кожевникова* | Радикальный национализм в России и противодействие ему. Сборник докладов Центра «Сова» за 2004-2007 гг. | С предисловием Александра Верховского | ISBN 978-3-89821-721-7

53 *Галина Кожевникова и Владимир Прибыловский* | Российская власть в биографиях I. Высшие должностные лица РФ в 2004 г. | ISBN 978-3-89821-796-5

54 *Галина Кожевникова и Владимир Прибыловский* | Российская власть в биографиях II. Члены Правительства РФ в 2004 г. | ISBN 978-3-89821-797-2

55 *Галина Кожевникова и Владимир Прибыловский* | Российская власть в биографиях III. Руководители федеральных служб и агентств РФ в 2004 г.| ISBN 978-3-89821-798-9

56 *Ileana Petroniu* | Privatisierung in Transformationsökonomien. Determinanten der Restrukturierungs-Bereitschaft am Beispiel Polens, Rumäniens und der Ukraine | Mit einem Vorwort von Rainer W. Schäfer | ISBN 978-3-89821-790-3

57 *Christian Wipperfürth* | Russland und seine GUS-Nachbarn. Hintergründe, aktuelle Entwicklungen und Konflikte in einer ressourcenreichen Region| ISBN 978-3-89821-801-6

58 *Togzhan Kassenova* | From Antagonism to Partnership. The Uneasy Path of the U.S.-Russian Cooperative Threat Reduction | With a foreword by Christoph Bluth | ISBN 978-3-89821-707-1

59 *Alexander Höllwerth* | Das sakrale eurasische Imperium des Aleksandr Dugin. Eine Diskursanalyse zum postsowjetischen russischen Rechtsextremismus | Mit einem Vorwort von Dirk Uffelmann | ISBN 978-3-89821-813-9

60 *Олег Рябов* | «Россия-Матушка». Национализм, гендер и война в России XX века | С предисловием Елены Гощило | ISBN 978-3-89821-487-2

61 *Ivan Maistrenko* | Borot'bism. A Chapter in the History of the Ukrainian Revolution | With a new Introduction by Chris Ford | Translated by George S. N. Luckyj with the assistance of Ivan L. Rudnytsky | Second, Revised and Expanded Edition ISBN 978-3-8382-1107-7

62 *Maryna Romanets* | Anamorphosic Texts and Reconfigured Visions. Improvised Traditions in Contemporary Ukrainian and Irish Literature | ISBN 978-3-89821-576-3

63 *Paul D'Anieri and Taras Kuzio (Eds.)* | Aspects of the Orange Revolution I. Democratization and Elections in Post-Communist Ukraine | ISBN 978-3-89821-698-2

64 *Bohdan Harasymiw in collaboration with Oleh S. Ilnytzkyj (Eds.)* | Aspects of the Orange Revolution II. Information and Manipulation Strategies in the 2004 Ukrainian Presidential Elections | ISBN 978-3-89821-699-9

65 *Ingmar Bredies, Andreas Umland and Valentin Yakushik (Eds.)* | Aspects of the Orange Revolution III. The Context and Dynamics of the 2004 Ukrainian Presidential Elections | ISBN 978-3-89821-803-0

66 *Ingmar Bredies, Andreas Umland and Valentin Yakushik (Eds.)* | Aspects of the Orange Revolution IV. Foreign Assistance and Civic Action in the 2004 Ukrainian Presidential Elections | ISBN 978-3-89821-808-5

67 *Ingmar Bredies, Andreas Umland and Valentin Yakushik (Eds.)* | Aspects of the Orange Revolution V. Institutional Observation Reports on the 2004 Ukrainian Presidential Elections | ISBN 978-3-89821-809-2

68 *Taras Kuzio (Ed.)* | Aspects of the Orange Revolution VI. Post-Communist Democratic Revolutions in Comparative Perspective | ISBN 978-3-89821-820-7

69 *Tim Bohse* | Autoritarismus statt Selbstverwaltung. Die Transformation der kommunalen Politik in der Stadt Kaliningrad 1990-2005 | Mit einem Geleitwort von Stefan Troebst | ISBN 978-3-89821-782-8

70 *David Rupp* | Die Rußländische Föderation und die russischsprachige Minderheit in Lettland. Eine Fallstudie zur Anwaltspolitik Moskaus gegenüber den russophonen Minderheiten im „Nahen Ausland" von 1991 bis 2002 | Mit einem Vorwort von Helmut Wagner | ISBN 978-3-89821-778-1

71 *Taras Kuzio* | Theoretical and Comparative Perspectives on Nationalism. New Directions in Cross-Cultural and Post-Communist Studies | With a foreword by Paul Robert Magocsi | ISBN 978-3-89821-815-3

72 *Christine Teichmann* | Die Hochschultransformation im heutigen Osteuropa. Kontinuität und Wandel bei der Entwicklung des postkommunistischen Universitätswesens | Mit einem Vorwort von Oskar Anweiler | ISBN 978-3-89821-842-9

73 *Julia Kusznir* | Der politische Einfluss von Wirtschaftseliten in russischen Regionen. Eine Analyse am Beispiel der Erdöl- und Erdgasindustrie, 1992-2005 | Mit einem Vorwort von Wolfgang Eichwede | ISBN 978-3-89821-821-4

74 *Alena Vysotskaya* | Russland, Belarus und die EU-Osterweiterung. Zur Minderheitenfrage und zum Problem der Freizügigkeit des Personenverkehrs | Mit einem Vorwort von Katlijn Malfliet | ISBN 978-3-89821-822-1

75 *Heiko Pleines (Hrsg.)* | Corporate Governance in post-sozialistischen Volkswirtschaften | ISBN 978-3-89821-766-8

76 *Stefan Ihrig* | Wer sind die Moldawier? Rumänismus versus Moldowanismus in Historiographie und Schulbüchern der Republik Moldova, 1991-2006 | Mit einem Vorwort von Holm Sundhaussen | ISBN 978-3-89821-466-7

77 *Galina Kozhevnikova in collaboration with Alexander Verkhovsky and Eugene Veklerov* | Ultra-Nationalism and Hate Crimes in Contemporary Russia. The 2004-2006 Annual Reports of Moscow's SOVA Center | With a foreword by Stephen D. Shenfield | ISBN 978-3-89821-868-9

78 *Florian Küchler* | The Role of the European Union in Moldova's Transnistria Conflict | With a foreword by Christopher Hill | ISBN 978-3-89821-850-4

79 *Bernd Rechel* | The Long Way Back to Europe. Minority Protection in Bulgaria | With a foreword by Richard Crampton | ISBN 978-3-89821-863-4

80 *Peter W. Rodgers* | Nation, Region and History in Post-Communist Transitions. Identity Politics in Ukraine, 1991-2006 | With a foreword by Vera Tolz | ISBN 978-3-89821-903-7

81 *Stephanie Solywoda* | The Life and Work of Semen L. Frank. A Study of Russian Religious Philosophy | With a foreword by Philip Walters | ISBN 978-3-89821-457-5

82 *Vera Sokolova* | Cultural Politics of Ethnicity. Discourses on Roma in Communist Czechoslovakia | ISBN 978-3-89821-864-1

83 *Natalya Shevchik Ketenci* | Kazakhstani Enterprises in Transition. The Role of Historical Regional Development in Kazakhstan's Post-Soviet Economic Transformation | ISBN 978-3-89821-831-3

84 *Martin Malek, Anna Schor-Tschudnowskaja (Hgg.)* | Europa im Tschetschenienkrieg. Zwischen politischer Ohnmacht und Gleichgültigkeit | Mit einem Vorwort von Lipchan Basajewa | ISBN 978-3-89821-676-0

85 *Stefan Meister* | Das postsowjetische Universitätswesen zwischen nationalem und internationalem Wandel. Die Entwicklung der regionalen Hochschule in Russland als Gradmesser der Systemtransformation | Mit einem Vorwort von Joan DeBardeleben | ISBN 978-3-89821-891-7

86 *Konstantin Sheiko in collaboration with Stephen Brown* | Nationalist Imaginings of the Russian Past. Anatolii Fomenko and the Rise of Alternative History in Post-Communist Russia | With a foreword by Donald Ostrowski | ISBN 978-3-89821-915-0

87 *Sabine Jenni* | Wie stark ist das „Einige Russland"? Zur Parteibindung der Eliten und zum Wahlerfolg der Machtpartei im Dezember 2007 | Mit einem Vorwort von Klaus Armingeon | ISBN 978-3-89821-961-7

88 *Thomas Borén* | Meeting-Places of Transformation. Urban Identity, Spatial Representations and Local Politics in Post-Soviet St Petersburg | ISBN 978-3-89821-739-2

89 *Aygul Ashirova* | Stalinismus und Stalin-Kult in Zentralasien. Turkmenistan 1924-1953 | Mit einem Vorwort von Leonid Luks | ISBN 978-3-89821-987-7

90 *Leonid Luks* | Freiheit oder imperiale Größe? Essays zu einem russischen Dilemma | ISBN 978-3-8382-0011-8

91 *Christopher Gilley* | The 'Change of Signposts' in the Ukrainian Emigration. A Contribution to the History of Sovietophilism in the 1920s | With a foreword by Frank Golczewski | ISBN 978-3-89821-965-5

92 *Philipp Casula, Jeronim Perovic (Eds.)* | Identities and Politics During the Putin Presidency. The Discursive Foundations of Russia's Stability | With a foreword by Heiko Haumann | ISBN 978-3-8382-0015-6

93 *Marcel Viëtor* | Europa und die Frage nach seinen Grenzen im Osten. Zur Konstruktion ‚europäischer Identität' in Geschichte und Gegenwart | Mit einem Vorwort von Albrecht Lehmann | ISBN 978-3-8382-0045-3

94 *Ben Hellman, Andrei Rogachevskii* | Filming the Unfilmable. Casper Wrede's 'One Day in the Life of Ivan Denisovich' | Second, Revised and Expanded Edition | ISBN 978-3-8382-0044-6

95 *Eva Fuchslocher* | Vaterland, Sprache, Glaube. Orthodoxie und Nationenbildung am Beispiel Georgiens | Mit einem Vorwort von Christina von Braun | ISBN 978-3-89821-884-9

96 *Vladimir Kantor* | Das Westlertum und der Weg Russlands. Zur Entwicklung der russischen Literatur und Philosophie | Ediert von Dagmar Herrmann | Mit einem Beitrag von Nikolaus Lobkowicz | ISBN 978-3-8382-0102-3

97 *Kamran Musayev* | Die postsowjetische Transformation im Baltikum und Südkaukasus. Eine vergleichende Untersuchung der politischen Entwicklung Lettlands und Aserbaidschans 1985-2009 | Mit einem Vorwort von Leonid Luks | Ediert von Sandro Henschel | ISBN 978-3-8382-0103-0

98 *Tatiana Zhurzhenko* | Borderlands into Bordered Lands. Geopolitics of Identity in Post-Soviet Ukraine | With a foreword by Dieter Segert | ISBN 978-3-8382-0042-2

99 *Кирилл Галушко, Лидия Смола (ред.)* | Пределы падения – варианты украинского будущего. Аналитико-прогностические исследования | ISBN 978-3-8382-0148-1

100 *Michael Minkenberg (Ed.)* | Historical Legacies and the Radical Right in Post-Cold War Central and Eastern Europe | With an afterword by Sabrina P. Ramet | ISBN 978-3-8382-0124-5

101 *David-Emil Wickström* | Rocking St. Petersburg. Transcultural Flows and Identity Politics in the St. Petersburg Popular Music Scene | With a foreword by Yngvar B. Steinholt | Second, Revised and Expanded Edition | ISBN 978-3-8382-0100-9

102 *Eva Zabka* | Eine neue „Zeit der Wirren"? Der spät- und postsowjetische Systemwandel 1985-2000 im Spiegel russischer gesellschaftspolitischer Diskurse | Mit einem Vorwort von Margareta Mommsen | ISBN 978-3-8382-0161-0

103 *Ulrike Ziemer* | Ethnic Belonging, Gender and Cultural Practices. Youth Identitites in Contemporary Russia | With a foreword by Anoop Nayak | ISBN 978-3-8382-0152-8

104 *Ksenia Chepikova* | ‚Einiges Russland' - eine zweite KPdSU? Aspekte der Identitätskonstruktion einer postsowjetischen „Partei der Macht" | Mit einem Vorwort von Torsten Oppelland | ISBN 978-3-8382-0311-9

105 *Леонид Люкс* | Западничество или евразийство? Демократия или идеократия? Сборник статей об исторических дилеммах России | С предисловием Владимира Кантора | ISBN 978-3-8382-0211-2

106 *Anna Dost* | Das russische Verfassungsrecht auf dem Weg zum Föderalismus und zurück. Zum Konflikt von Rechtsnormen und -wirklichkeit in der Russländischen Föderation von 1991 bis 2009 | Mit einem Vorwort von Alexander Blankenagel | ISBN 978-3-8382-0292-1

107 *Philipp Herzog* | Sozialistische Völkerfreundschaft, nationaler Widerstand oder harmloser Zeitvertreib? Zur politischen Funktion der Volkskunst im sowjetischen Estland | Mit einem Vorwort von Andreas Kappeler | ISBN 978-3-8382-0216-7

108 *Marlène Laruelle (Ed.)* | Russian Nationalism, Foreign Policy, and Identity Debates in Putin's Russia. New Ideological Patterns after the Orange Revolution | ISBN 978-3-8382-0325-6

109 *Michail Logvinov* | Russlands Kampf gegen den internationalen Terrorismus. Eine kritische Bestandsaufnahme des Bekämpfungsansatzes | Mit einem Geleitwort von Hans-Henning Schröder und einem Vorwort von Eckhard Jesse | ISBN 978-3-8382-0329-4

110 *John B. Dunlop* | The Moscow Bombings of September 1999. Examinations of Russian Terrorist Attacks at the Onset of Vladimir Putin's Rule | Second, Revised and Expanded Edition | ISBN 978-3-8382-0388-1

111 *Андрей А. Ковалёв* | Свидетельство из-за кулис российской политики I. Можно ли делать добро из зла? (Воспоминания и размышления о последних советских и первых послесоветских годах) | With a foreword by Peter Reddaway | ISBN 978-3-8382-0302-7

112 *Андрей А. Ковалёв* | Свидетельство из-за кулис российской политики II. Угроза для себя и окружающих (Наблюдения и предостережения относительно происходящего после 2000 г.) | ISBN 978-3-8382-0303-4

113 *Bernd Kappenberg* | Zeichen setzen für Europa. Der Gebrauch europäischer lateinischer Sonderzeichen in der deutschen Öffentlichkeit | Mit einem Vorwort von Peter Schlobinski | ISBN 978-3-89821-749-1

114 *Ivo Mijnssen* | The Quest for an Ideal Youth in Putin's Russia I. Back to Our Future! History, Modernity, and Patriotism according to Nashi, 2005-2013 | With a foreword by Jeronim Perović | Second, Revised and Expanded Edition | ISBN 978-3-8382-0368-3

115 *Jussi Lassila* | The Quest for an Ideal Youth in Putin's Russia II. The Search for Distinctive Conformism in the Political Communication of Nashi, 2005-2009 | With a foreword by Kirill Postoutenko | Second, Revised and Expanded Edition | ISBN 978-3-8382-0415-4

116 *Valerio Trabandt* | Neue Nachbarn, gute Nachbarschaft? Die EU als internationaler Akteur am Beispiel ihrer Demokratieförderung in Belarus und der Ukraine 2004-2009 | Mit einem Vorwort von Jutta Joachim | ISBN 978-3-8382-0437-6

117 *Fabian Pfeiffer* | Estlands Außen- und Sicherheitspolitik I. Der estnische Atlantizismus nach der wiedererlangten Unabhängigkeit 1991-2004 | Mit einem Vorwort von Helmut Hubel | ISBN 978-3-8382-0127-6

118 *Jana Podßuweit* | Estlands Außen- und Sicherheitspolitik II. Handlungsoptionen eines Kleinstaates im Rahmen seiner EU-Mitgliedschaft (2004-2008) | Mit einem Vorwort von Helmut Hubel | ISBN 978-3-8382-0440-6

119 *Karin Pointner* | Estlands Außen- und Sicherheitspolitik III. Eine gedächtnispolitische Analyse estnischer Entwicklungskooperation 2006-2010 | Mit einem Vorwort von Karin Liebhart | ISBN 978-3-8382-0435-7

120 *Ruslana Vovk* | Die Offenheit der ukrainischen Verfassung für das Völkerrecht und die europäische Integration | Mit einem Vorwort von Alexander Blankenagel | ISBN 978-3-8382-0481-9

121 *Mykhaylo Banakh* | Die Relevanz der Zivilgesellschaft bei den postkommunistischen Transformationsprozessen in mittel- und osteuropäischen Ländern. Das Beispiel der spät- und postsowjetischen Ukraine 1986-2009 | Mit einem Vorwort von Gerhard Simon | ISBN 978-3-8382-0499-4

122 *Michael Moser* | Language Policy and the Discourse on Languages in Ukraine under President Viktor Yanukovych (25 February 2010–28 October 2012) | ISBN 978-3-8382-0497-0 (Paperback edition) | ISBN 978-3-8382-0507-6 (Hardcover edition)

123 *Nicole Krome* | Russischer Netzwerkkapitalismus Restrukturierungsprozesse in der Russischen Föderation am Beispiel des Luftfahrtunternehmens "Aviastar" | Mit einem Vorwort von Petra Stykow | ISBN 978-3-8382-0534-2

124 *David R. Marples* | 'Our Glorious Past'. Lukashenka's Belarus and the Great Patriotic War | ISBN 978-3-8382-0574-8 (Paperback edition) | ISBN 978-3-8382-0675-2 (Hardcover edition)

125 *Ulf Walther* | Russlands "neuer Adel". Die Macht des Geheimdienstes von Gorbatschow bis Putin | Mit einem Vorwort von Hans-Georg Wieck | ISBN 978-3-8382-0584-7

126 *Simon Geissbühler (Hrsg.)* | Kiew – Revolution 3.0. Der Euromaidan 2013/14 und die Zukunftsperspektiven der Ukraine | ISBN 978-3-8382-0581-6 (Paperback edition) | ISBN 978-3-8382-0681-3 (Hardcover edition)

127 *Andrey Makarychev* | Russia and the EU in a Multipolar World. Discourses, Identities, Norms | With a foreword by Klaus Segbers | ISBN 978-3-8382-0629-5

128 *Roland Scharff* | Kasachstan als postsowjetischer Wohlfahrtsstaat. Die Transformation des sozialen Schutzsystems | Mit einem Vorwort von Joachim Ahrens | ISBN 978-3-8382-0622-6

129 *Katja Grupp* | Bild Lücke Deutschland. Kaliningrader Studierende sprechen über Deutschland | Mit einem Vorwort von Martin Schulz | ISBN 978-3-8382-0552-6

130 *Konstantin Sheiko, Stephen Brown* | History as Therapy. Alternative History and Nationalist Imaginings in Russia, 1991-2014 | ISBN 978-3-8382-0665-3

131 *Elisa Kriza* | Alexander Solzhenitsyn: Cold War Icon, Gulag Author, Russian Nationalist? A Study of the Western Reception of his Literary Writings, Historical Interpretations, and Political Ideas | With a foreword by Andrei Rogatchevski | ISBN 978-3-8382-0589-2 (Paperback edition) | ISBN 978-3-8382-0690-5 (Hardcover edition)

132 *Serghei Golunov* | The Elephant in the Room. Corruption and Cheating in Russian Universities | ISBN 978-3-8382-0570-0

133 *Manja Hussner, Rainer Arnold (Hgg.)* | Verfassungsgerichtsbarkeit in Zentralasien I. Sammlung von Verfassungstexten | ISBN 978-3-8382-0595-3

134 *Nikolay Mitrokhin* | Die "Russische Partei". Die Bewegung der russischen Nationalisten in der UdSSR 1953-1985 | Aus dem Russischen übertragen von einem Übersetzerteam unter der Leitung von Larisa Schippel | ISBN 978-3-8382-0024-8

135 *Manja Hussner, Rainer Arnold (Hgg.)* | Verfassungsgerichtsbarkeit in Zentralasien II. Sammlung von Verfassungstexten | ISBN 978-3-8382-0597-7

136 *Manfred Zeller* | Das sowjetische Fieber. Fußballfans im poststalinistischen Vielvölkerreich | Mit einem Vorwort von Nikolaus Katzer | ISBN 978-3-8382-0757-5

137 *Kristin Schreiter* | Stellung und Entwicklungspotential zivilgesellschaftlicher Gruppen in Russland. Menschenrechtsorganisationen im Vergleich | ISBN 978-3-8382-0673-8

138 *David R. Marples, Frederick V. Mills (Eds.)* | Ukraine's Euromaidan. Analyses of a Civil Revolution | ISBN 978-3-8382-0660-8

139 *Bernd Kappenberg* | Setting Signs for Europe. Why Diacritics Matter for European Integration | With a foreword by Peter Schlobinski | ISBN 978-3-8382-0663-9

140 *René Lenz* | Internationalisierung, Kooperation und Transfer. Externe bildungspolitische Akteure in der Russischen Föderation | Mit einem Vorwort von Frank Ettrich | ISBN 978-3-8382-0751-3

141 *Juri Plusnin, Yana Zausaeva, Natalia Zhidkevich, Artemy Pozanenko* | Wandering Workers. Mores, Behavior, Way of Life, and Political Status of Domestic Russian Labor Migrants | Translated by Julia Kazantseva | ISBN 978-3-8382-0653-0

142 *David J. Smith (Eds.)* | Latvia – A Work in Progress? 100 Years of State- and Nation-Building | ISBN 978-3-8382-0648-6

143 *Инна Чувычкина (ред.)* | Экспортные нефте- и газопроводы на постсоветском пространстве. Анализ трубопроводной политики в свете теории международных отношений | ISBN 978-3-8382-0822-0

144 *Johann Zajaczkowski* | Russland – eine pragmatische Großmacht? Eine rollentheoretische Untersuchung russischer Außenpolitik am Beispiel der Zusammenarbeit mit den USA nach 9/11 und des Georgienkrieges von 2008 | Mit einem Vorwort von Siegfried Schieder | ISBN 978-3-8382-0837-4

145 *Boris Popivanov* | Changing Images of the Left in Bulgaria. The Challenge of Post-Communism in the Early 21st Century | ISBN 978-3-8382-0667-7

146 *Lenka Krátká* | A History of the Czechoslovak Ocean Shipping Company 1948-1989. How a Small, Landlocked Country Ran Maritime Business During the Cold War | ISBN 978-3-8382-0666-0

147 *Alexander Sergunin* | Explaining Russian Foreign Policy Behavior. Theory and Practice | ISBN 978-3-8382-0752-0

148 *Darya Malyutina* | Migrant Friendships in a Super-Diverse City. Russian-Speakers and their Social Relationships in London in the 21st Century | With a foreword by Claire Dwyer | ISBN 978-3-8382-0652-3

149 *Alexander Sergunin, Valery Konyshev* | Russia in the Arctic. Hard or Soft Power? | ISBN 978-3-8382-0753-7

150 *John J. Maresca* | Helsinki Revisited. A Key U.S. Negotiator's Memoirs on the Development of the CSCE into the OSCE | With a foreword by Hafiz Pashayev | ISBN 978-3-8382-0852-7

151 *Jardar Østbø* | The New Third Rome. Readings of a Russian Nationalist Myth | With a foreword by Pål Kolstø | ISBN 978-3-8382-0870-1

152 *Simon Kordonsky* | Socio-Economic Foundations of the Russian Post-Soviet Regime. The Resource-Based Economy and Estate-Based Social Structure of Contemporary Russia | With a foreword by Svetlana Barsukova | ISBN 978-3-8382-0775-9

153 *Duncan Leitch* | Assisting Reform in Post-Communist Ukraine 2000–2012. The Illusions of Donors and the Disillusion of Beneficiaries | With a foreword by Kataryna Wolczuk | ISBN 978-3-8382-0844-2

154 *Abel Polese* | Limits of a Post-Soviet State. How Informality Replaces, Renegotiates, and Reshapes Governance in Contemporary Ukraine | With a foreword by Colin Williams | ISBN 978-3-8382-0845-9

155 *Mikhail Suslov (Ed.)* | Digital Orthodoxy in the Post-Soviet World. The Russian Orthodox Church and Web 2.0 | With a foreword by Father Cyril Hovorun | ISBN 978-3-8382-0871-8

156 *Leonid Luks* | Zwei „Sonderwege"? Russisch-deutsche Parallelen und Kontraste (1917-2014). Vergleichende Essays | ISBN 978-3-8382-0823-7

157 *Vladimir V. Karacharovskiy, Ovsey I. Shkaratan, Gordey A. Yastrebov* | Towards a New Russian Work Culture. Can Western Companies and Expatriates Change Russian Society? | With a foreword by Elena N. Danilova | Translated by Julia Kazantseva | ISBN 978-3-8382-0902-9

158 *Edmund Griffiths* | Aleksandr Prokhanov and Post-Soviet Esotericism | ISBN 978-3-8382-0903-6

159 *Timm Beichelt, Susann Worschech (Eds.)* | Transnational Ukraine? Networks and Ties that Influence(d) Contemporary Ukraine | ISBN 978-3-8382-0944-9

160 *Mieste Hotopp-Riecke* | Die Tataren der Krim zwischen Assimilation und Selbstbehauptung. Der Aufbau des krimtatarischen Bildungswesens nach Deportation und Heimkehr (1990-2005) | Mit einem Vorwort von Swetlana Czerwonnaja | ISBN 978-3-89821-940-2

161 *Olga Bertelsen (Ed.)* | Revolution and War in Contemporary Ukraine. The Challenge of Change | ISBN 978-3-8382-1016-2

162 *Natalya Ryabinska* | Ukraine's Post-Communist Mass Media. Between Capture and Commercialization | With a foreword by Marta Dyczok | ISBN 978-3-8382-1011-7

163 *Alexandra Cotofana, James M. Nyce (Eds.)* | Religion and Magic in Socialist and Post-Socialist Contexts. Historic and Ethnographic Case Studies of Orthodoxy, Heterodoxy, and Alternative Spirituality | With a foreword by Patrick L. Michelson | ISBN 978-3-8382-0989-0

164 *Nozima Akhrarkhodjaeva* | The Instrumentalisation of Mass Media in Electoral Authoritarian Regimes. Evidence from Russia's Presidential Election Campaigns of 2000 and 2008 | ISBN 978-3-8382-1013-1

165 *Yulia Krasheninnikova* | Informal Healthcare in Contemporary Russia. Sociographic Essays on the Post-Soviet Infrastructure for Alternative Healing Practices | ISBN 978-3-8382-0970-8

166 *Peter Kaiser* | Das Schachbrett der Macht. Die Handlungsspielräume eines sowjetischen Funktionärs unter Stalin am Beispiel des Generalsekretärs Komsomol Aleksandr Kosarev (1929-1938) | Mit einem Vorwort von Dietmar Neutatz | ISBN 978-3-8382-1052-0

167 *Oksana Kim* | The Effects and Implications of Kazakhstan's Adoption of International Financial Reporting Standards. A Resource Dependence Perspective | With a foreword by Svetlana Vlady | ISBN 978-3-8382-0987-6

168 *Anna Sanina* | Patriotic Education in Contemporary Russia. Sociological Studies in the Making of the Post-Soviet Citizen | With a foreword by Anna Oldfield | ISBN 978-3-8382-0993-7

169 *Rudolf Wolters* | Spezialist in Sibirien Faksimile der 1933 erschienenen ersten Ausgabe | Mit einem Vorwort von Dmitrij Chmelnizki | ISBN 978-3-8382-0515-1

170 *Michal Vít, Magdalena M. Baran (Eds.)* | Transregional versus National Perspectives on Contemporary Central European History. Studies on the Building of Nation-States and Their Cooperation in the 20th and 21st Century | With a foreword by Petr Vágner | ISBN 978-3-8382-1015-5

171 *Philip Gamaghelyan* | Conflict Resolution Beyond the International Relations Paradigm. Evolving Designs as a Transformative Practice in Nagorno-Karabakh and Syria | With a foreword by Susan Allen | ISBN 978-3-8382-1057-5

172 *Maria Shagina* | Joining a Prestigious Club. Cooperation with Europarties and Its Impact on Party Development in Georgia, Moldova, and Ukraine 2004–2015 | With a foreword by Kataryna Wolczuk | ISBN 978-3-8382-1084-1

173 *Alexandra Cotofana, James M. Nyce (Eds.)* | Religion and Magic in Socialist and Post-Socialist Contexts II. Baltic, Eastern European, and Post-USSR Case Studies | With a foreword by Anita Stasulane | ISBN 978-3-8382-0990-6

174 *Barbara Kunz* | Kind Words, Cruise Missiles, and Everything in Between. The Use of Power Resources in U.S. Policies towards Poland, Ukraine, and Belarus 1989–2008 | With a foreword by William Hill | ISBN 978-3-8382-1065-0

175 *Eduard Klein* | Bildungskorruption in Russland und der Ukraine. Eine komparative Analyse der Performanz staatlicher Antikorruptionsmaßnahmen im Hochschulsektor am Beispiel universitärer Aufnahmeprüfungen | Mit einem Vorwort von Heiko Pleines | ISBN 978-3-8382-0995-1

176 *Markus Soldner* | Politischer Kapitalismus im postsowjetischen Russland. Die politische, wirtschaftliche und mediale Transformation in den 1990er Jahren | Mit einem Vorwort von Wolfgang Ismayr | ISBN 978-3-8382-1222-7

177 *Anton Oleinik* | Building Ukraine from Within. A Sociological, Institutional, and Economic Analysis of a Nation-State in the Making | ISBN 978-3-8382-1150-3

178 *Peter Rollberg, Marlene Laruelle (Eds.)* | Mass Media in the Post-Soviet World. Market Forces, State Actors, and Political Manipulation in the Informational Environment after Communism | ISBN 978-3-8382-1116-9

179 *Mikhail Minakov* | Development and Dystopia Studies in Post-Soviet Ukraine and Eastern Europe | With a foreword by Alexander Etkind | ISBN 978-3-8382-1112-1

180 *Aijan Sharshenova* | The European Union's Democracy Promotion in Central Asia A Study of Political Interests, Influence, and Development in Kazakhstan and Kyrgyzstan in 2007–2013 | With a foreword by Gordon Crawford | ISBN 978-3-8382-1151-0

181 *Andrey Makarychev, Alexandra Yatsyk (Eds.)* | Boris Nemtsov and Russian Politics. Power and Resistance | With a foreword by Zhanna Nemtsova | ISBN 978-3-8382-1122-0

182 *Sophie Falsini* | The Euromaidan's Effect on Civil Society. Why and How Ukrainian Social Capital Increased after the Revolution of Dignity | With a foreword by Susann Worschech | ISBN 978-3-8382-1131-2

183 *Andreas Umland (Ed.)* | Ukraine's Decentralization. Challenges and Implications of the Local Governance Reform after the Euromaidan Revolution | ISBN 978-3-8382-1162-6

184 *Leonid Luks* | A Fateful Triangle. Essays on Contemporary Russian, German and Polish History | ISBN 978-3-8382-1143-5

185 *John B. Dunlop* | The February 2015 Assassination of Boris Nemtsov and the Flawed Trial of his Alleged Killers. An Exploration of Russia's "Crime of the 21st Century" | ISBN 978-3-8382-1188-6

186 *Vasile Rotaru* | Russia, the EU, and the Eastern Partnership. Building Bridges or Digging Trenches? | ISBN 978-3-8382-1134-3

187 *Marina Lebedeva* | Russian Studies of International Relations. From the Soviet Past to the Post-Cold-War Present | With a foreword by Andrei P. Tsygankov | ISBN 978-3-8382-0851-0

188 *Tomasz Stępniewski, George Soroka (Eds.)* | Ukraine after Maidan. Revisiting Domestic and Regional Security | ISBN 978-3-8382-1075-9

189 *Petar Cholakov* | Ethnic Entrepreneurs Unmasked. Political Institutions and Ethnic Conflicts in Contemporary Bulgaria | ISBN 978-3-8382-1189-3

190 *A. Salem, G. Hazeldine, D. Morgan (Eds.)* | Higher Education in Post-Communist States. Comparative and Sociological Perspectives | ISBN 978-3-8382-1183-1

191 *Igor Torbakov* | After Empire. Nationalist Imagination and Symbolic Politics in Russia and Eurasia in the Twentieth and Twenty-First Century | With a foreword by Serhii Plokhy | ISBN 978-3-8382-1217-3

192 *Aleksandr Burakovskiy* | Jewish-Ukrainian Relations in Late and Post-Soviet Ukraine. Articles, Lectures and Essays from 1986 to 2016 | ISBN 978-3-8382-1210-4

193 *Natalia Shapovalova, Olga Burlyuk (Eds.)* | Civil Society in Post-Euromaidan Ukraine. From Revolution to Consolidation | With a foreword by Richard Youngs | ISBN 978-3-8382-1216-6

194 *Franz Preissler* | Positionsverteidigung, Imperialismus oder Irredentismus? Russland und die „Russischsprachigen", 1991–2015 | ISBN 978-3-8382-1262-3

195 *Marian Madeła* | Der Reformprozess in der Ukraine 2014-2017. Eine Fallstudie zur Reform der öffentlichen Verwaltung | Mit einem Vorwort von Martin Malek | ISBN 978-3-8382-1266-1

196 *Anke Giesen* | „Wie kann denn der Sieger ein Verbrecher sein?" Eine diskursanalytische Untersuchung der russlandweiten Debatte über Konzept und Verstaatlichungsprozess der Lagergedenkstätte „Perm'-36" im Ural | ISBN 978-3-8382-1284-5

197 *Alla Leukavets* | The Integration Policies of Belarus and Ukraine vis-à-vis the EU and Russia. A Comparative Case Study Through the Prism of a Two-Level Game Approach | ISBN 978-3-8382-1247-0

198 *Oksana Kim* | The Development and Challenges of Russian Corporate Governance I. The Roles and Functions of Boards of Directors | With a foreword by Sheila M. Puffer | ISBN 978-3-8382-1287-6

199 *Thomas D. Grant* | International Law and the Post-Soviet Space I. Essays on Chechnya and the Baltic States | With a foreword by Stephen M. Schwebel | ISBN 978-3-8382-1279-1

200 *Thomas D. Grant* | International Law and the Post-Soviet Space II. Essays on Ukraine, Intervention, and Non-Proliferation | ISBN 978-3-8382-1280-7

201 *Slavomír Michálek, Michal Štefansky* | The Age of Fear. The Cold War and Its Influence on Czechoslovakia 1945–1968 | ISBN 978-3-8382-1285-2

202 *Iulia-Sabina Joja* | Romania's Strategic Culture 1990–2014. Continuity and Change in a Post-Communist Country's Evolution of National Interests and Security Policies | With a foreword by Heiko Biehl | ISBN 978-3-8382-1286-9

203 *Andrei Rogatchevski, Yngvar B. Steinholt, Arve Hansen, David-Emil Wickström* | War of Songs. Popular Music and Recent Russia-Ukraine Relations | With a foreword by Artemy Troitsky | ISBN 978-3-8382-1173-2

204 *Maria Lipman (Ed.)* | Russian Voices on Post-Crimea Russia. An Almanac of Counterpoint Essays from 2015–2018 | ISBN 978-3-8382-1251-7

205 *Ksenia Maksimovtsova* | Language Conflicts in Contemporary Estonia, Latvia, and Ukraine. A Comparative Exploration of Discourses in Post-Soviet Russian-Language Digital Media | With a foreword by Ammon Cheskin | ISBN 978-3-8382-1282-1

206 *Michal Vít* | The EU's Impact on Identity Formation in East-Central Europe between 2004 and 2013. Perceptions of the Nation and Europe in Political Parties of the Czech Republic, Poland, and Slovakia | With a foreword by Andrea Pető | ISBN 978-3-8382-1275-3

207 *Per A. Rudling* | Tarnished Heroes. The Organization of Ukrainian Nationalists in the Memory Politics of Post-Soviet Ukraine | ISBN 978-3-8382-0999-9

208 *Kaja Gadowska, Peter Solomon (Eds.)* | Legal Change in Post-Communist States. Progress, Reversions, Explanations | ISBN 978-3-8382-1312-5

209 *Pawel Kowal, Georges Mink, Iwona Reichardt (Eds.)* | Three Revolutions: Mobilization and Change in Contemporary Ukraine I. Theoretical Aspects and Analyses on Religion, Memory, and Identity | ISBN 978-3-8382-1321-7

210 *Pawel Kowal, Georges Mink, Adam Reichardt, Iwona Reichardt (Eds.)* | Three Revolutions: Mobilization and Change in Contemporary Ukraine II. An Oral History of the Revolution on Granite, Orange Revolution, and Revolution of Dignity | ISBN 978-3-8382-1323-1

211 *Li Bennich-Björkman, Sergiy Kurbatov (Eds.)* | When the Future Came: The Collapse of the USSR and the Emergence of National Memory in Post-Soviet History Textbooks | ISBN 978-3-8382-1335-4

212 *Olga R. Gulina* | Migration as a (Geo-)Political Challenge in the Post-Soviet Space. Border Regimes, Policy Choices, Visa Agendas | With a foreword by Nils Muižnieks | ISBN 978-3-8382-1338-7

213 *Sanna Turoma; Kaarina Aitamurto; Slobodanka Vladiv-Glover (Eds.)* | Religion, Expression, and Patriotism in Russia | Essays on Post-Soviet Society and the State | ISBN 978-3-8382-1346-0

ibidem.eu